AF584536

Tango Nuevo

UNIVERSITY PRESS OF FLORIDA

Florida A&M University, Tallahassee
Florida Atlantic University, Boca Raton
Florida Gulf Coast University, Ft. Myers
Florida International University, Miami
Florida State University, Tallahassee
New College of Florida, Sarasota
University of Central Florida, Orlando
University of Florida, Gainesville
University of North Florida, Jacksonville
University of South Florida, Tampa
University of West Florida, Pensacola

Tango Nuevo

CAROLYN MERRITT

University Press of Florida
Gainesville · Tallahassee · Tampa · Boca Raton
Pensacola · Orlando · Miami · Jacksonville · Ft. Myers · Sarasota

Printed in the United States of America on acid-free paper

This book may be available in an electronic edition.

17 16 15 14 13 12 6 5 4 3 2 1

Cataloging-in-publication information is available from the Library of Congress.
ISBN 978-0-8130-4219-0

University Press of Florida
15 Northwest 15th Street
Gainesville, FL 32611-2079
http://www.upf.com

This book is a part of the Latin American and Caribbean Arts and Culture publication initiative, funded by a grant from the Andrew W. Mellon Foundation.

For my parents, who sent me to dance class in the first place.
And for Steve, to many more years of dancing together.

Oh this is the animal that never was.
They hadn't seen one; but just the same, they loved
its graceful movements, and the way it stood
looking at them calmly, with clear eyes.

It had not been. But for them, it appeared
in all its purity. They left space enough.
And in the space hollowed out by their love
it stood up all at once and didn't need

existence. They nourished it, not with grain,
but with the mere possibility of being.
And finally this gave it so much power

that from its forehead a horn grew. One horn.
It drew near to a virgin, white, gleaming—
and was, inside the mirror and in her.

Rainer Maria Rilke, *The Sonnets to Orpheus II*, 4

The tango can be debated, and we have debates over it, but it still encloses, as does all that which is truthful, a secret.

Jorge Luis Borges, "A History of the Tango" (1999)

Contents

Acknowledgments

This book is my attempt to give voice to the many, varied, and contradictory experiences described to me and lived myself in the pursuit of Argentine tango. Because I want to understand the hold it has over me and so many others, I write in the hope of giving tango an existence independent of me, independent of all the dancers who create and re-create it every day. This book, then, is a tribute to the dancers, teachers, musicians, entrepreneurs, researchers, and others who shared with me a glimpse of their lives and their passion for tango.

While tango has brought both friendships and brief yet meaningful connections, the magic of El Galpon and the friends and acquaintances I met in Buenos Aires in January 2005 will always hold a special place in my heart. Singling out one tango instructor is equally difficult, for I have had the good fortune to study with many wonderful teachers. Though I took different lessons from afternoons at Rodolfo Dinzel's studio and classes with Gustavo Naveira and Giselle Anne, each transformed my understanding of tango in crucial ways. José Gobello and Olga Besio graciously provided letters of support for my early research, on behalf of the Academia Porteña del Lunfardo and Tango con Niños, respectively.

My life has been mysteriously intertwined with Meredith Klein's since she introduced me to the tango. She has been a tireless ally and confidant, and she and Andrés Amarilla were my family in Buenos Aires. I might not have lasted two years at "the end of the world" without Jorge Garnica and my *hermana del alma*, Silvina De Laurente. Michele Kadison and Chris Wenham kept me well fed and inspired during my second year in "mecca." The Philadelphia tango community welcomed me with open arms in 2002, and I can't imagine a better place for a beginning tango dancer. I am especially grateful to Lesley Mitchell and Kelly Ray, who were my first formal teachers, and to Lesley for introducing me to Buenos Aires. Countless family, friends, and fellow dancers have provided shelter, food, and good company over the course of this project. Special thanks to my parents, Kevin and Emily, and their Merritt brood, Jeannie and Eddie Burke, Marjorie and Lou Guth, Shari Kornelly, Harry Hoffman, Laura Digilio, Lester Tome, George Alley, Stacey and Ed Matthews, KC and

Chris Manning, Jason Nutile, Julie Orio, Merri LeDuc, Michele Kadison, Nancy Hirschorn, and John Chang for opening their homes to me, and to the many people who looked after my well-traveled cat.

I owe a great debt to Jayasinhji Jhala, Paul Garrett, Joellen Meglin, and Raquel Romberg. Each displayed a humanity that kept me interested in academic work, and their guidance and encouragement helped me develop much of the thinking that would eventually become this book. Raquel continues to be an inspiration within and outside of academia, and I am grateful that she pressed me to continue working on this book when I was nearly ready to give up.

My editor at the University Press of Florida, Amy Gorelick, guided me from proposal to publication, and her insights were critical to the crafting of this book. Marilyn Miller provided painstaking attention to an excerpt that appears in her edited volume, *Tango Lessons*; her tough questions stayed with me as I drafted this book. Likewise, Julie Taylor and Melissa Fitch were generous in their attention and encouragement. Ellen Wert would surely strike this sentence as overdramatic, but I would never have finished without her help. Not only did she reignite my passion for this project, but she provided an invaluable education in crafting disparate stories and ideas into a coherent whole. I am blessed to have found such a gifted editor.

A friendly face in Buenos Aires, Damian Lobato has become a friend and trusted resource since relocating to Philadelphia; he and Andrés Amarilla have helped me resolve countless questions related to tango history, terminology, and mechanics. Likewise, Elizabeth Cuidet and Gerardo Razumney never tired of my translation queries. Friends and colleagues Meredith Klein, Kristen Balmer, Lori Salmeri, Lester Tome, Michele Kadison, Jerry Klein, Jerry Handler, Martin Kläschen, Shari Kornelly, Lisa Jane Hardy, and Sarah Muir gracefully waded through various stages of proposals and drafts, making time when there was none, and offering thoughtful and thought-provoking critiques.

In 2009, tango brought me in touch with Steve, and my life has never been the same.

* * *

I appreciate the generous financial support of Temple University for providing funding for my early fieldwork, and Arcadia University's College of Arts & Sciences for helping to fund follow-up research in 2010. My family provided support in more ways than I can recount here; their generosity and faith made this work possible.

Finally, for reasons that will soon become apparent to the reader, I thank my fellow dancers—a smart, passionate, engaging, and opinionated bunch, indeed. The many conversations I have had on the sidelines and on the dance floor over the past several years have sharpened my observations and enriched my thinking. Thank you to everyone who helped me out along the way.

Prologue

Travels in Tango

Perhaps nothing in the contemporary culturescape is at one and the same time as specific and ubiquitous, as fiercely national and undeniably transnational, as local and global, as the tango.

Marilyn Miller, "Tango in Black and White"

Today, my children are killing you, tango.

Tango: Baile nuestro (Zanada 1988)

In 2000, I had the idea—when I started dancing—to get to know tango in the world. So I took a trip, just me and my guitar, to sing traditional tangos in the *milongas* in Europe and the United States . . . I would search the Web for the *milonga* that night; I'd go and introduce myself: "Hello, I'm Carlos, I'd like to sing for you . . ." I met people who invited me to other places, and just like that, I began to understand the global tango family. There's a network of people who share certain codes—and others not so much—but they're all united through tango. The experience was incredible because I felt at home wherever I went. To arrive in a *milonga* and be welcomed and to meet people right away . . . that helped me understand the global tango phenomenon a bit more.

Carlos Libedinsky, Argentine, composer, Narcotango (electronic tango band)

In the summer of 2004, I took a road trip with a tango friend down the west coast of the United States. From a tango festival in Seattle, we drove to Portland, stopping to dance for two nights in the *milongas* (tango social dances) before heading east to hike and camp. We left Bend, Oregon, about noon one day, with a five-hour ride ahead of us to the northern California campsite next on our itinerary. But somewhere along the way, the idea of driving all the way to San Francisco hit. It was Wednesday, and the Cellspace *milonga* would be starting at 9 p.m. If we drove straight through, we realized, we would make it just in time for a night of dancing. A quick review of our suitcases and laundry bags confirmed, one clean tango outfit each, and we were off. That we had nowhere to spend the night after nine hours of driving and three hours of dancing was the small inconvenience in this serendipitous alignment of time and place. For if you were a young tango dancer on the west coast in 2004, Wednesday was *the* day and Cellspace *the* place. Officially labeled an "alternative *milonga*," Cellspace was reputed to be among the few sites where you could find *tango nuevo*, or "new tango." A vague term at best, *nuevo* conjured images of a youthful crowd, adventurous music, gender-bending, playful dancing. At the heart of the struggle between "old" and "new" in tango, Cellspace was impossibly seductive.

On arrival, we learned that the organizer, an old friend of my travel companion, was out of town that night. No matter, we would simply introduce ourselves as friends, two tango gypsies in need of a warm bed in exchange for a free breakfast, an utterly mundane bargain in this world of traveling dancers. As my friend predicted, it was a cinch. Our host, Martin, offered his place immediately. Before we could even offer to treat him the next morning, he brought us breakfast in bed.

I haven't seen Martin since that morning. All in all, we spent less than twenty-four hours together. If he passed me on the street, I might not recognize him. Yet, seven years later, we are still in touch, occasionally chatting about tango in our respective cities, even sharing our writing and feedback with one another. Where such momentary connections often fade, our shared involvement in this world gave us a foundation that, despite the passage of time and the distance that separates us, has blossomed into something that technology alone seldom sustains.

I don't know whether the tango we were dancing at Cellspace that night was what some might call the "real" tango, a new tango, or something in between. There was certainly a healthy dose of alternative (non-tango) music played, I saw at least one woman leading, the dance floor looked a bit more like an American club than a decades-old Buenos Aires dance hall, and I probably did some moves I would not have done in the arms of older men in Buenos Aires a year earlier. But the principles of the dance that had served me in Argentina—leading and following, entering the music, connecting with my partner—served me in Cellspace.

What I do know is that I caught my first glimpse of Carlos's "global tango family" that night, where connections can be forged through the simple act of sharing a dance. My understanding of this network has only grown since then, through two years in the tango "mecca" of Buenos Aires and several other visits, and countless nights of dancing in Philadelphia, Boston, and a host of other cities across the United States. Like any family, the ties that bind us have evolved, been challenged, and been redefined. As I write today, that night reminds me of the many and varied rewards of this dance that extend far beyond the dance floor, that matter far more, and that will surely outlast debates over style and purity.

Locating Tango

Around any dance form exists a culture—think of those who are intensely involved in ballet, hip-hop, flamenco, or ballroom dancing, for example, whether as performers, students, or audience members. None, however, seem as loaded with possibility and mystique as tango. Nor, at this moment, does any other dance form have tango's global reach.

For one, tango seems accessible. It has humble origins; born in the immigrant slums of Buenos Aires and Montevideo, tango traveled to Europe along networks that included seaports and brothels, and was later revived in Argentina through venues including neighborhood social clubs. While there is a performance element (one that continues to grow), the dance invites and admits people of all ages and levels of skill and fitness. At its most basic, tango's "walk with finesse" is about two ordinary human beings meeting in an embrace. It is not unrealistic for a person in late middle age to decide, "I'm going to learn to tango," and do so, through a large and generous community of teachers and organizers of social dance the world over—and a burgeoning tango tourism industry that brings beginners and experts alike to study in Argentina.

Much of tango music and lyrics evokes loss and nostalgia, and the complicity of the dance is both enactment and antidote to that ache. The allure of tango is not sex, but sexiness. Not passion, but the reflection of passion. The beauty of tango is in the ephemera—the shared moments of the dance, always fading, never to be recaptured exactly the same—and in the possibility that awaits with each new dance. Like sex, the dance is different with every partner, and different with each encounter with that partner. Even those who lack special physical skills or training bring to the embrace their life experience—of hope, loss, passion, and poignancy. Like much of life, the dance is about improvisation within structure. A shared dance can spark feelings of "what if," "what was," and myriad possibilities in between.

Like much of what might look simple at first, however, tango can become an endless quest—for better skills in leading or following, for better moves, more receptivity to one's partners, better interpretation of the music. The lure of tango has been compared to a drug and to therapy, as learners and dancers find themselves quickly immersed in the dance and its local and international culture. Indeed, more than hobby, passion, or even obsession, tango can become a way of life. Tango can also be a powerful form of resistance to the isolation and disconnect of modernity. In an age where virtual often replaces face-to-face communication, tango offers practitioners the chance for physical contact in a safe environment, as well as an alternate space for self-fashioning, where they can construct their identity, engage with others, and build community in real time and space.

Tango is also a business. Worldwide, the business of tango encompasses schools, teachers, musicians, disc jockeys, organizers of festivals and *milongas*, clothing and shoe designers, performers, and theatrical production companies. Estimates put the tango industry at $400 million a year, with $100 million spent in Buenos Aires alone each year. In Argentina, where tourism is among the top industries and tango arguably the country's most famous export, the business includes all facets of hospitality, as tourists come from around the world for "tango tours," of a few days to weeks or even months. For a *porteño/a* (resident of the port city of Buenos Aires) with aspirations to the middle class, a career in some aspect of the sprawling tango trade is viable.[1]

With money and livelihoods at stake, it is no wonder that teachers, performers, and promoters are always looking for the edge that will set them apart from the rest, distinguish them from a stereotype they cannot or will not perpetuate, or lead them to a client or audience that might not have heretofore seen themselves in tango. The image of the middle-aged couple dancing a refined, deeply nuanced tango that reflects their many "hours," as one person put it, not only on the dance floor but in life, appeals to some. The image of the suave (perhaps older) man leading a gorgeous young woman is as much a reality in the *milongas* of Buenos Aires as it is a fantasy. So is the image of the older woman in fishnets and heels dancing the emotions of her life. Some younger dancers, many of whom bring physical training from other dance and movement disciplines, want the excitement of new moves, the inspiration of other music, and the freedom (or practicality or fun) of wearing casual or edgy clothing. Promotional images of professionals may hype sexiness as much as the dance itself.

That a dance and a culture exist inside the embrace of tango is something I understood from my first *milonga*. My understanding of each has only evolved since then, as I have pursued the tango across state and country lines over the past decade, like that night in San Francisco in 2004. It is what I describe here, through my observations as a dancer and an anthropologist. For contemporary tango exposes the complexity of cultural politics in a world where local practices can no longer be neatly separated from global forces, where individual behaviors and desires are shaped in an uneven yet constantly evolving set of relationships. A puzzle in its own right, contemporary tango reflects the labyrinth that is both modern-day life and human nature.

Tango as Dance, Tango as Culture

As a dancer and an anthropologist, I am both inside and alongside this puzzle. Indeed, the issue of *nuevo* emerged from my fascination with heated debates surrounding tango's capacity to grow and change, the general confusion that reigned around the category *nuevo* itself, and the dance's most recent global renaissance, so beautifully evoked in Carlos Libedinsky's words. From what one should feel in the dance, to how much and with whom and in what clothing and to what music one should dance, to who "owns" the dance or who has the right to define its future direction—and more: these are the myriad parts of the puzzle that is contemporary tango.

A dance of sorts in its organization, this book weaves in and around debates stemming from concerns of style and purity—matters of great concern exclusive to the global tango community—with the express goal of connecting tango's moment of great change to larger, more widely important issues. For I believe that Argentine tango is just one of many examples of tensions between old and new apparent across any number of realms, from language to architecture to cuisine to entire cultures or peoples. Primary among these are the weakening relationship between culture and place; the transformation of art, landscape, and experience into commodity and spectacle; shifting attitudes toward gender and sexual identity; the impact of technological innovation on human connection; yearnings for and constructions of "authenticity" and the subsequent tensions between preservation and evolution that underlie the survival of much cultural phenomena. Perhaps these tensions are not new, but the ways in which they play out are, and they reveal much about the world we inhabit today.

Like the tango embrace, the resulting text breathes: it departs from only to extend beyond the local questions of the dance. Or, said in the language of anthropology, my aim is to address macro-level questions through micro-level analysis. In these stories of tango are illuminations of life; that they are revealed through the particular practice of tango does not preclude their applicability outside of this community. In underscoring the connections between tango and life, I suggest that ethnography, with its attention to individual stories within a larger context, is particularly well suited to extrapolating lessons of the human experience, and moreover, to grounding studies of global phenomena by demonstrating the impact of larger structures and forces at the level of individual lives.

For example, the international tango community circulates around and is centered in the larger *porteño* tango scene. Moreover, Buenos Aires and Argentina feature prominently in the global tango imagination. Focusing on recent innovations in tango broadens perspective on the dance in its birthplace beyond narrow or stereotypical portraits. Yet reverence and respect have fueled its preservation and ensured its continuity with the past. By referencing the history and describing the contemporary situation of both the country and its capital, I note the interaction of local and global forces in tango's development, underscoring the ways in which ideas and representations of place continue to inform desires, attitudes, and behaviors. Powerful narratives linking authenticity and place drive global support of tango in its birthplace, yet these are also open to manipulation by local practitioners seeking to make a living in a world where "Argentine-ness" is an asset. Equal parts community and industry, contemporary tango offers a fascinating view into the practical realities of culture in the global economic sphere, and the ways in which it is shaped by and challenges the larger system.

While tango's appeal is arguably compounded by romantic ideas outsiders have about its place of origin, the dance's renaissance and increasing popularity worldwide since the 1980s (even more so since Argentina's economic crisis) have been advanced by inequalities in the global economy and the advantages individuals possess based on where they come from. But this "order" is shifting beneath our feet right now, evidenced not only in financial crises in Europe and the United States since 2007, but also in tango's most recent developments at home. That a *New York Times* article (Mount 2011) encouraged the United States to follow Argentina's example in economic matters, while the "newest" wave of young *porteño tangueros* embrace nationalism, together suggest that when relationships of power are in flux in the global economy, cultural politics evolve as well.

Travels in Tango

In writing this book, my methods were quite straightforward. Over the course of two years in Buenos Aires, I spent a lot of time in tango classes, *milongas*, and *prácticas* (tango practice events); I attended tango festivals, theater and dinner show productions, music concerts, and museums; I conducted research at the National Archives, the National Academy of Tango, and the Porteña Academy of Lunfardo;[2] I monitored Tango-L, an international tango listserv; I spent hours in front of Solo Tango, the cable channel dedicated to tango; I scoured newspapers, magazines, billboards, and building façades for stories, images, ads, and murals; and I interviewed social and professional dancers from Argentina and abroad, *milonga* and *práctica* organizers, tango artists, tango tour organizers, festival organizers, local tango entrepreneurs, and officials from the Ministry of Culture.

In addition to two years spent in Buenos Aires (2005–2007), I also draw on my early tango education in the United States (2002–2005); two brief visits in Buenos Aires, in 2003 and January 2005; my return to the United States (2007–2010); and a follow-up visit to Buenos Aires in June 2010.

Given the fluid nature of tango in Buenos Aires, my multiple exposure is critical to understanding the impact of global attitudes and desires upon the "local" scene in Buenos Aires. Indeed, foreigners feature prominently in my account. Though a fellow anthropologist warned me early on to stay away from the expats—as if the vast number of foreign tourists, visitors, and residents in Buenos Aires could be grouped together and disregarded en masse—the presence of non-Argentines in this book is inevitable. There is no single expat community in Buenos Aires, for the number of foreigners in the city has grown too large to admit an enclave. More importantly, the city's tango scene is increasingly shaped by their presence. As the influx of their bodies and their currency induces growth, their worldviews and desires influence the nature of that growth. So the notion of "staying closer to the source," that I could somehow grasp the authentic tango if I focused my observation and energy solely on Argentines, would be an injustice, a denial of the much more complex, disparate nature of the city's tango scene today.

By spending two years in Buenos Aires, I experienced firsthand the cyclical nature of tango there. Like the rituals and patterns that accompany planting and harvesting in a particular culture, there are seasonal shifts that shape this world—weeks when hordes of tourists descend upon the city, months when the *milongas* empty out and the city's professionals tour Europe, holiday breaks during the Northern Hemisphere's winter, when the "usual suspects" (including many professionals and skilled dancers) return from abroad. A theme I return to in the chapters to come, dancers are influenced by those around them and their perceived hierarchy within the scene, so the experience of dancing tango in Buenos Aires can vary greatly depending on the time of year.[3]

A Disclaimer

It is worth reiterating that my account of contemporary tango is a decidedly personal take on this world. Though I have been schooled to conduct research in the somewhat schizophrenic mode of "participant observer," the reality was altogether murkier given the physical, emotional, and psychological proximity demanded by the practice of tango. Thus, I must acknowledge my intimate involvement in this world, and admit that, like most people, I have certain biases. My gender, my age, my culture, my background: all these influence which people and stories I find interesting and how I interpret and pass them on. This book is not a memoir, but neither is it a comprehensive, objective portrait of tango today (a feat, I would argue, that is both impossible and presumptuous; indeed, I would advise suspicion of those claiming truth in tango).

The same disclaimer applies with regard to those whose voices I include. Their opinions should be viewed as such: necessarily subjective and theoretically open to change. Indeed, if you sat down with any tango dancer on two consecutive days, chances are he or she would respond differently to some of the same questions, especially if they'd danced in between. It is also important to note that I have framed their words. Each interview quote has been approved by the speaker; however, the interpretation, and the piecing together of these often disparate pieces, is ultimately mine.

Though I identify the origins of these voices, I don't believe that they can be neatly separated. Their attitudes and desires reflect the influence of larger norms related to place, but there is nothing static about tango or culture today. In my case, two years in the *porteño* tango community—

where many locals construct their lives around travel abroad and countless foreigners remain throughout the year—left me confused as to the significance of nationality today. That being said, an American passport incurs benefits that an Argentine passport does not, and my time in Buenos Aires did not erase these differences. My intention here is not to elide the position of individuals within the larger global political sphere, where place, citizenship, and nation-state do, in fact, still matter. In situating these voices, rather than try to encapsulate entire cultures in the observations of a handful of people, or suggest that all members of a global community stand on equal footing, I aim to give the reader a sense of the global scope of the tango scene, and to provide fodder for thinking about what happens when people from around the world come together and share ideas and dances.

It would be irresponsible not to acknowledge the advantages I possessed as a young woman in this world. I moved quite freely between the *prácticas* (specifically, those hosted and frequented by young dancers) and the *milongas* of Buenos Aires, and I was assured attention from leaders young and old in both settings. Had I been fifteen or twenty years older, this book would have been something very different. Like sports, dance is a realm that generally celebrates youth. However, Argentine tango stands out in this respect. Where the aging body draws attention for its rarity in American modern dance,[4] for example, tango is considered a respectable activity for people of all ages. While older men have it easier than their female counterparts in this world, nobody bats an eyelash at a grandmother in fishnets and high heels in the *milonga*. I have been asked time and again to reconcile these conflicting statements, and the truth is that I cannot. In tango, I see a world that ultimately favors men and an outlet where mature women may unabashedly revel in their sexuality. What I offer, then, are observations of and meditations on the significance of each.

How can I draw these observations while I remain intimately involved in the world I describe? Because contemporary anthropology has discarded the notion of complete objectivity and allows self-reflection, I am neither at the center nor the absent voice from above, but rather an occasional vehicle through which certain ideas are fleshed out. While I am by no means the first anthropologist to experiment with form, my situation in the community I research and my background and sensibility as a dancer make this particular ethnographic foray quite personal.[5] And thus, this book shifts forms, as often memoir as study.

Moreover, as anthropologist Paul Stoller puts it, the body is the site of "history from below" (1997: xvi). While books and words have much to tell us, there is a wealth of information that lies outside of official records. It is here that we find the stories of those living at the margins, and of the everyday people for whom, or about whom, history rarely speaks. Though tango has made its way into the canons of dance, music, and poetry, its roots lie here, in the bodies of those who had nothing. In this tradition, the body itself is at the center of this book, for tango continues to serve as a refuge for practitioners around the world, who alternately reflect, construct, and challenge the larger culture(s) they are part of in the act of dancing. As I approach this topic through my own bodily encounters in this world, this book is a testament both to the power of the body to house and to create knowledge, and to the importance of physical engagement with places and people as a means of gathering data.[6]

Dancing at "the End of the World"

Like *tango*, the very words *Buenos Aires* and *Argentina* tend to conjure often fantastical images among outsiders—alternately of vast plains and dancing cowboys, European sophistication and white slaves, charismatic first ladies and brutal dictators, exotic butterflies and glacial landscapes that drop off at "the end of the world." Central to the formation of country and capital, ideas about each place have fueled the tango's most recent global renaissance and they have worked to keep its heart centered at home. Moreover, these ideas have been cultivated at home and abroad, shaped and recalculated through Argentine interactions with and gestures toward the world beyond the Latin America it desperately tried to transcend. The struggle between "civilization" and "barbarism," as nineteenth-century liberal reformer Domingo Sarmiento so famously put it, ultimately drove Argentina's development—political, economic, and cultural—around Buenos Aires. The nation's internal glance has long been met with and fueled the *porteño* glance outward, to construct itself (and the larger nation it represented) in the image of Europe and, later, the United States. Also a projection, this external glance belies a conscious effort to be seen and to be recognized as equal by those who coined the terminology and thus drew the lines of these distinctions.

Geographically distant at "the end of the world," culturally familiar for all its European immigrants, yet never fully capable of shaking its indigenous and savage roots, Argentina functions as both mirror and foil. A promising example of the civilizing potential of European modernization, Argentina's attraction lies in its ultimate failings. Alluring in its familiarity, it is an "exotic other" that is easily accessed and consumed, and onto which Westerners may project their anxieties and fears, delighting in and reconfirming the differences at once.

Such gestures and projections occur in today's global tango community, whereas the form itself has been a site of identity struggle since its inception. A music and dance that developed through shocking transgressions of class, racial, ethnic, and gender boundaries, tango's evolution and survival are the fruit of local and global moves in response to these transgressions and to one another over the course of more than a century. Tango's eventual acceptance as a national symbol reflects the Argentine glance inward to define itself, and the *porteño* glance outward for legitimization, while debates over the evolution of tango in Buenos Aires raise questions about where power rests in global cultural networks. Moreover, as Savigliano (2005) points out, the category of "art" can easily disguise the privilege and inequality underlying cultural difference, and hide the exploitative potential of cultural commodification with its universal and transcendent connotations.

Though the word might be trendy these days, globalization is nothing new. But the degree and intensity of global interconnections that mark our modern lives distinguish today from the past. The impact of globalization on culture and its relationship to place has been a minor obsession among anthropologists for some time now (due, in no small part, to the role anthropologists have played in reinforcing the link between the two). The 1986 publication of Clifford and Marcus's *Writing Culture* represents a watershed moment with regard to the problems of this approach.[7] Among other things, the authors and their collaborators raised questions about the role of anthropology in constructing culture, the emphasis on objectivity in a highly subjective discipline, and the problems of studying local phenomena in an era of disappearing boundaries and increasing interconnectedness.

Building upon this interest in the relationship between culture and place, I trace tango in the circulation and intersection of global flows and local practices. Because globalization does not happen outside of preexisting relationships and structures of power, its effects are felt differently by individuals in different parts of the world. At the same time, contemporary culture does not adhere strictly to either geopolitical or Western value distinctions. Simply put, heightened globalization has yielded neither a neat hierarchy of cultures nor a loss of diversity, but rather less stability and greater complexity. The workings of contemporary tango—where power is also negotiated according to notions of culture and authenticity—speak to this situation, while the history of Buenos Aires and Argentina, as well as current shifts in the world economy, together prevent a straightforward mapping of hierarchies within the global tango community. As such, tango is a vehicle par excellence for exploring the intersections between the cultural, the economic, and the political spheres at a time of profound change.

Overview

Is there truly a *new* tango? What exactly is at stake in debates over defining tango? How will dependency on global interest and tango tourism impact the dance over time? Is there a point of saturation at which the city can support no more? Will the "traffic in tango" ultimately de-center the dance through the training and professionalization of ever more foreign practitioners? Does it rightly belong to some more than others? What do such global debates around cultural ownership mean given Argentina's history and today's postcolonial world? In raising such questions about Argentine tango, I aim to advance current debates in cultural politics, both in academia and in the public sphere.

I begin with my own travels in tango, introducing the intricacies of the dance through a tour of the recent past—from lessons with *yanquis* (North Americans) in Philadelphia, to the romance of Buenos Aires' *milongas*, to the explosion of its *práctica* and *tango nuevo* scene. I then offer a brief survey of tango's history, which, together with Argentina's, shed light on more recent developments in the dance. I pursue the contradictory interpretations of *tango nuevo* that I found along my way as dancer and investigator, mapping from its inception more than a century ago the tango's successive metamorphoses under the influence of globalization, fusion, and innovation. Parts of tango's puzzle are the elements of machismo and violence that survive in contemporary tango. Further complicating is commodification, one aspect of the dance's most recent global renaissance, where players round the world now lay claim to the dance, often with contrary motivations. I close with a discussion of recent changes in the dance via another "new" generation of dancers.

Writing about dance exposes the difficulty in reducing to words landscapes of movement and sentiment. However, in doing so as dancer and anthropologist, it is my hope to offer both a detailed exploration of the continued transformations of a beloved cultural tradition and an unflinching look at the complex motivations driving the global pursuit of this partner dance.

Notes on the Text

With the exception of names, Spanish words appear in italics, with definitions at their first appearance; I also include a glossary of Spanish words that appear often throughout the text, as well as some important dance terms. Aside from three noted instances, interviews with Argentines were conducted in Spanish and I provide English translation throughout. All translated text is noted either (τ), signifying my translation from Spanish; or (ε), indicating a response in English from a nonnative speaker of English. I include the country of origin and occupation of everyone I quote, identifying people according to their status at the time of my research.

While *maestro* (master) is often the preferred term, especially when referring to revered tango professionals over a certain age, the term does not have the same connotations in the masculine and the feminine. *Maestra/o* can be translated as "teacher," but Spanish speakers pointed out that the feminine version would be interpreted along the lines of "kindergarten teacher" rather than "master." Lacking the means to address men and women in this role with parity, I refer to all tango instructors and dancers simply as "tango professionals."

Though the practice has been questioned,[8] anthropologists often disguise entire places and populations in order to "do no harm"—to prevent any possible negative repercussions a person's words might one day incur. I struggled with this. Fellow anthropologists advised me to identify professionals whenever possible because of their stature, yet to protect the social dancers whose lives are anything but ordinary. This seemed inherently wrong on so many counts. For one, it seems to perpetuate a stratification I aim to avoid. Moreover, in tango, the line between social and professional is always shifting: your companion on the sidelines today may be teaching tango workshops next month. Most importantly, I felt it was crucial to consider and honor the wishes of those whose stories made this book possible.

For these reasons, I left the decision to those I interviewed. Some preferred that I use a pseudonym, while others were adamant that I use their real names. Those who wished to remain anonymous have been assigned first-name pseudonyms. I also often changed slightly their age, gender, nationality, or occupation, and I occasionally created dual or even multiple identities for one person. I use full names for everyone who asked to be identified.

Likewise, I have generally refrained from disguising tango sites. For one, the tango world and its events are quite public, and to varying degrees, commercial. Moreover, the venues themselves are often in flux; single sites play host to different events according to the day and time, *milongas* and *prácticas* may move location, while their organizers may shift and audiences evolve. As a result, my portraits are not only subjective but decidedly specific to a time and place.

If disguising people and places is a standard practice in anthropology, it also bespeaks a tradition of "othering" that has solidified the distance between anthropologist and community, and which may reinforce relationships of inequality. To "do no harm" assumes a vulnerability that I find presumptuous in the case of today's global tango community. Moreover, this stance precludes confronting our own vulnerabilities as researchers whose work arises from the dangerous (for unknown) territory of human relations. My approach—to write honestly and respectfully of a world I adore and analyze, and to disguise identities in certain instances—is admittedly imperfect, but the best solution I could find.

What I ask of you, the reader, then, is to play along; to open yourself to entry into this world, exposing your own vulnerability in the process, and to allow yourself to be moved by the characters and the stories within. Much like the tango, the experience I propose is ephemeral. Yet it is my hope that the power of these tales of tango will remain with you.

1

There Is No New Tango

In Argentina, everything can change, except the tango.

Astor Piazzolla, quoted in Ramón Pelinski, *El tango nómade* (2000)

There are many groups that have lost interest in making the music that musicologists expect from them. . . . Sometimes it's the anthropologist that gets more upset over the loss of identity than the culture itself. I don't know if it's a good thing or not, but if a people change it's because everything changes.

Carlos Reynoso, quoted in Sandra de la Fuente, "Los estudios culturales son una moda" (2007)

January 2005, El Galpon, Buenos Aires

He wore a fashionable sort of sweatpants, tie-dyed and low in the crotch, a ratty t-shirt, and sneakers. She wore a skimpy top that could pass for a bra, tight black leggings slit up the sides, rolled over to accentuate a long pelvis that swiveled and undulated, turning the most traditional of movements into more of an MTV affair. Low, red lights turned their sawdust- and sweat-coated bodies a beautiful pinkish bronze. The accordion-like cry of the bandoneon*—the signature tango instrument—cut the drone of drum and bass, nudging generic dance sounds toward territory that spoke of tango. His walk was pounding, his stride long and wide; his turns hinted at other dances as a leg trailed out in back attitude (extension with a bent knee) before traveling full circle to settle into a front* sacada *(displacement). The steps were familiar, but their execution, the music shaping them, the space surrounding them, and the bodies enacting them were anything but.*

Just days left to my tango vacation, I decided it was time for a private lesson. We negotiated a time and a price, and then I asked him about his dance. Aware that I was on treacherous ground, careful not to mention the word, I asked what he would call it. His smile turned stiff as he asked what I meant, but before I could respond he cut me off: "Mira *[Look],*" *he said,* *"call it what you want, but for me it's tango—*nada más *[nothing more]." End of discussion, he kissed me on the cheek and bade me goodnight.*

Seduction

Why do dancers in Argentina insist that there is "no such thing as *tango nuevo*?" How is it that outside Argentina, flying limbs, gender-bending, electronica, and bell-bottoms are all cited as evidence—for good or ill—of something new, yet inside Argentina defended as simply part of an evolving tradition known as tango by young *porteños*? What does it mean when these same Argentine dancers reluctantly employ the *nuevo* label to market themselves to foreigners?

In October 2005, I moved from Philadelphia to Buenos Aires to study Argentine tango, to collect stories, and to try to answer these questions. Armed with a couple of suitcases full of essentials, some (in)appropriately skimpy dance clothes, a humble collection of tango shoes that I hoped to expand, and a rather shell-shocked cat, I had a hunch that the glimmerings of growth and change I'd observed in the city's tango scene earlier that year were a sign of something worth looking into. As nearly every young, hip tango dancer I spoke with on that trip was so fond of saying, I wanted to "investigate the tango."[1]

For I had begun to make connections between my graduate studies in anthropology and my tango life. I was fascinated by questions of place. Through my newly trained eyes, I suddenly saw that the link between culture and place—always assumed and therefore unexamined—was indeed rather tenuous. I began to ponder what exactly made our practice in Philadelphia "Argentine," when the events were organized and the dancers, even those from Argentina, trained by North Americans. Aside from distinguishing our tango from its ballroom cousins, American and International tango, I wondered if there were traces of place in the dance. To what extent did tango foster a sense of connection to a distant homeland among the Argentines, most of whom freely admitted they might never have taken it up had they not left home in the first place? And just why was it so important to make the pilgrimage to Buenos Aires, after all? I had studied ballet more than half my life, yet it had never crossed my mind to take that study to Paris or Moscow. Still, less than a year into my study of tango, everyone was asking, "When are you going?" The Argentine men worked the hardest to seal my fate, whispering in my ear between dances, "When you come back, you'll be the best." They are notorious flirts, *los argentinos*; I don't doubt they whispered the same into every other *tanguera*'s (female tango dancer) ear. But the tango is fueled to a certain extent by fantasy, and flattery does much to spark that flame.

Of course, the seeds of that idea had been planted long before. In the summer of 2002, I got a ride from Boston to Philadelphia, where I would soon begin graduate school, from Meredith Klein. She had already been dancing tango for some time and had given me a crash course in tango just two years before this. But my first real *milonga* experience was that Friday night in 2002, when she dragged me to the University City Arts League, a community arts center housed in one of West Philadelphia's stunning old Victorians, and home, since the late 1990s, to a weekly meeting of the area's Argentine tango addicts. I wish I'd had the foresight to record all my impressions, but I simply had no idea what I was getting myself into at the time. You might say I wasn't looking for anything that night. You might also say, to paraphrase one of the cornier lines uttered by Pablo Veron's screen self in *The Tango Lesson,* that "the tango found me" that night.

I'd danced since the age of five, beginning with classical ballet before moving on to jazz and finally settling on modern dance. Later I dabbled in salsa and was even temporarily swept up in the swing craze of the late 1990s. But I was never entirely seduced by partner dance. I found ballroom oddly fascinating from a distance at best. I thrilled in being tossed around in the arms of a capable swing lead but could never dedicate myself to studying the form. Tango was different, though, and right from the start.

Long before imagining this book, I had always loved asking dancers what brought them to tango. Their varied responses reveal the sheer impossibility of indifference to the dance. A *tanguera* friend from Philadelphia confessed she had left a tango stage show horrified: she found the dance grotesque—a series of couples pushing, pulling, and fighting their way across stage. One of my first instructors, on the other hand, knew instantly that it would be big.

An organizer of one of Buenos Aires' *prácticas* told me he'd never really appreciated tango. His was the generation, born between the 1960s and 1980s, that grew up without tango, for whom the word conjured images of ill-fitting wigs, outdated suits, an embarrassing pastime reserved for shouting packs of *abuelos* (literally "grandparents," but more generally the elderly). When Mariano left Argentina at the age of seventeen to study in Europe, he carried one Astor Piazzolla[2] cassette with him. Listening to that music abroad, he told me, he understood tango for the first time. Half a world away, the hyperkinetic reality of the city's famously phallic *obelisco* (obelisk)—rising as if on a fault line, where the twenty-four-hour bookstores, theaters, and neon lights of Avenida Corrientes cut the sixteen lanes of traffic that are Avenida 9 de Julio—appeared before him with the sounds of "Libertango," Piazzolla's tribute to *porteña alegría*, or happiness in the city of Buenos Aires.

More than one dancer cited *The Tango Lesson*, Sally Potter's 1997 semi-autobiographical film that helped push tango dance and music even further into the global spotlight following its renaissance in the late 1980s. In fact, one woman recounted that she stopped the movie halfway through, ran to her computer, Googled "tango" and her city, found a private instructor, and danced seventeen out of the following twenty-one nights in two cities. Whatever the case, the dance seems to inspire an instant sense of attraction or revulsion, leaving little room for ambivalence.

My first encounter with tango was in the summer of 2000, when I saw Meredith perform. She danced with another woman, and although they exchanged lead and follow, Meredith followed more, closing her eyes when she did so. Something about the combination of the embrace and the closed eyes bowled me over. Not the dramatic, sideways-facing, cheek-to-cheek, arms shooting straight forward, staccato, marching dance that has shown up in countless films, this tango was softer. Sensual rather than sexual, the embrace—a hug, really—appeared to breathe. The movements arose in improvisation. Though there was a clear internal logic to it all, it was not rote execution. After years of dancing and watching dance, I felt that I was in the presence of something truly new, a communication free of speech and of sight, taking shape in that space—real or metaphoric, as they were often pegged together at the chest—between two people in that moment. I knew in that instant that I would dance it someday.

My boyfriend at the time thought so, too. Eyes slightly glazed, the faintest hint of drool forming on his lips, he turned to me emphatically, demanding more than suggesting, "You should do that—*with her*." The connection in the global imagination doesn't stray too far, the word *tango* generally conjuring images of sex, passion, and drama. In conversations with the uninitiated, the word tends to inspire a sense of awe, and with men, a renewed attention and interest, a second glance and reassessment, generally beginning with a question along the lines of "Isn't that really, um . . . *passionate*?"[3]

I had this image of Meredith in mind as I entered the Arts League two years later, the unmistakable sound of the *bandoneon* wafting down the stairs and enveloping me on contact. While I don't remember all the events of that first *milonga*, I can state with certainty that sex, passion, and danger were sadly absent from my seduction into tango. What I do recall is being showered with praise for the simple act of stepping back in response to a partner's step forward as I was walked around the room by the host of brave men eager to take me for a "test drive" that night. I remember a sense of fascination at this ritualistic dance cult, far removed from the downtown club strip, hidden among a string of fraternity houses, packs of undergrads streaming past on the sidewalk outside, hanging out of windows, and yelling at passersby.

Most of all, I was struck by the people. I felt immediately embraced by a friendly and mature community of dancers. Practitioners ranged in age from twenty-something all the way up to mid-eighties, and on that first night I met artists, doctors, lawyers, engineers, scientists, and more. The dance seemed to attract a mix of highly educated, middle- and upper-middle-class professionals and students, with a healthy percentage of expatriates, from Argentina and other parts of the world. Looking back, I'm sure I did little more than walk around the room with a bunch of middle-aged men a few times. And yet I was in heaven.

Over the next year, Friday nights were always reserved for tango. While I enrolled in a series of classes during that first year, I was not unlike many followers in that I picked up a lot just *milongueando*—sitting, watching, waiting, and stumbling, walking, and ultimately following in the arms of many a patient leader. Here I learned the tango etiquette of dancing in *tandas*, a musical set of three to four songs of tango, *vals* (waltz), or *milonga* (the generally faster, often happier of the three varieties of tango music), separated by a *cortina*, a splice of non-tango music that signals the end of the *tanda*, allowing couples to part ways and begin again with someone new. After a few blunders, I learned to reserve thanks for the end of the entire *tanda*, rather than after a single dance. (A polite exit strategy, saying "Thank you" after a single song or two but before the *tanda*'s end, is a means of softening the harsh message that you just can't bear to stick it out for three songs with your partner.)

I also grew accustomed to close encounters with men about my father's age, for the scene was not a young one overall. From the entirely asexual practice embrace, where partners stand face-to-face holding elbows, contact reduced to the forearm, I quickly learned to rest my right cheek to my partner's, to wrap my left arm around his neck, resting my right hand about shoulder height in his left, so that my right elbow bent softly at my side, to gently peg my chest to his, my right side slightly apart from my partner, so that our embrace opened into a slight *v*, and to close my eyes, shutting out the noise of the room around me so as to "hear" the lead more clearly. In the six days separating one Friday from the next, I began to crave the feel of a man's arms around me, moving me through space to music from another time and place.

On Saturdays, I occasionally hitched a ride out to the Main Line for a guided *práctica*. On Sundays, I went to a rotating series of *milongas* hosted by different instructors and held in a different location each week. On Wednesdays, I might stop by the *milonga* above a French-Asian fusion restaurant in downtown Philadelphia.

In retrospect it's hard to pinpoint what exactly got me hooked. The positive reinforcement, the excitement of a new social scene, the dance itself: all were potential candidates, but there was something in the *idea* of tango that held me in its grip long before I would execute anything mildly resembling the image of the dance that was in my mind. The tango is famous for its melancholy lyrics, and the sadness in the music spoke to me. I liked the challenge of improvisation and the absence of mirroring movements in the embrace. As one *tanguera* succinctly put it, "If this was a dance about patterns, I wouldn't be here" (Laura Pellegrino, American expat). The inward focus of the dance—where the energy is centered into the couple, as opposed to out into an audience, yet the couple feeds from the presence of other couples on the floor and the watchful eyes of those on the sidelines—appealed to the dancer in me who had grown shy of formal performance.

Tango, Old and New

Less than a year into my study of tango, I enrolled in a Spanish conversation class and made my first trip to Buenos Aires on a two-week tango tour led by my Philadelphia teacher. We stayed at a tango *pensión* (guesthouse) in the heart of San Telmo, one of the city's historic tango districts. Run by a *tanguero*, the *pensión* was one of many such tango residences in the city supported by the year-round influx of foreign dancers. Indeed, the tango experience began within the walls of the *pensión*, where you could rent the practice room for private use, take group classes with the owner, or hone your sense of balance and axis in yoga classes. Extending from our front door, welcome packets and city guides mapped the location of the dance through the different *barrios* (neighborhoods) of the city, highlighting the sites of the most popular *milongas*, *prácticas*, classes, and shoe stores. Even the resident cat, Astor—in honor of Astor Piazzolla—seemed to be in on the game, marking the *pensión* as unmistakably tango territory.

With the help of earplugs and sleep masks, we magically transformed into nocturnal beings, for while *milongas* in Philadelphia close down by 1:00 a.m., their counterparts in Buenos Aires are just getting started at that hour, with dancers arriving about midnight and later, often staying until the sun comes up. Over the next two weeks we hit the *milongas* every night and some afternoons as well, attended group and semiprivate lessons, shopped for tango shoes and clothing, took in a tango *cena* show (dinner show), ogled tango legend Horacio Salgán's hands through binoculars at one of his last concerts before the famed Club del Vino closed its doors, stocked up on tango CDs, and consumed quantities of local beef, wine, and *dulce de leche* that were kept in check thanks to this fierce itinerary of tango consumption.

Though I met dancers my own age, the *milongas* we attended were largely populated by middle-aged and older practitioners, and in these sites the codes of the *milonga* were still in full force. While I was already prepared for the counterclockwise line of dance, the practice of dancing in *tandas*, and the breaks provided by *cortinas*, the ritual theatrics of the *milongas porteñas* were more extensive. A window onto the past, these traditions, firmly grounded in the history of the city, had been carried over decades from one generation of *tangueros* to the next. Here I learned to change shoes in the bathroom, for it was considered in bad taste to do so at the table. I struggled with the subtleties of the *cabeceo*—the invitation to dance initiated by shared eye contact, often across a crowded room. It might include the slightest of nods or the tiniest of twirling gestures with the hand, or even mouthing "*Bailamos?*" (Shall we dance?). I realized that if I didn't start making eyes at these older men, I wasn't going to dance at all. I learned to stand graciously through the first thirty seconds of a song, to stop my awkward fidgeting and glancing round the room if we'd run out of small talk, while my partner took in the first few bars of music—quite likely identifying the orchestra, singer, and year of the recording—before embracing me and beginning the dance. I stopped pulling away and allowed myself to be firmly escorted off the floor after a *tanda* with a man about my grandfather's age, smiling politely as he provided commentary on my abilities to my table companions. I learned that if I shared a table with a man I entered the *milonga* with, I might not receive any invitations to dance, for it would be assumed that we were a couple, that I "belonged" to him.

One of the more striking revelations of my first visit was the number of foreigners dancing tango in Buenos Aires. Not just the ten-day tango tour crowd, many had rearranged their lives to stay a month to a half-year in Buenos Aires; others were racking up frequent flyer miles making the trip multiple times a year; still others had come to Buenos Aires on holiday and never left. I met an airline attendant who'd devised an ingenious setup, scheduling herself on a weekly flight to Buenos Aires so that she could dance year-round in "mecca," as it is often called. While the large foreign community reinforced the idea that place does matter—that there was something to be gained by pursuing the dance in its birthplace that might not be found elsewhere—foreigners and locals alike noted that the trend seemed to be on the rise, presenting a certain threat to the "authenticity" of the tango experience in Buenos Aires. Over the course of twelve days, my most regular dance partners were an Ecuadorian-American law student on semester abroad, an Italian architect by day and tango instructor by night, and (finally) a retired Argentine mechanic. Though my Philadelphia partners reassured me of the return on my investment, insisting that my dance had leaped years in a matter of days, I suspected they'd be a tad disenchanted were I to reveal the nationality of the arms that embraced me each night in Buenos Aires. So I kept that bit of my trip to myself.

Over the next year, I began to hear the term *tango nuevo* tossed around more and more. I traveled from Philadelphia to dance in Providence, Rhode Island, a few times. Home to a thriving community of young *tangueros*, Providence was then considered an enclave for experimentation in the United States. Hosts of dancers from all along the eastern seaboard and beyond regularly made the trek for the monthly all-night *milonga*. Those in the know could spot the occasional carpool of young tango fanatics en route on I-95 north or south one Saturday a month, desperate to dance until the sun came up, just like they do in Buenos Aires. Inside could be observed a sizable crowd of mostly twenty- to forty-something *tangueros*, dancing to music ranging from Osvaldo Pugliese[4] to Astor Piazzolla to Tom Waits.

Here was a space where eager young dancers were pushing the tango beyond its traditional limits. Men and women switched the roles of leader and follower. Couples broke and inverted the embrace, freely importing from other dance forms like swing, salsa, blues, and contact improvisation. And the dress was anything but traditional. Women paired slinky dresses over bell-bottoms, jeans and sneakers abounded, and from tattered cargo pants emerged the conversation-stopping Comme il Faut, the limited-edition stiletto heels that brought tango shoe design into the twenty-first century, mixing colors and patterns previously unheard of on the *milonga* floor. (Before the advent of U.S. resellers, Comme il Faut were the prize souvenir of the *tanguera*'s journey to tango mecca, a sign that she had "accumulated mileage" on Buenos Aires' dance floors, and evidence of her ability directly correlated to the outlandishness of the design.) The event grew so popular that Providence's organizer invested in an old mill building and converted it into a dance hall, complete with futons for overnight guests and her own living quarters with space for visiting tango celebrities and friends.

A tango road trip down the Pacific coast in the summer of 2004—from a tango festival in Seattle to *milongas* in Oregon, San Francisco, and Los Angeles, where I found myself surrounded by hordes of enthusiastic, creative young dancers—solidified my fascination with this growing trend, which seemed to me to be decidedly youth oriented and North American, or at the very least not very Argentine.

And then Meredith, the friend who'd introduced me to tango, essentially changing my life forever, called. She hadn't been to Argentina yet, and she needed to get away. I was her only tango friend blessed with the generous four-week holiday break reserved for university folk . . . Would I join her for a month in Buenos Aires?

To be honest, I wavered at first. I wanted more of what I'd found in Providence and on the Pacific coast. What I'd come to understand as *nuevo* seemed reserved to these isolated pockets of young, eager dancers lucky enough to have cultivated or to be in the midst of a community open to experimentation, and the less lucky "festival brats," forced by their combined passion and unfortunate geographic situations to succumb to a livelihood of chasing the tango.[5] Based on my own trip and the information filtered through *tangueros* "in the know," tango in Buenos Aires remained largely traditional. Or so I thought at the time.

Cromagnon, Underground *Milongas*, and New *Prácticas*

In the end, I relented. Seduced by the romance of the city, the cheap airfare, and the prospect of heat in winter, I found myself back in Buenos Aires in January 2005, this time for a month. On January 3, at an hour that would soon become ungodly for waking but just right for retiring after a night of dancing, we touched down at the airport, the country's deceptively tranquil port of entry, about thirty-five kilometers outside Buenos Aires in the sleepy suburb of Ezeiza. The ride into the city was a pleasant shock to my northern bones; my body was stiff from a sleepless, eleven-hour overnight flight, still in the huddled posture of defense it naturally assumes from Halloween to Memorial Day after a lifetime of New England winters. Within seconds we had rolled the car windows down, our faces screaming for sun, the saturated heat of January in Buenos Aires seeping into every pore, the hour barely 9:00 a.m. Giddy from the exchange rate and the heat, we marveled at the availability of fresh fruit at every corner and feasted on a breakfast of mango and papaya while poring over the *Tango Guide* left by the last guests in our apartment, plotting our strategy for the next month. The fantasy came to a halt, however, when news of the Cromagnon tragedy arrived.

A popular nightclub in the working-class *barrio* of Once, Cromagnon was the site of a devastating fire that claimed the lives of 194 young people on the night of December 30, 2004: the club had lacked sufficient fire exits. In the midst of what is normally the sleepy winter holiday season, the city was reeling. The government's response was to impose a shutdown on all clubs—including the *milongas*—until they had been inspected and confirmed to be up to code. On the very day I'd arrived for a monthlong tango vacation, I found the doors in mecca slammed shut in my face.

Tango-L, the international tango listserv operated out of the United States, became our CNN. Dancers from around the world posted queries on the inspection crackdown and anticipated date of *milonga* reopenings. Some of these were tango tourists who'd saved for months, even years, to travel to the dance's birthplace, others simply enthusiasts who liked to keep up with the latest goings-on in Buenos Aires, manifesting their membership in a global tango community via the Internet. Meanwhile, "authorities" on the situation sent ever-changing reports on which clubs would risk opening their doors, which had been raided by police, and eventually, with news of a handful of large dance halls that lay just outside official city limits, where locals and visitors who shared a desperation to dance might go to get a tango fix.

The posts on Tango-L were not insensitive to the horror of the tragedy. Tango dancers from around the world shared in the Argentines' sadness and outrage, extended their sympathies, and applauded the city's efforts to put safety first. After nearly a month of shutdowns, however, many noted the economic damage suffered by the organizers, waitstaff, and others whose livelihood depended on the city's 80 to 130 weekly *milongas*, while also lamenting their own rotten luck if they happened to have found themselves on a tango tour of Buenos Aires in January 2005.

But the situation wasn't as desperate as a follower of Tango-L might have believed. In the absence of the traditional *milongas*, I was witness to and participant in a makeshift community of dancers—primarily young, both foreign and Argentine—who transformed *prácticas* into informal (read: illegal) *milongas* and hosted private dance parties. *Prácticas* by and large remained open during the *milonga* shutdown. It was here and in classes that we got wind of the parties, or *milongas clandestinas* (underground *milongas*), being held in El Galpon, a cavernous former industrial space in the still-raw outer edges of the *barrio* of Palermo. As more and more *milongas* closed their doors, El Galpon became our haven, its charmless façade concealing a hidden gem that January. At the far end of a treacherous passageway of broken tiles lay the run-down old factory floor that had hosted raves, underground performances, and now *milongas clandestinas*, the ceiling ascending to the heavens, the weak plywood floor permanently covered with dust, the red lights never glowing stronger than dim.

Thick concrete walls blocked out the oppressive January heat but not the ever-present fear that this space too would soon disappear. At the same time, the lack of seating and a musical program free of *tandas* broken by *cortinas*, heavy on electronic and alternative music, combined to create a space that my body recalls as nonstop motion, sweat, and grime.

The videos I shot at El Galpon are a blur of pastels—it being the height of summer—that dissolve as the camera focuses to reveal a room full of scantily clad, sweat-drenched, playful young bodies. Absent is the special mix of order, severity, and reverence that marks the *milonga* floor. The tango face, a serious expression that may range from concentration to trance to bliss, is seen to break into a full smile, laughter, at times even chatter. Dancers in wait sprawl alongside the piles of backpacks, street shoes, and gym mats that line the front end of the space, the bodily connection to the floor inspiring some to stretch out in straddle position, keeping their muscles warm and their hips loose, open, and ready for the next dance. Others on the sidelines demonstrate moves from contemporary dance. On the dance floor, some attempt to integrate contact improvisation into their tango, flipping their partners upside down and the embrace on its head.

All of the things that I associated with *tango nuevo* at the time and that I had heard did not exist in Buenos Aires were there at El Galpon. Women were leading and men were following; there was no identifiable dress code; both sexes unabashedly and verbally invited one another to dance; with no *tandas* or *cortinas*, couples were free to dance as little as a song or two or as much as an hour or two (or three) at a time; the music ranged from traditional tango to Piazzolla to electronic tango to alternative; dancers were expanding upon the vocabulary of traditional tango—opening, breaking, and inverting the embrace, playing with off-axis movement, doing lots of *colgadas* and *volcadas*, introducing concepts and movements borrowed from other dance forms.

And there were hordes of young people. In contrast to what I had seen in August 2003, and to reports I'd received from others since, there appeared to be a growing, thriving community of young Argentine dancers. No longer content to sit and wait for the dance floor to clear at 4:00 a.m., they had slowly been creating their own spaces within which to dance, socialize, and experiment in ways more befitting their ages, desires, schedules, and attitudes than the traditional *milongas*. They called these events *prácticas*.

By no means a novelty in the tango world, *prácticas* are a firmly rooted tradition in tango, known in both lore and current practice. As the number of younger *porteños* dancing tango has increased, however, a new type of *práctica* has emerged. In contrast to practice sessions held in *academias* (tango schools) these new *prácticas* function as alternatives, no longer solely supplements, to the *milongas*, providing a space for both social encounter and tango dancing, where the strict codes of the *milonga* do not reign, for an entirely new set of codes has arisen to take their place. This is not to say that overlap does not exist. Many of these young dancers strip out of jeans and practice sneakers only to dash across town, reverse-Cinderella-style at midnight, trading rags for something a little more formal, while others traverse both worlds with less regard for codes (much to the dismay of many traditionalists). Nor does it mean that there aren't plenty of younger *porteños* and foreigners pursuing an altogether more traditional training. What was evident during this month in January 2005, however, was the opening up of new spaces in the city's tango scene, organized by and catering to younger dancers, where the dance vocabulary, the music, and the codes were undeniably expanding.

When we weren't at El Galpon, we were at El Motivo[6] on Monday nights, Práctica X on Tuesdays, and Tango Moderno on Thursdays, all relatively new *prácticas* hosted by younger dancers. Word spread and we found our way to the private tango parties occasionally held in the Cupula;

named for its spectacular domes and turrets, the building itself was famed among *tangueros* for one apartment that had been rented by dozens of teachers and tour organizers over the years, and another that had been refurbished by an American expat and outfitted with a stunning wood floor just in time for the *milonga* moratorium. And on Saturday nights, it seemed as if every dancer in the city descended upon La Calesita, the edenic outdoor *milonga* that lay in the midst of a large sports club and park in the *barrio* of Belgrano, just beyond the Hipódromo and outer reaches of Palermo.

Despite having one of the least pleasant dance surfaces in the city—a round slab of concrete that wreaked havoc on shoes, knees, backs, and the ability to pivot—La Calesita's surroundings were magical. Once waved (little more than the guard's vague gesture into the darkness ahead) through the formidable stone archway secured by iron gates, with only the faint sounds of the tango to guide you, the *milonga* lay beyond a patchwork of empty lots and grass, in a clearing perfectly enclosed by a circle of trees, a *parilla* (grill), picnic tables, and chairs. Beneath a canopy of green, colored Christmas lights illuminated the dance space, strung from the dried-up fountain at its center, around which dancers circled in counterclockwise rotations, to the trees that marked the *milonga* limits, and beyond which the occasional pair could be observed strolling for a bit more privacy. La Calesita was the biggest party in tango that January. More than the setting, the beauty of this place lay in the depth and diversity of its crowd. With nowhere else to go, the most unlikely of compatriots shared the floor, packing it to the rim from midnight until 5:00 a.m.: young rebels, die-hard old-timers, professionals back from their most recent tours, desperate tourists, even locals for whom the tango was a hobby at best. La Calesita woke me from the makeshift bubble of *prácticas* and parties that had arisen in the absence of the *milongas*, putting me in touch with one of the more wonderful aspects of Argentine tango today: its truly intergenerational character. On our last night, I lingered on past 7:00 a.m., finally succumbing to that uniquely sweet brand of tango exhaustion as the last bits of darkness dissolved with the return of the sun.

The *milonga* moratorium had been in effect nearly three weeks when the police raided Club Villa Malcolm in the early morning hours of Saturday, January 22. At the time home to El Motivo's *práctica*, the club was hosting the displaced Salon Canning *milonga* that Friday. Fed up, dancers responded by "cutting the avenue" in protest. Redirecting traffic, they sang and danced in the streets until 5:00 a.m. That Sunday *La Nación* ran an article dedicating a few lines to the protest (2005). But the main goal of the piece was to "out" the *milongas clandestinas* being held in El Galpon and in the Cupula loft. The owner of El Galpon put an immediate stop to the parties, and I haven't been back to the Cupula since.

On January 28, the day I flew home, the city announced that the *milongas* were free to reopen in accordance with the 1998 law that established tango cultural patrimony.[7] The social clubs, dance halls, *confiterías* and salons housing *milongas* were declared "exceptional." Following registration with the city, they would be exempt from many of the rules regulating dance clubs. But over the next few months, tales of frustration continued to arrive via Tango-L, warning that a handful of *milongas* remained closed. The horror of Cromagnon fresh in the public memory, organizers were careful to adhere to capacity restrictions, leaving crowds of unhappy dancers outside their doors each night. Further, new music requirements were established as part of the *milongas*' exemption. (In one rather bizarre example of strict surveillance of the city's dance clubs, police shut down an afternoon *milonga* when they heard *cumbia* music during a *cortina*. Apparently, the city's finest weren't schooled in the codes of the *milonga*, and had no idea that snippets of non-tango music actually regulated the entire flow of this most *porteño* of dance events.)

Meanwhile, alternative tango spaces were poised for growth. Mere months after El Galpon's closing, Gabriel Glagovsky, one of the forces behind events held in the space, started his own *práctica* in Club Villa Malcolm on Friday nights, with a Wednesday night practice and occasional Saturday party soon to follow. El Motivo and Práctica X continued to grow in popularity. The Tango Moderno *práctica* changed nights and moved to a trendy bar in Palermo Viejo. Tango Soho lasted a year in the charming dance hall of a Palermo Soho restaurant before moving to Villa Malcolm on Thursdays. La Vikinga, an "alternative" *milonga* where *tangueros* could dance to electronic and non-tango music, soon sprang up in the city center, and La Marshall, the increasingly popular *milonga gay*, moved a third time to acquire more space. While certainly not the sole impetus for the growth of this alternative scene, the Cromagnon tragedy undeniably opened a temporary space for less formal, more experimental tango venues. At the same time, a rising community of younger dancers and teachers gained more visibility, and they have since carved out an even larger niche within the *porteño* tango community.

In the short span of less than a month, everything had changed. Or had it?

In discussions with the young *porteño* dancers I met that month, I was surprised to find wide-scale rejection of the term *nuevo*. When asked what they dance, nearly all replied "Tango," and if they were pressed to clarify or if offered "*tango nuevo*," their typical response ran along the lines of "Look, call it what you want, but for me it's tango." While asserting their determination to investigate and expand the dance's possibilities, they remained adamant in defining their practice as tango, situating their dance within a larger historical tradition, where that tradition had been founded and survived based on its very capacity for improvisation, renewal, and change. In fact, most attributed to foreigners this emphasis on terminology and distinction of styles. Yet, despite a philosophical rejection of the *nuevo* label on the one hand, many admitted the term held a certain marketing cachet, and confessed to reluctantly employing it in order to attract foreign students—a necessity for the Argentine seeking to make a living in tango.

And thus arose the impetus for this book: the incongruence of these conversations, my observations of a noteworthy experimental niche in the *porteño* tango scene, and my previous ideas surrounding what *tango nuevo* meant. While many Argentines professed discomfort with the label, dancers from abroad found the term *tango nuevo* a mystery—hard to pin down, different depending on whom one spoke to, where they came from, and whom they admired in the tango world, but an arguable phenomenon, trend, or style nonetheless. Meanwhile, the forces of globalization were leaving an ever-growing imprint on the *porteño* tango community. Tango tourism had already exploded in the wake of the country's 2001 economic crisis and ensuing peso devaluation, which made possible "consumption" of the city at a fraction of its former price.[8] A $100 million per year industry by 2010, tango's exponential growth in Buenos Aires owes much to the jacked-up purchasing power of foreign currencies. At the same time, the growth of tango communities the world over is creating ever-greater opportunities for Argentine professionals to travel and teach abroad. This heightened circulation—and the potential disturbance it posed to long-standing ideas about culture, its relation to place, and just who may lay claim to it—interested me.

So it was that I found myself back in Buenos Aires in October 2005, to "investigate the tango," in all senses of the phrase, and to attempt to piece together the puzzle that *tango* had become.

2

Finding Tango

From the Golden Age to the Twenty-First Century

The relationship between periphery and center is not sufficiently explained by accounts of suffocating Eurocentrism or analyses of defiant colonial resistance. At the very least, they fail to capture the complexity of Argentina's relationship to Europe. . . . Argentina both feeds and feeds off Europe's view of it, and Europe produces and consumes an Argentina that acts as a pivot between the exotic and the familiar.

Amy Kaminsky, *Argentina: Stories for a Nation* (2008)

Es más importante entender que recordar, aunque haya que recordar para entender. [It is more important to understand than to remember, but to understand you must remember.]

Susan Sontag, quoted for *Malvinas: Islas de la memoria*
(2007 exhibit at the Centro Cultural Recoleta) (author's translation)

August 2006, National Archives, Buenos Aires

I arrive early to get a spot in the photo collection, and tell the archivist I'm looking for images of tango. To my surprise, he tells me they don't have much, then asks, "Music or dance?" To my response, "Dance," he brings one small box containing eight envelopes and a set of plastic gloves.

Visiting the National Archives is not unlike sitting at my grandmother's kitchen table, poring over those shots that never made it into the neatly arranged family albums. In each envelope, arranged in no particular order, many void of any identifying details, are the various "tango dance" pictures held by the country that claims tango a national symbol. A good 50 percent are pictures of folklore performances, there are a handful of interesting tango images, and, for reasons I can't explain, the box includes about a dozen shots of ballerinas in the woods. When I finally submit my order form, I ask whether I can pay the twenty peso fee when I pick up my negatives. Payment on delivery is fine, I am assured, but cash is out. While they need the money, he tells me, the Archives cannot accept cash. Instead, I am to reimburse Argentina for the use of images of its national treasure in the form of Bic pens.

In classes and in discussions with professionals, I am to hear time and again that the history of tango is, in many ways, a collection of myths, opinions, and hearsay. Undocumented by its originators and at the mercy of those who wrote history, tango did not fare well. Given its lower-class origins, its scandalous profile, and its fall from grace during the mid-twentieth century, one has to wonder whether the lack of archival material reflects the nation's stance—still unsure—on tango.

Or are the archivists taking a progressive stance? For the tango is a living tradition, not a mere relic from the past to be neatly "preserved." As today's young dancers so eloquently demonstrate in their words and their movements, tango is alive and well. No need to pack it away in a shoebox.

In the dancers' playful experiments, I see the thirst for innovation that drove generation after generation of their forebears—documented on film, some held in private collections, screened for me by more than one tango professional. From El Cachafaz and Calderón, to José and Lita Mendez, Petróleo, Copes and Nieves, el Pibe Palermo and Norma Soto, Virulazo and Elvira—it is not only skill, but difference and novelty that set them apart. At the same time, traditionalist criticisms of today's innovators reflect the history of tango's struggle, across time and space, to be recognized, understood, not left for dead.

A Little History

> Its own extent is the evil from which the Argentine Republic suffers; the desert encompasses it on every side and penetrates its very heart; wastes containing no human dwelling are, generally speaking, the unmistakable boundaries between its several provinces. Immensity is the universal characteristic of the country: the plains, the woods, the rivers, are all immense; and the horizon is always undefined, always lost in haze and delicate vapors that forbid the eye to mark the point in the distant perspective, where the land ends and the sky begins. On the south and on the north are savages ever on the watch, who take advantage of the moonlit nights to fall like packs of hyenas on the herds in their pastures and on the defenseless settlements.
>
> Domingo Faustino Sarmiento, quoted in Nouzeilles and Montaldo, *The Argentina Reader* (2002)

The history of tango is well-covered territory, and the subject of many deft analyses.[1] Still, a precise history is impossible for the simple fact that the form itself and the populations who created it were considered so undesirable by those recording history at the time. Historians and dancers alike note that tango's origins are traced in the scant written and photographic documentation of the time, but also in a certain amount of myth, conjecture, and hearsay. Arguably part of its mystique, such mystery and contesting accounts continue to plague the dance's more recent history, as the chapters to come illuminate. I do indulge in an overview of tango history here, alongside a brief review of Argentine and *porteño* history, in order to situate the reader in what must be acknowledged as occasionally unsettled territory. In tracing contemporary trends within their larger historical context, I aim to locate today's global tango community in relation to its Argentine roots.[2] I also introduce three key factors central to the origins and continued development of the dance and the music, which lie at the heart of current debates surrounding *tango nuevo*: fusion, innovation, and foreign influence.

Tango's history reflects the history of a nation built through an outward glance, and it parallels the ongoing tension between the country and its capital, Buenos Aires, in defining its identity. Sarmiento captures Argentina's struggle to define itself against the encroachment of what he saw as its naturally savage state at a critical point in its history. After Argentine independence from Spain in 1816, a struggle for self-definition played out between the Federalists, who imagined a nation of autonomous provinces, and the Unitarists, who advocated a centralized political system with power concentrated in Buenos Aires. Sarmiento's vivid framing of the country's vastness as its "evil" was the plea of an impassioned Unitarist who saw Argentina's salvation in a civilizing project of European immigration, educational reform, modernization, and capitalist expansion. By the late 1800s the Unitarist vision had begun to take hold in many ways. The country experienced unparalleled economic growth thanks to significant British investment and expanding beef and wheat exports, and it received more than three million immigrants between 1871 and 1914. Though immigration was linked with progress and "whitening," the new arrivals were largely poor laborers from Southern and Eastern Europe, the majority settling in Buenos Aires. Failing Sarmiento's "civilizing" prescription, they laid the groundwork for social transformation and growing class struggle in the capital.

During the late-nineteenth-century wave of industrialization, the port city of Buenos Aires in particular was inundated by European immigrants, *gauchos* (cowboys) migrating from the *pampas* (plains) in search of work, and former African slaves. Buenos Aires was nicknamed "Babilonia" for the dizzying array of peoples who suddenly populated its streets, while the contradictory narratives of the ruling oligarchy and the growing cadre of disenfranchised immigrants shaped turn-of-the-century *porteño* culture. The goals of modernity and progress were reflected, as they were in many emerging Latin American capital cities of the time, in urbanization projects modeled on those of Western European cities. When, in the early 1900s, Argentina became one of the world's wealthiest nations, Buenos Aires was called the "Paris of the South," as sections of the city were razed and remapped to mimic the grand avenues of Haussmann's City of Lights, and high-end European shops sprang up on the central Calle Florida, tantalizing the newly wealthy and upwardly aspiring with the promise of cosmopolitan consumerism.

Meanwhile, the newly arrived underclasses suffered miserable living and working conditions in the other Buenos Aires, those sections of the port city ignored by the "civilizing" mission of modernization but ripe for another import: anarchism. Tango emerged from this mix of displaced lower-class *porteños*, and in its infancy, it was practiced in the *arrabales* (slums located on the outskirts of the city), *conventillos* (tenement houses), and brothels. Scholars have traced the dance to sources as varied as the mazurka, the polka, the Cuban habanera, and the Afro-Argentine *candombe.* Fusion via parody was central to the development of the dance: the city's *compadritos* (hoodlums) lifted and mocked movements of the black "tango," an improvised dance rooted in *candombe* and danced apart, to create the *milonga,* precursor to the tango, an improvisational dance executed in an embrace. Influences in sound are traced to the habanera, the *tango andaluz* (Andalusian tango), and the *payadores'* (cowboy minstrels) *milongas,* the folk songs imported from the *pampas.* Accounts of the tango's musical development reveal a highly improvisational exchange between dancers and musicians on the fringes of late-nineteenth-century Río de la Plata society.

It is important to note that tango emerged through interaction between the cities of Buenos Aires and Montevideo, Uruguay, situated on the opposite shore of the Río de la Plata.[3] Though the dance, its music, and its poetry ultimately flourished to a much greater extent in Buenos Aires, Uruguay can likewise claim the dance, as it did most recently in the application submitted jointly to include tango on the UNESCO List of the Intangible Cultural Heritage of Humanity.

While the word *tango* tends to conjure images of an exclusively heterosexual brand of passion, the dance's early development was largely through male-male partnering. Reflecting the demographics of Buenos Aires at this time, when male immigrants were coming in search of work, often leaving their families behind, this also explains the tango's scandalous profile, for in its early years it was considered unfit for "ladies."[4] Women's contributions to the dance's origins and development are recorded within the context of the brothels, where tango was rumored to be a means for men to compete for women, a scarce commodity in those early years. These accounts of male-male dancing highlight the competitive and improvisational spirit underlying the dance's origins—an important link between old and new. Accounts from dancers and historians alike suggest the survival of this competitive tradition well into the twentieth century, and many of today's young *tangueros* point to the spontaneity and innovation of these early days as evidence of their adherence to the "authentic" spirit of traditional tango in continuing to push the dance's boundaries. Tango music and lyrics in these early years, in the late 1800s into the first decade of the 1900s, were likewise playful, bawdy, and often humorous, a strong contrast to the genre's ultimate identification with the more somber themes of love, loss, nostalgia, and displacement from the era of Carlos Gardel forward.

Like the "savage" expanse that so terrified the country's nineteenth-century reformers, the tango—because of its association with the places of lower-class work and living, "undesirable" populations, dangerous ethnic and racial mixing, and women who exercised power through sexuality—was a source of anxiety for those who would make Buenos Aires an elite global city on a par with London or Paris. This other Buenos Aires—where the underclasses suffered in close quarters, but also in proximity and full view of the luxury of the oligarchy—bred intense political radicalization. Workers' strikes were a frequent occurrence in the first decade of the twentieth century, and the government responded with repressive, anti-immigrant and anti-worker policies and violence.[5] Though Radical Party president Hipólito Yrigoyen introduced important social reforms during his first presidency (1916–1920), his progressive mission was marred by pressure from all sides, including foreign capital interests. Xenophobic, antiunion policies remained intact, while the government continued violently suppressing workers' strikes, culminating in the "Semana Trágica"

("Tragic Week") of January 1919, which left hundreds dead and more injured, and during which police raids on working-class enclaves resulted in a remarkable 50,000 arrests.

Meanwhile, British capital funded railway construction that extended the city's limits. As capitalist expansion facilitated the growth of a fledgling middle class, government policies supported families and home ownership. The policies encouraged working- and middle-class *porteños* to settle in these new suburbs, considered a salve to the ills of *conventillo* culture and part of a larger effort to quell the political radicalism in the working-class enclaves. As second-generation immigrants formed families in the new suburbs, they also formed deeper ties to the city through the *barrios* themselves, thanks to the leisure time afforded by workday reductions. This connection to the land and to the *barrio* would become a central theme in tango lyrics, as well as a means of asserting two contrasting worlds in Buenos Aires: the democratic *barrio* and the decadent *centro* (city center).

An important theme in tango lyrics, the cosmopolitan center was also a critical site, geographically and philosophically, in the tango's development. After it gained popularity in the dance salons and academies of Paris, London, and New York in the early 1900s, the tango became an acceptable symbol of the city, and thus the nation. The appropriation from abroad, especially Paris, fed aspirations of social status. Though Britain was Argentina's largest trading partner at this time, Parisian society represented the height of cultural sophistication. The phrase *riche comme un Argentin* (rich as an Argentine) became popular parlance to label somebody "filthy rich," as newly wealthy, upward-striving Argentines descended upon Paris and modeled themselves after the French. An annual sojourn and schooling in Paris became rituals of cultural distinction and markers of social status among this Latin American nouveau riche. The relationship with Paris was key not only for Argentines but also for the tango, as evidenced in the more than 300 compositions dedicated to the French capital. Legend places initial contact in the port of Marseille, where, in 1906, Argentine sailors are said to have left behind two classic tango scores (and supposedly returned with "white slaves").[6] In any case, the musicians, dancers, and wealthy Argentine males who frequented brothels back home together introduced Paris to the tango shortly thereafter. Admired as a relic of Latin American exoticism, tango took Europe by storm as it was sanitized and codified for the dance-academy circuit. Igniting Parisians' peculiar love for the dance, tango solidified an already important connection between the two cities. That connection would sustain the dance, as well as some of Argentina's citizens, through tough times in the future.

That the tango was accepted by the *porteño* masses who viewed the oligarchy's Eurocentrism with a degree of contempt reveals the strength of their own aspirations: middle- and working-class *porteños* were as upwardly aspiring as was the oligarchy. While many sought to distance themselves from the tango's profile in its early years—immigrant, anarchist, lower class, salacious—its acceptance by the *porteño* elite served as a nationwide stamp of approval, framing the tango itself as upwardly mobile. A cosmopolitan cultural product that reflected a new Argentina, the tango became a medium through which the masses could record and reflect on their own lives. Thus began the *Época de Oro* (Golden Age) of tango, thirty or so years from the 1920s–1950s, during which dance halls and cabarets spread throughout Buenos Aires, *clubes de barrio* (neighborhood social clubs) hosted giant tango parties, tango orchestras flourished, and many of the most enduring musical recordings were made.

As codification—the development of a standardized vocabulary and rules that can be taught in a classroom setting—made the dance both acceptable and a commodity, the evolution of the *tango canción* (tango song) marked the era of *tangos para escuchar* (tangos for listening), which further made the tango respectable for the fact that it was now also a spectator activity. While early instrumentation included guitar, flute, violin, harp, and clarinet, the introduction of the German *bandoneon* was key in solidifying the tango's signature sound. Just as the substitution of *bandoneon* for flute introduced a melancholy element to the music, the playful and bawdy lyrics of the earliest tangos evolved in the hands of lyricist Pascual Contursi around 1914. In contrast to the boastful, first-person celebrations of the *compadrito* common in the earliest tangos, Contursi elaborated stories, used second-person narration, and introduced nostalgia, sentimentality, and the overriding theme of lost love to the tango song.[7]

These evolving tango lyrics spoke to the reality, and the anxieties, of the newly suburbanized working and middle classes. Glorifying the suburban landscape, the innocence of *barrio* life, and the love of the mother figure (alternately the one and only true female or the first in a long line of women who deceive, promising a world that does not exist), their tone was overwhelmingly melancholic, lamenting not only love lost but also, eventually, the disappearing *barrio*. Perhaps more importantly, these lyrics painted a reassuring portrait of gender relations in a city where rapid growth, industrialization, and early feminist movements had upset what still had been assumed to be the natural order of things. Cautionary tales of women who sought to escape domesticity, the simplicity of *barrio* life, or poverty, many tangos spoke of the moral decay of the *centro*, the emptiness of champagne and cabarets, and the shame of being "kept" in a playboy's love nest.[8]

The shift in tango lyrics of this time reflects the ultimate failure of the nation's suburban fantasy. Despite certain gains under his leadership, incomes fell as the cost of living rose during Yrigoyen's first presidency. The male of tango lyrics became a tortured figure. Unable to confront the true source of his dashed dreams (state-sanctioned abandonment of workers and failure of the government's middle-class program), the male character in the new tango songs either blamed conniving, heartless women or wallowed in passive, self-pitying bouts of nostalgia. As Bergero explains, "The nostalgic, deflated men of the tango are conscious of their marginality and failure, for which they blame themselves and/or treacherous women, rather than facing the real cause of their abrupt displacement: the dissymmetry between the enabling narratives that tantalize them and the disappearing realities of everyday life" (2008: 289).

Indeed, the working classes suffered during the 1920s, through a combination of factors, including cyclical unemployment crises, leading up to the 1929 global depression and the first of what would become a series of coups. Uriburu's 1930 coup initiated a return to conservative power, and it began the period now known as the *decada de infame* (decade of infamy), during which workers' unions and conditions in the *barrios* and for the working classes further declined.

Against this backdrop, tango temporarily declined. Its revival in the early 1930s has been attributed, in part, to the timely and politicized lyrics of Enrique Santos Discépolo, whose "Yira, Yira" (1930) and "Cambalache" (1935) famously recounted the bitter disillusion, impoverishment, and conservative manipulation of the system that marked the time. But tango would ultimately thrive by the late 1930s; propped up by the local film industry and supported by the isolationist years of World War II, it became a dance and music of the masses, reaching its peak during the early years of Juan Domingo Perón's presidency, a time of renewed prosperity for the nation. Alongside the *tango canción*, tango music evolved to accommodate its growing popularity as dance, notably in the rhythmic compositions of Juan D'Arienzo, Rodolfo Biagi, and Angel D'Agostino, and in the case of Carlos DiSarli, the striking integration of melody and rhythm. By the 1940s, athletic clubs were contracting ensembles of fourteen musicians and turning soccer fields and basketball courts into giant dance parties, while downtown theaters removed seating to make way for tango dance contests, advertisements for tango dance parties filled local newspapers, and tango orchestras were booked a year in advance.

A combination of factors contributed to the tango's decline beginning in the late 1950s, coinciding with a period of growing political, economic, and social turmoil that culminated in the horrific *proceso* (El Proceso de Reorganización Nacional, the National Reorganization Process) of the military dictatorship that ruled from 1976 to 1983, having seized power from Perón's widow Isabelita in a March 1976 coup.[9] Some contend that Perón's 1949 decree that Argentine music constitute 50 percent of the music played on the radio positioned the subsequent rise of Argentine folk music at the expense of tango. Growing numbers of ethnic minorities were migrating from the interior of the country to Buenos Aires at this time, prompted by Perónist policies of inclusion and social welfare, and this new urban class preferred folk to tango, the music of racist, anti-Perónist, middle- and upper-class *porteños*. Compounding these demographic, political, and cultural shifts, the tango's emphasis on social justice and poverty—an important theme alongside that of nostalgia and lost love—was increasingly at odds with the improved living conditions enjoyed by lower-class *porteños* under Perónism.[10]

Meanwhile, other Latin rhythms like bolero, rumba, and samba were gaining popularity, and American rock 'n' roll was exploding on Argentine radio waves, on television, and in film. Both trends further fed growing perceptions of tango as old-fashioned, kitsch, depressive, and maudlin. Responding to this shift, RCA is said to have destroyed a warehouse full of original tango recordings to make rehearsal and storage space for more lucrative pop endeavors in the 1960s. Recalling the latter years of tango's decline, artist Jorge Garnica notes that by the 1970s, young *porteño* artists and scholars were hosting anti-tango conferences that attacked the genre's "exaltation of pain," and arguing for art forms that more appropriately reflected their modern lives. All of this occurred against a backdrop of economic decline and, from Perón's overthrow in 1955, increasing political unrest. In particular, the collapse of post–World War II European markets for Argentine agricultural exports fed Perónist exploitation of the very working class Perón had risen upon, which only facilitated his ouster amid a crumbling economy and ever-declining living standards (Harnan 2002).

The 1950s saw the close of many of the cafés, dance halls, and salons that had offered one orchestra after another on a daily basis while, strapped for cash, the neighborhood clubs scaled down or eliminated the dance parties that had once filled soccer fields. As the social landscape changed, tango music changed along with it. This was as much a response to the larger economic climate as to the availability of recorded music—especially the treasured recordings of the 1940s, composed with dancers in mind—and the affordability of sound systems. The *orquestas típicas*—quintessential Golden Era tango bands of ten to fourteen musicians—were replaced by trios, sextets, and octets. Such composers as Horacio Salgán and Atilio Stampone marked the arrival of the tango vanguard, while singers, among them "El Polaco" Roberto Goyeneche, Julio Sosa, and Edmundo Rivero, changed the nature of the tango song, their interpretations crafted with listeners rather than dancers in mind.[11]

By far the most important figure of the avant-garde movement was Astor Piazzolla, who revolutionized tango music in a prolific career that spanned more than fifty years. A classically trained musician who first picked up the *bandoneon* at the age of eight, Piazzolla was famous for creating complex compositions rejected as "undanceable" by traditionalists, for bringing the tango into contact with other music, and for importing ideas and instrumentation from other genres into the tango.[12] Largely responsible for keeping the tango alive among international audiences, Piazzolla's music inspired rancorous debate at home, where the most common criticism, "*Eso **no** es tango*" (That is *not* tango), can still be heard today. Decades before the most recent renaissance of tango dance, Piazzolla coined the term *tango nuevo* to refer to the music of his newly assembled quintet back in 1960. His famous lament, "in Argentina, everything can change except tango," is interesting for its insufficient scope today, for resistance to change knows no boundaries in the global tango community.

From Perón's ouster in 1955, Argentina entered a period of political and economic unrest marked by cyclical recessions and recoveries, inflation, under- and unemployment, and a decline in the standard of living that had long supported claims to Argentine exceptionalism in Latin America. Political instability intensified with the repressive era of the "Argentine Revolution," initiated with the 1966 coup led by General Juan Carlos Onganía and followed by two internal coups before culminating in a return to Perónism and, following two incredibly brief interim presidencies, Juan Domingo Perón's reelection in 1973. A short reprieve greeted the Argentine populace in 1973, as wheat prices soared, inflation fell, and fiscal growth doubled in comparison to preceding years. But Perón had staked his comeback on politically shaky ground. Playing his left- and right-wing supporters against one another, he ultimately cracked down on leftist militants while turning a blind eye to violence carried out by a covert right-wing operation with ties to the police. When Perón suffered a heart attack and died in office in July 1974, his widow Isabelita assumed the presidency, and the country quickly stumbled into chaos. As Argentina was ravaged by violence, with inflation at over 300 percent by 1976, the junta seized power under the guise of restoring order to the country, by waging war against its own citizens in order to rid Argentina of its "subversive" elements.

During the reign of the junta, from 1976 to 1983, tango as dance further declined. Government policies, including curfews and at one point the prohibition of meetings of more than three people, sent the dance largely underground. At the same time, there are testaments that the "true *milongueros*" (men who live for the *milongas*)[13] never stopped dancing and that while the events were scaled down and evolved in format, there were *milongas* during the 1960s and 1970s.[14] The dance was also kept alive by a handful of professionals who got their foundation in the *milongas* of the 1950s and 1960s and who found work abroad, in Buenos Aires' few *casas de tango* (tourist show houses), on the occasional television program, and in the *tanguerías* (café concert and tango bars) that arose in the 1970s. This was the era of Juan Carlos Copes and María Nieves's "tango ballet" productions. International star of stage and screen and global ambassador of tango, with Nieves, Copes brought tango to American audiences on Broadway and the *Ed Sullivan Show* in the late 1950s and early 1960s. On local television programs and in the *tanguerías* of the 1970s, Copes and Nieves were among the few professional dancers who struggled against popular perception to secure the tango's place in the *porteño* culturescape.

One of the great teacher-choreographers, Antonio Todaro, who is credited with teaching many of the star stage performers of the 1980s and early 1990s, ran a tango school together with Raul Bravo for seventeen years in the 1960s and 1970s. In an interview, Bravo attests to the suffering he endured as a tango teacher, an occupation that was frowned upon by society and official authorities alike. He notes that much learning went on in the context of *prácticas*, and that from the 1940s through the 1980s, tango professionals who taught at academies were not respected (Ueki 2009). While several of today's renowned professionals studied tango with Rodolfo Dinzel at the National School of Dance in the early 1980s, Dinzel himself told me that there were few professional couples in Buenos Aires in the late 1970s, and that there was "nowhere to study." He also claimed to be an anomaly as a young man in the *milongas* in the late 1960s, when the tango was considered a shady activity, and the youngest dancers were in their sixties.

From this tangled web of accounts, it is clear that tango as social dance largely fell out of fashion in Buenos Aires from the 1960s; this is supported by conversations with young adult and middle-aged Argentines who considered themselves part of the "lost generation" of tango. While it never fully disappeared, it was kept alive as social dance by a small number of mostly older, working-class diehards. It was not until the country's return to democracy in 1983 that the dance truly began to reclaim a more prominent place at home, and through a series of events in Argentina and elsewhere, it entered a global renaissance that has continued without stop.

Most accounts of tango's reemergence underscore the role of internationally touring stage shows in reviving the dance, echoing tango's earlier rebirth at home following success abroad. According to this view, once again, external acclaim made the dance legitimate, suggesting that Argentina still looked outward for cultural legitimacy. *Tango Argentino*, which premiered in Paris in 1983, and featured professional couples including Copes and Nieves, Nélida and Nelson, Carlos and María Rivarola, and revered *milongueros* Virulazo and Elvira, was the first of many such stage shows produced with the express purpose of reintroducing international audiences to the tango. Spectacularly packaged programs of tango music and dance that present the movement vocabulary, clothing, sentiment, and lyrics as iconic representations of Argentina's history, these shows continue to play a large part in reinforcing the idea that an "authentic" version of tango can be tied to a particular place. It was off stage, however, that cast members sparked the growth of tango communities, in the post-show classes, demonstrations, and workshops offered in each city and town they stopped in, from New York to Paris to Tokyo.

But tango had been alive and well in Paris long before *Tango Argentino*, evidence of the particular bond between France and Argentina, and of the importance of external influence in tango's history. After World War II, Argentina was again flush with cash, and the country supplied much-needed food and credit to war-torn France, a favor that Paris rewarded by naming both a street and a subway station for the nation. While the end of Perónism in 1955 marked a period of profound transition for both the tango and Argentina, the music and dance flourished in Paris, where the innovation that incited rancorous debate at home was readily embraced.

In Paris, Astor Piazzolla, on scholarship and desperate to become a classical composer, was, fortunately, persuaded by his famed teacher, Nadia Boulanger, of his true gift. Inspired by the city and encouraged by the Parisians' taste for innovation, Piazzolla composed and recorded a tango disc with a string orchestra that made him famous in Europe. Though he left Paris in 1955, this formational period of experience and achievement truly marked a "before" and "after" in tango music and solidified Piazzolla's commitment to "new" tango music. In his wake, such artists as Susana Rinaldi, Cuarteto Cedrón, Juan Carlos Carceres, Juan José Mosalini, and others formed an important community of Argentine exiles and Europeans who kept the tango alive, and in Piazzolla's tradition, moving forward in Paris. A haven for Argentines during the repressive years of the brutal military dictatorship that ruled from 1976 to 1983, Paris received many who fled the country whose identity had long been constructed around its European immigrants.[15] In the Coupole dance hall, in the political lyrics of Cuarteto Cedrón, in the *tanguería* Trottoirs de Buenos Aires (named for "Veredas de Buenos Aires," the tango penned by longtime exile Julio Cortázar), tango was alive in Paris, and it became a medium through which Argentine refugees could reflect on their identity and the condition of living yet another exile.[16]

Although the story is a lesser-known tale, tango was undergoing a parallel rebirth at home. After Argentina's return to democracy in 1983, the government created the Programa Cultural en Barrios (Neighborhood Cultural Program) in 1984, with the goal of encouraging *porteños* to reclaim public space following years of repression, fear, and devastation. The program breathed new life into Buenos Aires' crumbled social landscape by creating a network of neighborhood cultural centers where residents had access to free classes, from drawing to photography, music, and tango. In the headquarters, located in the heart of Buenos Aires' theater district at the Centro Cultural San Martín, future "*nuevo* father figure" Gustavo Naveira taught his first tango classes with his then wife and dance partner, Olga Besio.

Having only begun dancing with a university club in 1981, Naveira confessed he'd felt terrified at the prospect of teaching. Except for the classes he'd taken with Rodolfo Dinzel, one of the only professionals teaching tango at that time, at the National School of Dance, there had been almost nowhere to practice and dance tango socially. The *milongas* as they are today did not exist. By the end of the Golden Era, the few clubs that did offer *bailes con orquesta* (dances with an orchestra) featured tango only along with jazz and varied other music; tango dancing was not the centerpiece of these events as it had once been. During those early years of tango's revival at home, Naveira and his friends went to *peñas*, folkloric music and dance parties, just to be able to dance the ten or fifteen minutes of tango that was the customary break in the evening.

As it turned out, Naveira's teaching debut was well timed, benefiting from what Daniel Rodhegiero called "a general need to participate" with the return of democracy (Wikler-Luker 2007). The classes were a huge success. Drawing crowds of 200 or more, Naveira and Besio were often forced to turn people away at the door. Initially a four-week trial, the San Martín gig turned into a five-year engagement. Soon, Naveira and Besio were teaching and performing all over the city, and Naveira left his studies in economics to dedicate himself full-time to the tango.

At the same time, the fledgling neighborhood centers began to offer tango classes as well. And it was then that the *milongueros* resurfaced (or, as some have argued, became visible again). Of the men who'd been raised on the tango, many hadn't danced it in more than twenty years. Some became instructors in these neighborhood classrooms; others helped secure the dance's comeback by supporting the *milongas* that slowly started again in *clubes de barrio*, dance halls, and cafés. Just as the neighborhood centers piqued renewed interest by seizing upon a collective desire "to do," they also had a hand in relegitimizing the tango, for the very fact that it was being presented in a classroom setting.

It was in these local sites, I was to hear from many, that the tango awoke from its nearly thirty-year slumber. While *Tango Argentino* may have set the stage for a global renaissance, it would have no center, no soul, they argued, were it not for the revival of the dance as social encounter in its birthplace. So it is that many Argentines proudly assert their hand in the tango's comeback, resisting the well-worn narrative of the country's outward glance, instead staking full claim to one of the few remaining resources left after the 2001 economic crisis.

On the Rectification of the Names

After my interview with Gustavo Naveira, a friend directed me to the writings of Carlos Alberto Estévez, or "Petróleo," a dancer who gained fame in the 1940s. Nicknamed for his devotion to a cheap, dark wine dubbed *petróleo* (gasoline) in *lunfardo*, Estévez was a bank clerk by day and dancer by night who chronicled the changes taking place in the dance at that time. At the height of the Época de Oro, he noted an explosion in formalized dance instruction, accompanied by a period of remarkable choreographic innovation, where old steps were left behind, replaced with the new figures and postures that "reign up to the present day": [17]

> The Tango Academies begin to proliferate in neighborhood clubs: "Rosas de Abril," "Nelson," "Federal," "Papelera," etc., etc., and "*el tango nuevo*" begins to grow. . . . The tango dance enters an evolutionary phase, it changes, it is the beginning of a period of great choreographic advancement; those dance glories of yore are forgotten, for now there are others with the goods to take their place. . . . They were Academies of men, the seeds of future dancers, where all who shared a passion for the dance came, and a feeling of progress and innovation hung in the air, for the simple fact that they rendered yesterday's movements old today. (τ)
>
> Quoted in Angió (date unknown)

Also dubbed "El Bailarín Imposible" ("The Impossible Dancer"), Petróleo formed part of the Club Nelson Men, a group of twenty-three male dancers who met regularly to practice, their goal being innovation and their inspiration coming from all manner of sources, from Andalusian zapateo to ballet and lindy hop. Cited by one dancer as the breeding ground for the *fantasía* style of tango[18] that includes low lifts and jumps, Club Nelson evokes the playful carousing that marked El Galpon when I visited Buenos Aires decades later.

If a new tango had in fact already emerged—in the dance more than half a century ago with Petróleo's generation, and in the music with Piazzolla as early as 1960—how much weight could the term hold in describing contemporary trends in the dance? Many *tangueras/os* argue that the changes the term denotes are no longer so new at all. In that case, perhaps post-*nuevo* would be a better name. But this brings up the question of which *nuevo* the "post" is referencing, and the usefulness of the term *new* to describe a moment or a feeling within a tradition still very much alive, and therefore inevitably, though certainly not quietly or necessarily easily, evolving.

Browsing the *New York Times* one day, I came across a reference to Confucius's thoughts on "the rectification of the names." Confucius believed that humanity's problems lay in an attitude of carelessness toward words and their meanings. To repair the social order, he argued, we must begin by reuniting words with their proper significance (Pollan 2007). Over the course of two years in Buenos Aires, I set myself this task with regard to *nuevo*. In the end, I found that the answer lay beyond the data itself. Rather, it emerged over time, with the perspective I gained through distance and experience, a decent education in the history of the dance, and the eventual knowledge that people are motivated by larger circumstances to present themselves and their opinions in particular ways. (By virtue of their status, for instance, tango professionals have much at stake here.) Most importantly, my tango investigation pointed to a confluence of factors that have combined over the past thirty years to keep the dance alive, where the familiar themes of fusion, innovation, and foreign influence appear anew.

"A Clown" Makes Good: From Cochabamba to a Tango Alphabet

> Recently, the term *tango nuevo* has been used to describe a style of dance that's a bit more free, with bigger steps, that isn't always on the floor, that allows another type of movement, that allows an exchange of lead and follow. . . . But this isn't a new tango, because we were doing that fifteen years ago with Gustavo [Naveira] in Cochabamba. And most of the people who teach this passed through Cochabamba at one time or another. So, it's nothing new. I think people began calling it *tango nuevo* because they couldn't come up with a better way to say that while there are certain differences, in reality, it still has much in common with traditional tango. (τ)
>
> Olga Besio, Argentine, tango professional

In an interview with a young *porteño*, he described the initial disdain of many old-guard dancers toward Naveira in his early years, the late 1980s and early 1990s. "*Es un payaso!*" (He's a clown) they would yell in the milongas. Naveira himself admits to being one of the only twenty or so *pibes* (kids) in the tango scene back then. Fabian Salas was another, and they soon developed a close friendship based on what Naveira calls an "incredible affinity" in the way they understood the dance. Moreover, Naveira told me, there was plenty they didn't understand. They were young, restless, and hungry. They wanted to know the tango inside and out, to master the steps that stumped them, to try out new ideas, to get at a sort of "tango common practices," to deconstruct and build the dance anew. Their shared passion resulted in the now-famed Cochabamba "investigation" group of the mid- to late 1990s.

Naveira was already a renowned tango instructor in Buenos Aires. His weekly *práctica* was considered one of two main gathering points for many of the serious dancers at the time. (The other was with Mingo Pugliese, among the youngest dancers to have participated in the Club Nelson sessions of the 1940s.) Through the investigation group, a constantly rotating research lab that many of today's star teachers once passed through, a new way of thinking about and teaching the tango developed. Not surprisingly, accounts from the dancers associated with the group vary in the details of its composition, its timing, and the contributions of different attendees. But in our conversations, all concurred on the results: rather than a new style of tango, or even new steps, what Naveira and Salas achieved with the help of the other dancers who passed through their group was a new understanding of the physical mechanics of the dance.

In deconstruction and construction, by the mid-1990s they rejected teaching through a prearranged collection of steps; instead, they broke down the larger figures or patterns to explain the dance through its simplest elements: front, side, and back steps. Based on the system developed earlier by Rodolfo Dinzel and described in his 1997 book *El Tango: Una Danza*, every movement of either the leader or the follower is some version of a front, side, or back step. The steps are executed in either a parallel system (leader and follower step together with the opposite foot) or crossed system (stepping with the same foot), the movements of each dancer framed as a constant rotating around the other. The magnitude of this conceptual overhaul is striking for its implications in the classroom, at the level of innovation, and in practice.

The change in instruction was revolutionary. Demonstration and reproduction of sequences, collections of steps that together generally range from one to a few eight-count phrases of music, remains one of the most common teaching techniques. Many students are introduced to the tango via the "eight-count basic," a figure that takes the couple through a box shape on the floor in one eight-count phrase of music. Interestingly, the proliferation of this standard entrée into the dance has been traced to the post-dictatorship stage show (specifically, *Tango Argentino*, the show that wowed Parisian audiences in 1983, and the many internationally touring stage productions of tango music and dance that have come in its wake), whose cast members sought an efficient means of transmitting some sense of the dance to foreigners. It has been derided by many older Argentine dancers as "academic," a classroom construction with little foundation in the dance itself. On the other hand, teachers who utilize the basic step argue that it provides an easy map for beginning dancers, and a logical framework for building one's dance, for all future steps can be explained as emerging from some part of the basic. They argue that while Naveira's deconstruction opens the door for creativity, such freedom is useful only when it can be exercised within a larger context, the structure of traditional tango, which begins from this basic step. Oftentimes, students are taught the two roles of the sequence as distinct choreographies: leader and follower stand on separate sides of the room and learn their steps outside the embrace. When leader and follower come together, they incorporate the pattern. Although they may be able to reproduce the steps, they haven't necessarily learned to transmit (lead) or interpret (follow) them. In many cases, they have learned to dance alone while in someone else's arms.

A certain amount of choreographic incorporation is essential. Without an agreed-upon vocabulary, practitioners would not be able to share a dance. Moreover, executing a step or sequence on one's own allows the dancer to feel the movement, something that does not always happen immediately in the embrace, especially for beginner dancers. Having a figure to execute also teaches dancers to move—to be responsible for themselves, and especially as follower not to expect the leader to push one through space.

However, teaching through replication of a pattern sidesteps the improvisational core of tango. Naveira and Salas's deconstruction reveals the building blocks of larger patterns. Several young dancers who had first studied with other instructors before studying with Naveira described their confusion and frustration at the choreographic approach:

> When I started out, my *maestro* would show us a sequence, a mini-choreography. It took me so long to figure out that I was supposed to improvise. I didn't know in the beginning because nobody told me. If you want to understand the dance, in my opinion that's the worst way to teach—with sequences. Especially with a beginner. They need to know the rules of the dance, and from there they can create, they're free—they're not prisoners of the tango. (τ)
>
> Pablo Inza, Argentine, tango professional

The "rules," as Inza calls them, are the building blocks: the front, side, and back steps. With sequences broken down to their smallest units of meaning, students are no longer limited to replication; they are equipped with the tools to understand, even dissect, patterns and to create their own. Luciana Valle, a participant at Cochabamba and cofounder of the popular, female-run *práctica* and academy El Motivo, described this as a shift from teaching "words" to teaching "the alphabet":

> Before we used to speak by words; now we teach the alphabet and you do your own words. Before people used to dance by steps—this is a turn, this is an *ocho* . . . but if you wanted to do something inside the turn you couldn't because you only knew the whole pattern, like with a word. . . . From the point of view of teaching, there's nothing like teaching the people to create their own steps. If you teach the structure of the dance, you give them the power. If you teach them a step, they always depend on you because they need you for a new step. (τ)

As noted above, this deconstruction ushered in an era of unparalleled invention. Federico, an Argentine dancer who participated in the investigation group in the late 1990s, describes how the dancers searched for common practices in order to "open their minds." Abstaining from certain tendencies, he said, they uncovered new solutions to familiar problems: "We discovered that the turn is really organic and the natural thing to do when you're learning, and we were always creating with the same formula. So we stopped turning. We stopped turning in order to focus on new things" (ε). Federico suggested that the sheer quantity of innovation may have led to the term *nuevo*. Once the fruit of inspiration, new sequences were now the product of a seemingly endless multiplication of possible combinations, resulting in a seemingly infinite supply of novel movement compositions, leaving traditionalists befuddled:

> Seven years ago, tango dancers made one step a month if they were really creative. Before that creating tango steps was all about inspiration. [Antonio] Todaro[19] had a lot of inspiration and imagination and creativity, but now we have this tool. And I think many people call it "*nuevo tango*" because they couldn't understand how all those steps just appeared. And many people didn't have the ability to recognize it as tango, they didn't realize it was the same thing that they were looking at. (ε)

From innovation that suggested an inexhaustible supply of step combinations came sophistication. Simplifying and standardizing tango pedagogy thus facilitated the development and sophistication of the dance in a remarkably short period of time. The new approach quickly produced autonomous students who were able to improvise, play, and introduce their own ideas into the dance—to an extent that raised eyebrows among traditionalists.

3

What's So New about *Tango Nuevo*?

To talk of authenticity has invariably involved referring to tradition as an element of closure and conservation, as though peoples and cultures existed outside the languages of time. It is to capture them with the anthropological gaze, where they are kept in isolation and at "critical distance" as though they do not experience movement, transformation.

Iain Chambers, *Migrancy, Culture, Identity* (1994)

Defining *Nuevo*

Now when I see neotango, I don't really agree with it. A lot of technique, acrobatics . . . but where is the feeling? (τ)

Juan Carlos Copes, Argentine, tango professional

Nuevo means to me that I'm on my own axis, and nothing more really.

Ginger, American expat, chef

Tango nuevo is the theoretical understanding. Style is a different thing. I don't think *tango nuevo* is a style.

Sarah Bonnar, Australia, tango professional

I think that *tango nuevo* is something commercial—it's marketing. And it's a title that originated abroad. (τ)

Karina Colmeiro, Argentine, tango professional

So-called changes of direction, an open embrace with a shared axis, a different connection between the couple and more flexibility in combining the steps of traditional tango, together create a dance that both looks and feels different. (τ)

Patricia Lamberti, Argentine, tango professional and former co-director of Academia de Estilos de Tango Argentino

If you look at the history of tango, new things appear all the time . . . a new way of dancing, the frame of the embrace, how you hold the woman—so many new things, and they were always trends. (τ)

Rodolfo Dinzel, Argentine, tango professional

Now after Naveira, we have a language, a vocabulary, and that was a revolution for the dance. . . . It was about research in the probability of tango as a dance. (ε)

Federico, Argentine, tango professional

For me, *tango nuevo* is a label for selling something. . . . It suggests that what is old isn't good, because we're always looking for something new. And, really, in my opinion, the term says nothing. . . . It's as if *tango nuevo* doesn't even exist. (τ)

Dana Frígoli, Argentine, tango professional and co-director, DNI Tango School

It's more open, more fluid and more . . . aerobic. You need to have a lot of energy; it's a younger person's tango, that's constantly developing.

Nancy, American expat, actress

I only know that people associate an open embrace dance with it. I never use the term *nuevo* tango because I think there's a kind of misunderstanding. . . . Maybe for me it would mean by flexibilizing the embrace, you open up more possibilities in terms of moves, nothing more. (ε)

Matthias Kroug, German expat, scientist

There are lots of jumps, lots of gymnastics in *tango nuevo*—*los chicos* [the kids] are lucky to be young and they dance a tango with lots of jumps. (τ)

Roberto Dentone (Argentine), *milonguero* / tango professional

It's kind of what's evolved from the dance. . . . In its application I think it's lost an essential quality that is tango.

Naomi, American, tango professional

No one called what he [Naveira] was doing "new tango" at that time and I imagine he wouldn't call it that, either. To me, he developed new codes and a new structure to an already-existing vocabulary. It was kind of revolutionary in a way, and then gradually, people took off with it.

Brooke Burdett, American expat, tango professional

I think the act of naming it had more to do with the appearance of electronic tango orchestras. They haven't been around that long yet. As far as what it refers to in the dance, it's not very new at all. (τ)

Olga Besio, Argentine, tango professional

It's a catch phrase. It's an easy way to describe an evolutionary process. . . . The minute you label it, it ossifies it in a sense—it freezes it in time. And already we're out of whatever nuevo tango is, we're into something else.

Michele Kadison, American expat, choreographer and writer

> I think the big difference between *tango nuevo* and whatever you want to call the other tango is that it's really not improvised and there's no connection to the music. . . . They'll dance to the Rolling Stones or disco music. And then for the most part, they all dance the same—it's a series of steps.
>
> Deby Novitz, American and Argentine resident, *milonguera* and clothing designer

> That it's influenced by other things—other kinds of dance. That it's a bit more tolerant, that it's allowed to move a bit more, that it's not the classical or traditional style. It tries to break a bit the classical posture, because the steps are always the same; you're not really changing anything. (ε)
>
> Karina, Swiss expat, lawyer

> It's more playful, more liberating for the body; it has a sensuality that's more fit for a young body. It encourages a more dynamic use of space, a happiness—a happier form of movement. (τ)
>
> Jorge Garnica, Argentine, artist

June 2007, Café Pharmacie, Buenos Aires

How to approach a topic you aren't even sure exists? I am struggling with this question when I meet Raquel, a friend and mentor visiting Buenos Aires, for coffee. I confess to feeling blocked, trapped even, in the solitary process of writing. Terrified at the prospect of all those hungry eyes—my tango friends and acquaintances eager to get a peek at my take on their world. And what of the others, the ones I don't know? Tango dancers are a critical bunch, as I've gathered from following Tango-L these past few years. What's more, I'm stuck on the very definition of the topic I myself chose. Whenever I sit down to write about tango nuevo, *I come up with a different story.*

"So write that" is her simple reply.

* * *

For all the argument that it's an empty term, that there is no new tango, *que no existe* (it doesn't exist), *nuevo* has sneaked its way into existence by generating all this debate in the first place. By and large, the Argentines I spoke with rejected the term as an inappropriate modifier for describing contemporary trends in the dance. An exception would be those who disapprove of the changes to a tradition they hold dear and wield the term to discredit it by separating the *nuevo* from the "traditional," the "real," or the "authentic" tango. On the other hand, those who reject the term are undoubtedly strategizing as well. Staking their particular claim to the dance, they are situating their modern-day investigations and experimentations within a larger cultural and historical trajectory, according to which the tango remains somehow "Argentine."

Interestingly, many of these same dancers are often categorized as proponents or practitioners of *tango nuevo*. For example, José Garofalo, organizer of the popular downtown *milonga* Porteño y Bailarín, told me that on a recent tour of the United States, his classes were marketed as *tango nuevo* on the west coast and *tango milonguero* on the east. Lamenting the rigidity of such labels, Garofalo confessed that he does, in fact, fall under both categories if they must be used. Also president of the group that organizes the experimental Cambalache tango festival, Garofalo adapts his teaching to the audience: "That's the paradox, that you can't be innovative and conservative at the same time, and I'm a bit of both: traditional on the floor and innovative in terms of what I want on the stage. I think it's just as ridiculous to teach people a 'new tango' that they aren't physically capable of using on the dance floor as it is to demand that stage dancers move like *milongueros*."

Meanwhile, other dancers evolve their thinking over time, or evolve their marketing strategies according to the situation. I distinctly remember a conversation I had with Federico, a young *porteño* dancer back in January 2005: When I asked whether he danced *tango nuevo*, his response was an emphatic "No." He told me that for him tango had always meant "crazy things," that as a child he witnessed old people doing "crazy things" on the dance floor, and that he associated a close embrace and simple movements with *bolero* rather than tango. Yet less than one year later, Federico, by then a rising professional preparing for an international tour, had appropriated the term *tango nuevo*, and his Web site referenced his facility in both traditional and *nuevo* tango.

In our follow-up interview, Federico described *tango nuevo* as a code or structure to analyze the possibilities of the dance in a mathematical way, in order to create new, weird steps. Despite his dramatic change of tune, Federico's response elucidates an important distinction between *nuevo* as a system of analysis and the consequences of using that system in the dance itself. His about-face also illustrates two important points: the term itself is open to change, and it may be interpreted and valued distinctly according to place or situation. In this case, in preparation for a world tour, a rising professional reevaluated the currency of the term and fashioned a new definition that transcends the visual cues so often associated with *nuevo*. When I asked Federico whether he would market his classes as *nuevo* when he travels to the United States, his response reflected Argentine ambivalence with the term:

> For me, *nuevo* is the way I can compose weird steps like linear *boleos* (throw of the leg), back *ganchos* (leg hooks)[1] with changing directions in a very mathematic way that can create new things, but in the U.S. people associate *nuevo* with some tricks in the way you dance and some way of dressing. . . . I don't use wide trousers, and I will not use them ever—I think they're horrible! I don't throw my weight back when I dance and I will not do it ever! And if you don't do those two things, are you a *nuevo* dancer in the U.S.? It starts to be confusing. (ε)

* * *

Like nearly every Argentine dancer I spoke with—whether they agree with the use of the term or not—Federico traces this change in thinking about the dance to the investigations led by Gustavo Naveira and Fabian Salas in the 1990s. While interviews with foreigners produced a wider range of descriptions as to what constitutes *nuevo*, Naveira and Salas were constantly referenced as a point of origin. Naveira and Salas, however, have always been outspoken in their rejection of the term *nuevo* to refer to their dance. Despite his being called "the father of tango nuevo," Naveira told me, "the term means nothing, absolutely nothing" to him, and he hasn't the faintest idea where it originated. He added that the term seems an effort to separate the tango that is danced today from that danced before at the level of style—to create a new style of tango—and that he perceives such a separation to be a great error. As I heard in countless interviews and conversations, the tango has evolved and changed, which is nothing new: it has been evolving and changing since its inception, they say, and *ojalá* (God willing) it will continue to do so.

"There Are No New Steps!"

(quoted in Luhrmann, *Strictly Ballroom*)

Indeed, Naveira and Salas insist that the tango they were dancing *was not new*, that they did not introduce any new steps into the dance's vocabulary. What they did, however, was mine the annals of the dance's history to revive movements that had fallen out of practice. *Colgadas* and *volcadas*, for example, are often cited as "new moves" that appeared with the arrival of *tango nuevo*; however, many Argentines young and old told me that these movements had long existed—they might not have been labeled or executed in the same manner that they are today, but the principle behind the step itself was already there. Naveira and Salas also searched for novel ways to execute familiar movements, introducing a wider range of qualities of movement in tango dance (and encouraging others to continue doing so), which made certain moves look new or unfamiliar.

Further, they were young. They were the kids, youthful in energy and spirit, and they had come of age in a different era than had the *milongueros*. Of a different generation, one acquainted with a broader set of cultural references from their formative years, they simply moved differently. As Luciana Valle observed,

> We cannot dance the way that we used to dance fifty years ago because we are not the same human beings. The relationship between men and women is not the same as it was fifty years ago, and the relationship of every human being with their own body is not the same. . . . The health, the sports, the yoga, everything that people do now was something that people [didn't] do fifty years ago, so how can we dance the same? It's impossible. (ε)

Moreover, young people with training in other movement disciplines were picking up the tango, and they brought with them an intimate knowledge of the body, as well as a new vocabulary for talking about the body in movement. In a conversation with me, one young *porteño* traced the consolidation of the dance's evolution to the precision with which newly arrived female *tangueras* with backgrounds in classical ballet, modern dance, and other dance forms could identify and verbalize the mechanics within the embrace:

> When people began to arrive from contemporary dance, pop, folk—traditions that already had a detailed description for every movement—we could begin to understand how tango movements worked. And I think this had a lot to do with the women: they could understand how the proposal or the lead functions, they could intuit how the movements arise and unravel. . . . Naveira developed it, but it was the women who really made it work. (τ)
>
> Raul Masciocchi, Argentine, tango professional and *práctica* organizer

The contribution of these female dancers, combined with the entry of dancers from movement disciplines that include contact improvisation and martial arts, has facilitated a rethinking of the art of lead and follow. Fusion of elements from other partner dances—among them zouk, swing, rock 'n' roll, salsa, and samba—is evident at many levels, perhaps most fundamentally in the rupture and inversion of the embrace and the introduction of underarm turns. These dancers also had new ideas about how the body may move in tango. By playing with such elements as dynamic, momentum, speed, intention, focus, and emotion, they facilitated an expansion in the qualities expressed in tango dance, thus compounding the generational distance separating them from their elders.

Among the more successful young couples to build a business around a decidedly modern aesthetic are Dana Frígoli and Pablo Villarraza. Founders of a very successful tango academy, DNI, they have a committed core of young teachers who are all trained in the same method and who promote the same fluid, romantic, spiraling brand of tango in exhibitions, in the classroom, even in photographs. The style is marked by *disociación* (separation at the torso, of the ribs and chest from the hips and legs to allow torsion), and Frígoli's study of yoga, ballet, and contemporary dance is evident in their circular partnering, jumps, and extension-rich movement. Moreover, outside training is encouraged to the extent that Frígoli and Villarraza provide onsite yoga, ballet, and contemporary dance classes.

Indeed, such "preparation" for tango is increasingly popular these days. Yoga, stretch, and conditioning classes are offered at many of the popular tango schools and academies, and flyers for supplemental training abound at Buenos Aires' *prácticas*. However, when I broached this topic with young dancers, all adamantly stated that such outside training is not *necessary* for tango. Local narratives ground *tango nuevo* in investigation and deconstruction, resisting connections to dance vocabulary or steps. Nonetheless, growing cross-promotion of training certainly lends support to the argument that *nuevo* is exclusive in the level of physical ability it demands, while traditional tango is open to anyone regardless of age or dance background because its essence is simply "walking with more finesse," at heart the kinesthetic interpretation of feeling.

This is not to suggest that traditional tango is "simple," or that complexity, dexterity, and artistry are absent from it. A quick glance through tango's history belies reducing traditional tango to walking. For instance, in the 1933 film *¡Tango!*, El Cachafaz punctuates his stylized walk with small jumps and whipsmart, waist-high kicks that catch Carmencita

Calderón's waist in a fleeting front attitude. José and Lita Mendez's flashy *canyengue* moves in *Derecho Viejo* (1951) are full of *boleos*, while his solo leg twists suggest *boleos* bred with the lower-body wriggling of the Twist or the hokey pokey. Likewise, the rebellious investigations of the Club Nelson men and Federico's description of his elders' "crazy moves" on the dance floor are evidence that the history of tango is not only one of constant re-creation, but blatant displays of prowess. Acknowledging this history, my point here is to draw attention to the accessibility of traditional tango in its origins as a popular form, where "simply walking with more finesse" is an entirely acceptable approach to the dance, but by no means its only manifestation.

Tango's evolution during the late twentieth century has also encouraged a relaxation in attitude, something a new generation has seemed to embrace. In my interview with Pablo Inza, he noted that this conceptual overhaul has freed the tango from a tendency toward absolutism: "In the past, I heard something much more strict like 'Not like this' or 'That's wrong,' and I believe we're a little more open today. I'm not going to tell you that anything goes, but I think we're more open-minded. We're open to the possibility that there is more than one way to do something" (τ). What's more, young *tangueros* have begun to strip the dance of false emotion. The *cara de tango* (tango face), the exaggerated facial expression of passion that continues to reign on stage and screen, has largely fallen out of use in exhibition performances by professional couples at social tango events:

> Before, you would see the "tango face" in exhibitions, the man looking like he was in love with the woman, the passion . . . now you don't see that anymore. When there's an exhibition, it's the couple dancing, nothing more. And that's wonderful. . . . I don't have to put on the *cara de tango* to move someone with my dance. The story isn't in the face; it's there in the couple, in their bodies. I don't have to look at you a certain way. So, I think there has been an evolution in the dance. (τ)
>
> Pablo Inza, Argentine, tango professional and *práctica* organizer

This expansion in vocabulary and quality of movement can also be traced to the tango stage show and the importation of stage elements into social dance. *Tango Argentino*, the production so often credited with generating the global revival in tango dance, was noteworthy for the maturity and experience of its dancers. This show is often described as the most authentic version of tango to appear on the stage, a spectacle that gave audience members a glimpse of the "true tango"—closest in spirit to social Argentine tango. Though many of the original cast had, in fact, made a name for themselves on the stage, and the choreography included moves unsuitable for a *milonga*, the overall feel of the show was more of an "elegant, dignified, respectful dance on the floor" (Gazenbeek 2008: 12). The shows that have followed it, however, feature younger dancers and, especially in the case of the women, dancers with training in ballet, folk, or contemporary dance, even sometimes little to no prior experience in social tango.

The years since *Tango Argentino* first toured have seen a steady integration of non-tango movements into performance tango and an overall more acrobatic image of the tango on stage. The *fantasía* vocabulary that evolved from the competitive spirit of the 1940s *nuevo* pioneers already included low lifts and jumps; however, the higher lifts, jumps, and extensions that have come to define *tango escenario* (stage tango) have been employed to enlarge the dance, expanding the vocabulary in both volume and expression to accommodate for the distance between dancer and audience imposed by a proscenium setting.

This tango has come full circle, landing back in the rehearsal sessions of young *tangueros* who fuse social, stage, and other dance vocabularies in exhibitions. Moreover, such cross-pollination manifests itself in the growing *práctica* scene, where spacious venues encourage young bodies to borrow from these exhibitions, to further explore the boundaries of tango in a social context. Foreign influence plays out here as well, for the tango show finds the bulk of its audience support either abroad or in tourism, while the growth of exhibitions (an important means of gaining exposure and drumming up business) and the need for ever-novel exhibition choreography can also be tied to the growing global industry centered in Buenos Aires.

"*Así bailaban mis abuelos*" (My Ancestors Danced Like This)

(Mariano Del Mazo and Adrián D'Amore, *Quién me quita lo bailado* [2001]).

> Sometimes people forget that one of the characteristics of tango, of the essence of the dance, is creativity, improvisation, change. (τ)
>
> Olga Besio, Argentine, tango professional

> It's important to remember that the drive to invent and reinvent is very much the "traditional" spirit of Argentine tango.
>
> Sharna Fabiano, *The Rise of NeoTango Music* (2007)

Time and again, I heard the word *evolution* to describe the changes taking place in tango. Rejecting the term *nuevo* for the division the word implies—between the tango of today and that of before—many of the Argentines I spoke with argued that change and development are the inevitable products of survival, evidence that the tango is still very much alive. Situating their practice within a larger historical trajectory, they pointed to descriptions of Petróleo's generation, highlighting the striking parallels in youthful energy and tireless investigation. In recounting that familiar story of *porteños* who gathered on street corners, continually challenging one another in an endless bout of one-upmanship, many Argentine *tangueros* find their artistic ancestry:

> There was always experimentation in tango. There was a time when men got together, on a street corner or in someone's patio, to practice and exchange steps. Okay, today we're many more, there are lots more people dancing tango in many different places. But more than new, I would say . . . this has always existed in tango, it's just that now it's on a much larger scale, so people call it "new tango," but I would call it experimental. For me it's tango . . . it's tango in a creative phase. (τ)
>
> Gabriel Glagovsky, Argentine, tango professional and *práctica* organizer

Like Federico, the young *porteño* dancer who initially rejected the *nuevo* label for its denial of tango's rich experimental past, many pointed to the tradition of *campeonatos* or *concursos* (competitions or contests) in the history of tango as proof of the constant search for novelty and improvement: "Years ago, there were always competitions in Buenos Aires. There were contests and the best couple would be selected. So, this desire—to do things differently, to evolve, to want to be the best—it was always there. What happened, I think, is that after Naveira, the concepts began to take on an order" (τ; Raul Masciocchi, Argentine, tango professional and *práctica* organizer).

This "order"—the one thing that so many agree is new—is something that Naveira himself acknowledges publicly; on his Web site, he is "the pioneer of a new technique of teaching the tango," and his investigation and analysis "have revolutionized tango dancing towards the end of the 20th century" (2011). But the idea of an order also represents an important break with the past for the very possibility of classroom instruction. In my interview with Olga Besio, she described the dearth of instruction when they began dancing together in the early 1980s. Not only had the dance fallen out of practice, with very few classes available, but it was believed that the tango was not "teachable":

> The tango wasn't very well-regarded then. Folk dancers used to say that tango was something else entirely, it was the dance of low-lifes. . . . There was nowhere to go to learn tango. Either somebody from your family taught you, or a friend or an acquaintance, but there were no places to learn to dance, there were no schools, no courses. . . . Back then, many people said you couldn't teach tango, that it wasn't something that could be taught. . . . Actually, everybody said that. (τ)

The writings and interviews left by the *tangueros* of yore and the *milongueros* of today speak to the survival of the dance through "acquisition." An entirely nonacademic process, tango was passed down from one generation to the next through contact with the dance itself. They didn't need prefabricated choreography and complex concepts. The dance was simple. They learned by watching and doing: "I danced tango and *milonga*, but naturally, nobody taught me. I saw people dance and I learned. There were great dancers in that time. When you have the knack for learning a dance, you don't need to go to a school to learn a style. I had sisters at home, so we practiced there" (τ; Oscar Héctor Malagrino, Argentine, *milonga* organizer). Another point stressed by traditionalists that feeds from such stories is the notion that a "real" tango dancer is not formed in the classroom. The ultimately personal expression of a feeling, a *milonguero* cultivated his dance through careful observation on the street, or if he was of age, in the *milongas*. From there, he would take what he saw and construct his own dance, practicing under the watchful eyes of family, friends, neighbors, and peers.

The late Carlos Gavito noted that in the absence of women and dancing schools, young boys were bodies to be practiced on, and moreover, tools for innovation. Not yet old enough to be allowed into the *milonga*, his apprenticeship began with the role of follower until he was able to turn the tables and practice on another young boy:

> In those days, tango was practiced between men. The older men would use boys, who were placed in a standing position, mimicking the women, and the men would practice their steps. They would say

> "Hey boy, come, stand here, put your foot here, and now there" and they would try new steps and new ways. So at the beginning I was just a body, but I paid attention to the steps and when I was fifteen, I did the same with a younger boy. It was then my turn to practice steps. In those days there were no dancing schools, and no television, so a kid like myself would have soccer during the day, and tango in the late afternoon.
>
> Gavito, quoted in Quiroga (2001)

Juan Carlos Copes, on the other hand, began at a later age, and his entry into the tango world sounds much like an anthropologist's entry into a foreign culture: a fascinating encounter with another world, where one learns through watching before doing, successful participation dependent upon observation and incorporation: "The best thing would be to make the rounds one by one to all the *milongas* they could, to 'study' the subject up close and to slowly start incorporating this art that seemed so unattainable. . . . [They] smoked more than they danced. They sat and watched this foreign ritual, like someone at a party he wasn't invited to" (τ; Del Mazo and D'Amore 2001: 41–42).

Testaments from those present during the 1940s, the era in which Petróleo declares *el tango nuevo* appeared, highlight the goals of innovation and personal style above all else. His colleague "Lampazo" (José Vazquez), for instance, labels Petróleo "a tremendous creator," a dancer of unparalleled inventive skill (quoted in Angió). If we are to believe such testimonies, these dancers not only ushered the tango into its modern era, but they were rebels, their insatiable passion for the dance leading them to break with what had come before. This passion is important, for it links the efforts of Petróleo and his contemporaries, as well as the figures recognized and lauded as *milongueros* or elder *tangueros* today, to the more recent generations of dancers local and global who continue looking for new ways to interpret the tango. The investigations initiated by Naveira and Salas in the 1990s and the more recent explosion of classes and practice groups organized by young dancers are all similarly grounded in the goals of exploration and innovation: to more deeply understand the mechanics and possibilities in the dance, and to continue reinterpreting the dance in ways that are appropriate for contemporary bodies and minds.

This legacy has interesting implications today. On the one hand, there is the narrative of tango through acquisition. Wrapped up in this narrative is a healthy disdain for classroom instruction, its very structure stripping the dance of its essence and reducing it to the rote execution of steps. The "step" itself is often the center of this debate. Gavito, for instance, famously argued that the essence of tango is not the steps but that which exists in between, the pauses: "Anybody who pretends to dance well never thinks about the step he's going to do, what he cares about is that he follows the music. You see, we are painters, we paint the music with our feet" (quoted in Quiroga 2001). Revered for his elegance, simplicity, and dramatic pauses, Gavito embodied this attitude in countless performances and interviews, in turn, spreading it to a huge global fanbase over the course of a very successful career.

On the other hand, the growth of the global tango industry has created enormous opportunities for these same dancers to cash in on their experience through the classroom. This contradiction became apparent when I observed Roberto and Camila, a couple then in their 70s, teach a class at the (now defunct) Academia de Estilos de Tango Argentino, the government-funded tango preservation program that connected young dancers with *milongueros*. In an interview, one of the program staff described the program's goal and methods as "preservation through mimicking." Its young participants were directed to "literally copy" what they see, to absorb and preserve the style of a different *milonguero* week after week. During the question-and-answer period following their class, however, Roberto and Camila told their young pupils to do just the opposite: to "find their own dance."

This history of learning through acquisition is often invoked to pit feeling against mechanization in instruction, the argument being that post-Naveira instruction has reduced tango to physics and analysis at the cost of heart:

> [Naveira's] kind of teaching is so detrimental to those for whom the music is the foundation of the dance. He is missing the essence of tango. For me, his most revealing comment is: "At a certain moment, there arose the need to technically identify every single thing done in dancing." There arose that need in him, evidently. But goodness only knows where he got the notion that anyone else needs their rainbows unweaving.
>
> Tango-L post, 2008

Criticism of post-Naveira instruction is by no means reserved to traditionalists. A young *porteño* dancer whose movement, clothing, and music preferences all reveal an openness to experimentation attacked the tango vanguard on this point exactly: "For me, the avant-garde tendency in tango is to make it more scientific—or more than scientific; I would say mechanical. The modern tendency is pure mechanics to me, and the dancers working from that focus become more and more mechanical. And the more mechanical you become, the less feeling you have. For me, the more brain you put into something, the less heart it can have" (τ; anonymous).

Meanwhile, countless dancers from Argentina and abroad heralded Naveira and Salas's investigations for effecting clarity, rejecting such attacks as simplistic and countering that emotion and thought are not mutually exclusive. No longer smoke and mirrors—as it was presented in other classes in the 1990s—the dance is demonstrated to operate through a rational physics of movement:

> That [physics of movement] was what was missing at that time. Things were explained in a very irrational way, and they were explained "like this"—and when you asked how—[they said] "like this" and they showed it. There weren't words, there was no language for explaining things and when they spoke they made it even more confusing. So it was better to hear "like this" and to watch and try to understand what they did, but there was no logic. But the dance possesses an internal logic. . . . By putting it into a system and understanding what you're doing is demystifying the dance—and this allowed people to be dancing in very little time. What once took a long time to learn you could now understand quite quickly. (τ)
>
> Cecilia Gonzalez, Argentine, tango professional

Though so many of Argentina's young dancers now bring to tango a movement background, often with more than one specific movement vocabulary and technique, they do not bring to it the cultural references to the dance and music that their elders experienced. Further, the younger generation has very different ideas about what it means to incorporate and execute a movement technique. Add to that the fact that since the late 1960s partnered social dance had fallen out of vogue with the rise of American and Argentine rock and punk music, and the revolution represented by Naveira and Salas's new pedagogy becomes more clear.

Once vague, metaphoric, and mysterious, tango instruction is now clear, straightforward, and logical. Now that dancers have the tools to create their own dance, the learning process is quicker, encouraging the investigation that feeds more innovation. However, there is an important distinction between understanding how a dance functions and *actually dancing.* Absorbing instruction and applying that knowledge to replicate, deconstruct, and create new figures or movements will train one's body to know a dance. But the spontaneous creation of a wordless conversation on the dance floor retains an air of mystery: it is neither entirely penetrable nor explainable. The embodiment of Isadora Duncan's philosophical defense of her calling, "If I could tell you what I mean there would be no point in dancing," dancers communicate and share things in dance that cannot be reduced to words:

> But to have an experience . . . nobody can teach you that. . . . And to see him [Naveira] dance, you realize there's much more that isn't the what but the how—and that can't be explained. You either feel it or you don't, you communicate it or you don't. And it's possible that the people who can transmit that in their dance will have a hard time explaining it to you in words or exercises. So there's a point at which the *maestro* can't help you anymore. You're on your own and you have to do the work. You have to put yourself into your dance—your own personality, your own feelings, your own body, your own life. . . . And that's what's missing, that experience of putting one's self into the dance, even though we learn so quickly now. So it takes time . . . it has to do with hours, the hours you build up on the floor, the hours of life and experience. That's not something that can be taught. (τ)
>
> Cecilia Gonzalez, Argentine, tango professional

Esa ansiosa búsqueda de la libertad (That Anxious Quest for Freedom)

> You have to believe in yourself and not so much in the one who's teaching you. It's okay to believe in your teacher, but over time as you improve, you have to have faith in yourself. . . . If I believe in someone else I'll keep doing what he does, but if I believe in myself I can do anything, because I go on discovering. . . . I'd rather watch some fool doing crazy things on the floor, because at some point he'll do something, he'll surprise me and I'll learn from that—it will give me an idea. (τ)
>
> Claudio, Argentine, tango professional

It is through such a deep technical understanding of the body's movements, combined with a tireless exploration of the myriad physical or choreographic possibilities, that over time the dancer approximates "freedom."[2] A common theme in the writings of tango dancers past and present, *libertad* (freedom), is expressed in terms of both empowerment—the product of Gonzalez's "hours," or miles, accrued on the dance floor, it is the power one feels with mastery of a form and the ability to create it anew—and singularity, where one's dance is a distinctly personal expression, "freeing" the dancer from mentors and peers. As María Nieves recounts, "Every Saturday and Sunday there were different steps. A good *milonguero* couldn't dance the same all the time. It was very rare that one would copy another. If you liked a step somebody else did, you watched, you picked it up mentally, but you wouldn't do it the same, you tried to do something different with it. Because to copy was horrible" (T; quoted in Del Mazo and D'Amore 2001: 45).

Inherent within the discourse of *libertad* are the notions of improvisation and innovation, and it is this ability to create that makes the dancer not only an actor but a protagonist. More importantly, as Juan Carlos Copes points out, the opportunity to be somebody, fleeting as it may be, is central to the appeal of tango, especially for the average Argentine as the country entered another period of decline in the 1950s: "I saw how they used the dance to become someone within the larger situation of social marginalization that they lived in. It was there [in the *milongas*] that I learned lessons that would be key in my career. One was that the tango is a free dance, where the imagination reigns" (T; quoted in Del Mazo and D'Amore 2001: 42).

In the record left by dancers from the 1940s through the *milongueros* and elder *tangueros* of today, innovation is referenced at the level of choreography and "style," where style is a personal rather than a formal trait. A frequent point of contention raised by traditionalists centers on this notion of style. Citing the growth of a tango industry, the proliferation of classes and teachers, and a classroom focus on the replication of figures (though generally broken down into their smallest parts), such attacks against *nuevo* tend to frame it as a style that subsumes and links its members through a shared vocabulary of steps, in the process limiting *libertad*, or the development of one's own dance.

But the efforts of such a personal journey are evident in the dance of many practitioners often lumped together under the *nuevo* label. While Naveira confessed to having learned much from his teachers, he also told me that he has gone "*tan por la rama*" (so far out on a limb) that he has a hard time identifying his dance with that of his mentors. Enrique and Lucia, whose Tango Búsqueda was once described to me as "beyond *nuevo*"; former partners Norberto "El Pulpo" Esbrez and Luiza Paes, known for their labyrinthine legwork; and Chicho Frúmboli, famed for his unparalleled musicality and inventiveness: these are just a few examples of younger dancers who truly separated themselves from mentors and peers.

Interestingly, in our interview, Luiza Paes echoed the sentiment expressed by traditionalists, equating the growth of the tango industry with an increasing lack of diversity. Locating their singularity in their distance from Buenos Aires (in 2006, they lived and worked in Buenos Aires, after having met and worked together in Brazil for several years), she argued that their long stint outside Argentina gave them the freedom to develop a tango unlike that of any other couple. Still, despite claims of growing homogeneity, many young Argentines emphasize an equally lonely path toward individuality. When I asked Santiago Pegue, a twenty-two-year-old Argentine dancer who stands out immediately in the *prácticas* not only for his looks—asymmetrical mohawk, bell-bottoms, sneakers, and hat—but also for his fluid, contemporary-influenced approach to tango, about his teachers and his dance, he asserted independence: "They didn't teach me what I do, I discovered it on my own. The professor is me. I'm the one investigating" (τ).

July 2006, the Tango Life, Buenos Aires

About nine months into my first year in Buenos Aires, and my doubts over leaving only seem to grow with each passing day. The fact that it is the most brutal time of year when I begin to feel this reconfirms my certainty. True, Buenos Aires can't hold a candle to Boston in the category of winter, but the humidity, the old stone buildings, and the insufficient heating combine to keep me constantly chilled. You feel it in the tango scene too. The milongas *and* prácticas *are quieter. Many professionals are smartly touring in warmer climates. Many tourists are holding off for the late August tango championship.*

Still, I resist the temptation of warmth and cable tv tonight, and under the cover of numerous layers of tops and bottoms alike (to be removed or not, to a point, according to the temperature and my luck), head out to a práctica *at 10:30 p.m. After sitting for quite a while—happy that legwarmers are back in style, glad I chose that scarf that doubles as shawl—chatting with friends and watching the floor, eventually I get a couple of dances in.*

I walk out with Patricio, a young Argentine businessman who, despite being a frequent enough presence in the prácticas *and* milongas, *still seems a bit of an outsider. There are plenty of young* porteños *for whom tango is a hobby, but Patricio is different: he seems both enamored and critical of this world at once. It is likely one of the reasons we get on so well.*

When I confess to anxiety over leaving, he looks sideways at me. What better audience to test out the plans I've concocted, in preparation for a phone call with my family, to justify one more year? I've managed to get some translation and editing work on the side, I tell him. If I'm earning U.S. currency and living in Buenos Aires, I'll have more time to devote to my book.

More than unconvinced, he seems genuinely disappointed; as if seeing me in a new light for the first time, where suddenly I am just another in the ever-growing trove of foreign tangueras, *living and breathing the tango day and night, year in and year out. My research has always set me apart, made me sensible, somehow more respectable in Patricio's eyes. Now he questions whether it is all a front, whether I am not just seeking a refuge from reality in tango. "This isn't Buenos Aires, Carolyn—partying all the time," he barks. Seeing me recoil, he softens his voice, but not the message: "You're putting your future on hold if this is what you're planning on doing with your life."*

Like critics of today's young tangueros, *he is unimpressed. He questions me to think hard, to take account, to explain just what all this "investigating" is really about.*

Tango "for Export"

As Naveira and Salas's tango revolution opened the floodgates to innovation and "investigation," Argentina was poised for a rather unpleasant revolution of its own. In 1991, under President Carlos Menem, the Convertibility Law pegged the Argentine peso in a one-to-one fixed-rate relationship to the U.S. dollar. A host of factors in the late 1990s precipitated the country's economic crisis and a series of currency devaluations and adjustments in late 2001 and early 2002, including rising unemployment, the appreciation of the peso in relation to its trading partners' currencies, Brazil's economic crisis, the 2001 devaluation of the peso for foreign trade, a series of debt restructurings, and bank runs with declining confidence in the peso and rumors of default.

When the government froze bank accounts in December 2001, limiting withdrawals to small sums in pesos, Argentines took to the streets in protest. These were the famous *cacerolazos* (protests of banging pots and pans) that brought middle-class Argentines to the street, in a moment that united citizens across the divides of social class as everyone braced for the inevitable crash of the convertibility system. With no relief in sight, the protests grew violent, and when martial law was declared, the situation grew dire as protesters broke windows, destroyed billboards, graffitied buildings, and set fires.

Between December 21, 2001, when President Fernando de la Rúa resigned, and January 2, 2002, when Eduardo Duhalde was sworn into office, the country went through three interim presidents. In the months that followed, the peso flip-flopped between a two-to-one and a four-to-one relationship to the U.S. dollar, finally stabilizing in a nearly three-to-one relationship to the dollar in 2003. While it moved toward a four-to-one relationship in the late 2000s, this was accompanied by rising inflation. However, the combined impact of these trends is hard to gauge in the face of declining trust in the Instituto Nacional de Estadística y Censos, the national statistics and census bureau, since a host of analysts were let go or resigned following the institution of a new method for calculating inflation, introduced by a government appointee.[3]

So what does Argentina's crisis have to do with tango today? In a sense, everything. Notwithstanding the lasting damage it incurred, with time, the crisis became a boon for tango in Buenos Aires. In short, devaluation encouraged the growth of a global industry centered on the dance's birthplace for the simple fact that consumption was now drastically discounted for the foreign dancer. Moreover, it isn't just the dance, but the lure of the country and its capital that draws foreigners.

Like Paris in the 1920s or Prague in the 1990s, Buenos Aires in the early 2000s became an expat haven, a "playground for Europeans and Americans looking to relax or reinvent" (Mount 2006). More than the great prices, it is the tantalizing mix of danger and familiarity the city offers up, as Mount (2006) so perfectly captures in a *New York* magazine piece that also touts the city's "bikini-clad women" eager to befriend wealthy foreigners:

> There are other cities across the globe that offer relatively inexpensive living, of course: Mexico City, Rio de Janeiro, São Paulo, Bangkok. But potential expats generally cross them off the list because prices have started rising (Mexico City) or they're too culturally

different (Bangkok) or because the rich–poor conflict makes being a "rich American" too dangerous (Brazil). Buenos Aires mixes a potent cultural cocktail: low prices, a familiar-but-different (and sexy) vibe, good weather, great food, and the chance to start over.

In the years leading up to the crisis, tango played a role in selling foreign investors on the idea of business ventures in Argentina. Blustein (2005) recounts that teams of bankers descended upon the city in the 1990s to meet with economists and political bigwigs by day only to be wined, dined, and inevitably escorted to a tango show by night. As a former J. P. Morgan employee explained it, seduction lay beyond the dollar signs; foreign bankers were pulled in by the entire package: "they wouldn't only buy the bonds, but the whole country, the concept" (quoted in Blustein 2005: 34).

Outside Argentina, tango communities arose the world over thanks to touring stage shows like *Tango Argentino* (1983), *Tango X 2* (1988), *Tango Pasión* (1993), and *Forever Tango* (1996). At the same time, films like Sally Potter's *The Tango Lesson* (1997) and Carlos Saura's *Tango* (1998) further fueled global interest in the dance, the music, the country, and its capital. Potter's film also introduced viewers to some of the most beloved traditional tango recordings, while Yo-Yo Ma's rendition of "Libertango," the finale on the disc, and his Grammy-winning disc-length homage to Piazzolla, *Soul of the Tango* (1997), reintroduced global audiences to tango at the peak of the world music craze, reinforcing its "high-culture" profile via connection to the master cellist.

The transformation of Argentina's economy also situated tango as a veritable national product, arguably its best-known export aside from beef. Much as the dance has served as a refuge time and again for its marginalized practitioners, so tango became the country's passport to protagonism in the wake of the crisis. And as this social activity has become every day more an industry, a pathway to livelihood in a struggling economy, *tangueros* young and old have smartly become entrepreneurial. After the crisis, foreigners could suddenly afford to come to Buenos Aires to immerse themselves in tango for periods stretching into weeks, months, even years. The result is a scene that continues to grow, whose client base can accommodate diversity, where twenty-two-year-old tango professors represent the promise of capitalism: "choice."

Santiago, the twenty-two-year-old with the mohawk, is a marvelous dancer. In a 2009 performance with Cecilia García, the pair brought Philadelphia's tango community to their feet in a standing ovation that seemed unlikely to end. His considerable skills aside, though, it is interesting to ponder where today's young innovators might be without tango's newfound cachet, and more generally, where tango might be today without the crisis. To set oneself apart is a means of branding, a necessity in any market. In this sense, *tango nuevo* is not just the dance and all its changes but also the commodity that tango has become. Many of the "autonomous students" that emerged from Naveira and Salas's tango investigations have become tango professionals themselves, encouraged by and reinforcing the growing global client base, who in turn encourage the expanding local industry that now encompasses not only schools, social dance events, and *cena* shows but also hotels, shoe and clothing outlets, tour companies, taxi dancers, music stores and bookstores, and more.

It has arguably also encouraged traditionalism as a counterpoint, the other end of the spectrum in the tango marketplace. While there is evidence that tango as dance never fully disappeared, there is also a healthy debate surrounding the veracity of certain professionals who claim *milonguero* status or who promote their dance as rooted in tradition, the argument being that all manner of events—from the invasion of foreign music and media, the counterculture and the decline of partner dance, political repression, the terror of the *proceso*—created a rupture in tango's history. Tango as commodity invites entrepreneurs of all stripes; it is not only the young and the rebellious but also the more conservative who seize its promise. And in the global community, it is not only innovation but also tradition that is replicated, that traverses borders in the bodies of Argentine professionals, foreign devotees, and mediated performances.

* * *

Beyond the growth of schools and classes in Buenos Aires, the explosion in online media technology has encouraged a culture of tango education through imitation. The speed with which steps and trends now move across borders (and back) has increased to "immediate" thanks to sites like YouTube and Facebook, and a general attitude of openness to being filmed and having that film posted online, arguably another new trend and a notable shift in Buenos Aires' tango culture. In 2003, I was warned that photography was strictly forbidden in the *milongas*, for attendees might be somewhere, and perhaps with someone, they shouldn't be. In 2005, no one minded my videotaping at El Galpon for my research, so long as I requested permission; less than a decade later, cameras and video recorders are ubiquitous in classes and an unremarkable presence at many *prácticas* and *milongas*. YouTube has become a virtual one-stop shop for the tango enthusiast, the volume of footage from *milongas*, *prácticas*, classes, exhibitions, and stage shows reaching staggering proportions. Ready access to this footage allows developing dancers to find inspiration, to take ideas, and to craft their dance after someone they may never meet in person.

While a certain degree of imitation is necessary in developing one's vocabulary, homogeneity is also a reflection of the relative youth of the contemporary tango scene, and the relative immaturity of many of the dancers who have entered the scene since its revitalization. As Cecilia Gonzalez points out, the systematization of instruction allows dancers to get out on the floor much more quickly than ever before, but mastery of the form and "freedom" from one's teachers and peers are the rewards of a longer journey. At the same time, the entry of dancers trained in other disciplines continues to feed an expansion in movement quality and vocabulary. This expansion in movement vocabulary combines with the growth of more spacious venues encouraging a culture of demonstration, where many cite pressure to display their chops, as Korey Ireland, an American tango professional, attests in describing one of the new *prácticas*: "[ ] event is the environment where you kind of show off what you're doing, and hopefully you're doing things that other people can't do. And so you kind of establish your credibility. . . . It's a place to practice but it's also a place to be seen." Oddly enough, Ireland's description evokes the same quest for freedom, or singularity, that marks the testaments left by the dance's forebears, while also giving credence to the common complaint that *nuevo* is little more than showing off fancy steps.

The new pedagogy and expansion in vocabulary have also encouraged greater appreciation for repetition in the classroom. In a conversation with me, Pablo Inza recounted how frustrating his early training was, for as María Nieves points out, a *milonguero* seldom dances the same twice: "He gave us steps and we practiced them. . . . When I asked him to show the sequence again he showed something similar but not quite the same; he explained the steps but not how to do them" (τ; Argentine, tango professional and *práctica* organizer). In contrast, Naveira's classes are a showcase of precision and musicality, evidenced in the ease with which he and wife Giselle Anne break down and re-create each sequence with exactitude. Thus, for the professional, the ability to demonstrate each step as always the same is highly valued in the classroom context, while for the social dancer, the ability to execute a given step the same is demonstration of progression.

To ask today's young dancers to move beyond the steps to "what exists in between" is a tall order given the recent arrival of so many. Such transcendence is achieved through lifelong pursuit and tireless dedication, a product of one's "hours," maturity in the form and in life. Emotion, metaphor, and philosophical waxing—all have their place in the art of dance, and I do not argue that they be taken lightly. But philosophical treatises may also be a convenient means of obscuring physical limitations. For the veteran or lesser-skilled dancer, the simplicity-authenticity link is perhaps a rather ingenious means of repackaging diminished or as-yet-unrealized physical capabilities under the guise of "feeling."

The feeling-versus-mechanics debate raises a crucial question, though: namely, what is tango? Many contend that it is not just steps but feeling, in the tradition of composer Enrique Santos Discépolo, who famously called the tango *un pensamiento triste que se baila* (a sad thought danced). Others highlight the importance of the embrace. I have often heard the dance described along the lines of "walking with more finesse." But are these descriptions to be interpreted as restrictive definitions, or as suggestive openings? How do we define the limitations of the dance? How far may it evolve before it becomes something other or new?

The rupture of the front-front orientation of the embrace (leader and follower facing each other) is often cited as evidence of a break from traditional tango. However, tango history abounds with examples of alternative approaches to this facing of leader to follower in tango. Early photographs and promotional sketches highlight the influence of Hollywood and ballroom dance as they raise questions about the "novelty" of *nuevo*. Descriptions of Petróleo's generation evoke a rule-breaking gang of young men. Images and writings present Antonio Todaro's fondness for positioning both leader and follower facing in the same direction, and a recent video of the late *milonguero* Pupi Castello shows him leading a young *tanguera* from behind, her back to his chest, in a popular Buenos Aires *milonga*.

I raised the question of the embrace in my interview with Pablo Inza, who tested the boundaries of tango to great effect with his former dance partner Moira Castellano. Inza's early study in the patio of a *milonguero*'s home is undeniable. His walk, his embrace, his playful attention to the music all combine to give his dance a feel that is undeniably tango. On the other hand, their inversion and rupture of the embrace, Moira's rebounding *gancho* extensions, and her Martha Graham–like contractions all point to her extensive background in classical and contemporary dance. Responding to my question about the embrace, Inza highlighted the importance of intention in defining the dance: "In contemporary tango, we might break contact, but only to pick it up again, not to lose it. We stay connected. There might be an instant where we're no longer embracing, but we keep looking for one another. The idea of dancing with that person is still there" (τ). Another young *tanguero* argued that limiting tango to the embrace reflects a rather impoverished perspective. Like the time and place that gave birth to tango, the dance itself should be open to evolution:

> It's like Discépolo said: tango is a thought that you dance. The tango is what drives you to dance, it's not the embrace. Honestly, it would be a real shame if it were nothing more than the embrace. If it were just that it would be so simple. I think tango is everything, it's a way of life. . . . The tango is Argentine, and if Argentina can evolve, so can the tango. I like modern life, what's happening here and now, living in this time. . . . I don't dance a tango of the future, I dance the tango of today. (τ)
>
> Santiago Pegue, Argentine, tango professional

Such comments point to the problem that dogs the idea of authenticity. Attempting to define culture according to tradition or limiting it to what may be deemed authentic often denies the very life and energy necessary to survival. For the survival of any tradition necessarily implies choices, improvisation, and renewal, rather than mere repetition over time.

This idea comes up in countless conversations with young dancers and musicians, who argue that knowledge of and respect for the tango's roots do not preclude development and transformation. As American *tanguera* Sharna Fabiano eloquently frames it, being authentic demands respect for the past and accommodation to the present: "Remaining authentic means having a real connection to the past, being educated and sensitive to it, finding a link with the present, and then moving forward to include what we are feeling now about the human experience" (quoted in van Kokswijk 2006).

Emerging from what seemed an irreversible relegation to the status of kitsch, the tango is thriving for the simple fact that so many people, young and old, are dancing it again. But the promise of survival lies with the young. Grounded in the understanding effected through years of investigation, they are injecting the tango with the life that only youth can bring.

Rather than new, however, it is changed, updated, contemporary—the intention remains *tango*. Most importantly, the renovation at the heart of contemporary tango is sincere to the essence of the dance—improvisation, innovation, and change:[4]

> But that doesn't mean that the word *tango nuevo* is correct. They created a way to approach the dance, and of course the dance has changed, the dance has progressed, the dance has new moves, some of them due to the fact that people are starting to understand what they do. When you understand what you do, you own the dance, so you can create more dance. (ε)
>
> Luciana Valle, Argentine, tango professional and *práctica* organizer

Darwinism, Tango, and *La revancha de la práctica* (the Return of the *Práctica*)

> I think it is perhaps the most important thing happening in tango today: the recuperation of a practice space that had been lost. (τ)
>
> Pablo Inza

In my interview with Naveira, he suggested that tensions in the tango scene emerge not from these changes per se, but rather from the harsh reality of evolution—that someone or something always gets left behind:

> Not only has it evolved, but it keeps getting better and better. And this is a problem for many people, because not everyone is prepared, not everyone is in the condition to keep up with these improvements. Anyone who isn't open to diversity, to the enrichment of the choreography, to the development of the dance—it's convenient for them to frame this new situation as just another new style. (τ)

As these "improvements" have incurred greater complexity in tango movements, and more young dancers have entered the scene, the *práctica* has made a comeback. While the number of young *porteños* dancing tango had increased by the time of the Cochabamba group in the 1990s, there were almost no sites geared toward young dancers because there were so few of them. One exception was Parakultural, an underground theater and performance space whose artsy crowd initially opposed the introduction of tango. Now in a new space dedicated to tango, Parakultural's popular Salon Canning *milonga* regularly draws a mix of young, old, foreign, local, professional, and social dancers. Another is La Viruta. Initially more of a *práctica*, it acquired prime space when it moved to the spacious basement of a Palermo Viejo cultural center in 1997. La Viruta was once described to me as the "*shopping* of tango" (tango mall); indeed, its success lies in its accessible pricing and atmosphere. The classes, *milonga* and *práctica* fees, food, and alcohol are dirt cheap, and beginners are encouraged to get out on the floor right away, resulting in an often chaotic scene.[5] A favorite among young dancers, it has flowered into the city's largest *milonga*, club, and tango academy, catering to some 250 students a day and offering four *milongas* a week by late 2007.

But the majority of the *milongas* remained governed by the old guard during those early years, and as more and more kids infringed upon their territory, the *milongas* became sites of tension, where the clash was between generations:

> In the beginning, there were few young people dancing, so the older people had more power. They were powerful. And when you went dancing, it was all according to their rules. So you had to adapt yourself to the rules imposed in that place, by these people. And they were incredibly rigid . . . protective . . . it was like they wanted to protect something that they possessed. They didn't want anybody else to come and change things. And they played with them. I think they had fun with this. When young people showed up, they shoved them off the floor with their elbows—hard. (τ)
>
> Cecilia Gonzalez, Argentine, tango professional

Asserting their dominion much as an animal marks its territory, the elder dancers enforced tradition through seniority and majority rule. With time, however, the rivalry on the floor settled into less-contested coexistence. Several dancers describe the eventual transition in a handful of *milongas*: as the night wore on and space cleared, *los pibes* had a bit more freedom to open the embrace, to execute the *boleos*, *ganchos*, and *volcadas* that a packed floor could not accommodate, and to play, to experiment, and to make mistakes without the pressure of the elders' watchful eyes and biting tongues.[6] As the number of young people dancing steadily increased, however, the need for new spaces became more pressing. As Luciana Valle recalled, she and her friends longed for venues with codes that would reflect their modern sensibilities: "Obviously, there was a need of a lot of young people that wanted to go dance . . . with more space, with more relaxed codes, with better ambience, with a better mood, you know? With people that are friendly—they are the way that they are outside the dance, too" (ε).

This desire resulted in El Motivo, the *práctica* that opened its doors in late 2004 at Villa Malcolm, the Palermo Viejo social club that has since become a sort of *práctica* central, playing host to several other new events. El Motivo found quick support among the city's burgeoning young *tanguero* population. Within six months, El Motivo was drawing 100 dancers a week, and a host of other *prácticas* have opened since. More than sites for practice, these events have grown to the extent that they transcend the historical implications of their label. Meeting a need, they have become alternatives to the *milongas*, social venues for tango dancing organized and attended primarily by dancers in their twenties through forties.

Not only in name, it is also in the establishment of an entirely new set of rules that the *prácticas* break with tradition. From earlier hours (most begin between 8:00 and 10:00 p.m. and close between midnight and 3:00 a.m.)[7] to the absence of *tandas* and *cortinas* as well as the *cabeceo*, the altered codes are intended to create a more relaxed environment. As one organizer put it, the *prácticas* are events for "normal" people, where "normal" stands in opposition to *milonguero*:

> In my *práctica*, you invite the person to dance directly. It's informal. You can dance as much as you like. There are no *tandas*, no *cortinas*, people go out on the floor and dance five, six, seven songs. I dim the lights, so you don't see any one dancer in particular. The lights are bright in the *milongas*, and everyone goes out to show off. . . . They're all places for dancers of a certain level, the *milongas*. I organize a place for dancers, normal people. Not for people who stay out until 7 in the morning, drinking coffee, doing coke,[8] whatever. (τ)
>
> Anonymous, Argentine, *práctica* organizer

Moreover, the sites themselves reflect the tango philosophy of those within. While Buenos Aires' *milongas* are often housed in dance halls, salons, and *confiterías* that harken the tango's Golden Era, whether in their architecture, design, or decor, the sites of the city's *práctica* scene demonstrate a deliberate disregard for such traditional tango aesthetics. When I arrived in late 2005, for example, the dance floor of one quite popular *práctica* was flanked by enormous file cabinets. At the same time, however, young Argentine *tangueros* are proud of their cultural heritage and eager to situate their dance within a larger cultural trajectory. This is exemplified by the mural project that was completed in Villa Malcolm, the Palermo Viejo social club–turned–*práctica* central, just before I left Buenos Aires in late 2007. A collage of famed Golden Era musicians and bandleaders who performed in the club, along with their names and performance dates, the mural is just one example of tango's large footprint on the city, and of the difficulty in neatly separating the new from the traditional.

The relaxed etiquette of the *práctica* scene extends to physical appearance and grooming, too. The *prácticas* are sites for young people, and attendees look and dress the part. Sneakers, jeans, cargo pants, bell-bottoms, backless tops, body piercings, tattoos, dreadlocks, hats: there are no rules governing appearance in the *prácticas.* Fashions tend to reflect what is popular on the streets, and to evolve just as quickly.

A tongue-in-cheek note posted on a tango e-zine sums up traditionalist resistance to the changing face of tango:

> Advice for giving tango nuevo classes, and to exponentially increase student enrollment, at least for a bit.
>
> 1. Bathe little.
> 2. Shave even less.
> 3. Wear clothes three sizes too big.
> 4. Get yourself an old sweatshirt, or a pullover with big stripes.
> 5. Put something on your head (a headband, pick, etc.)
> 6. Keep your partner at a distance of at least 2 meters.
> 7. Use fat, colored sneakers—never shoes (how old-fashioned!)
> 8. Make a face that says: "What a drag! When will this end?"
> 9. Don't ever play Di Sarli, Troilo, Pugliese or any of those other dinosaurs.[9]
> 10. Wear earrings, wristbands, piercings, *tatuajes* (sorry, "tattoos"), etc.
> 11. Smoke, drink, and take whatever comes your way.
> 12. Do not respect any milonga codes (how outdated!)
> 13. Move with no sense of rhythm, as illogically as possible.
> 14. Don't look at your partner ever again.
> 15. Rant and rave against everything, saying: "I'm investigating."
> 16. Keep your hair long and greasy, and if you dye it, only ridiculous colors will do. (τ)
>
> Asociación Civil Intertango, *Tango y Cultura Popular*, No. 72, July 2006

Though suits and fishnets might be less common in the *milongas* these days, there remains a higher degree of formality surrounding appearance in these sites. Indeed, a friend told me that her father-in-law, whom she described as "one of the old *milongueros*," had not danced in two years because he didn't own a proper suit. There are plenty of young people at the *milongas*, however, and there is plenty of crossover from the *prácticas* to the *milongas*. While some young dancers adapt their attire and etiquette, others are testing the boundaries, as a recent Tango-L post laments:

> "Scenes from the *milonga*"
>
> Friday she was wearing camouflage leggings, her first pair of Comme il Faut shoes, and a hodgepodge of summer tops. She used to dress more appropriately for the *milonga*, but she's one of the trendsetters toward the grunge style in the *milongas*. . . . She hasn't learned that she should change into her dance shoes in the ladies' room. That's like changing in the gym before or after exercising rather than in the locker room. She's dancing practically every *tanda* with her eyes closed, so she hasn't had an opportunity to learn much by watching. You'll see her dancing early at Leonesa and later at Lo de Celia. She's the one with all the butt action.
>
> Tango-L post, 2007

The rules are open to change as well. Long high on the list of traditionalist taboos, dance sneakers have gained legitimacy of late, thanks to a growing customer base who demand comfortable shoes—from stage dancers who must practice many hours a day, to professionals who spend hours teaching before going out social dancing at night (a necessary part of promotion), to foreigners from communities where the codes are less rigid. The ultimate sign of acceptance came when famed dancer El Flaco Dany lent his face to Fabio Shoes' ad campaign. The city's first major manufacturer of tango sneakers, Fabio has crafted a "classical" sneaker for the *tanguero* concerned with "dancing with codes"; as the company's Web site notes, it is named "El Cachafaz," in honor of the legendary tango dancer.

Sharing a cab ride home with me one night, a fellow expat complained about the current trend in tango fashions. Wide, flowy pants are in, and these conceal the one thing he really wants to see: the feet. Indeed, this image of the tango—of two chests pegged together, utter restraint from the head to the waist, belied by slicing legs and naughty footwork—has evolved.[10] The entry of so many dancers from other movement disciplines has encouraged attention to the body in its entirety, not just the feet and legs. From the opening and inversion of the embrace; increasing exploration of *alteraciones* (changes in direction); emphasis on *disociación* to the point of extensive and dramatic torsion; and the overall trend toward fluidity, elasticity, and circularity: the body's range of motion in the embrace has expanded. This expansion in quality and range of movement has both admitted and encouraged new fashions. Wide pants, for example, accentuate a sense of flow and roundness, softening rough edges and sharp movements; they trail behind and heighten leg extensions, highlighting a sense of rebound, and they enlarge the couple's presence while "containing," maintaining the sense of partnership in the very circularity they insinuate.

A New Tango or a New World?

Rather than the conceptual and pedagogic overhauls cited by Argentines, many foreigners focus on visual cues—movement vocabulary, dress, etiquette—and music when asked to define *nuevo*. Moreover, they argued in interviews, a relaxation in codes makes tango more attractive to young people:

> On a very simple level, I think it's a way of making tango appealing or cool in contrast to the "old-man tango"—you know, in contrast to the tango of our grandparents.
>
> Korey Ireland, American, tango professional

> There's a sense that tango's not cool and that *nuevo* is the answer to that. You know, "you can look like a rock star and still dance tango!"
>
> Deborah, American expat, tango professional

While Argentines might reject the *nuevo* label to stake their claim to the dance, foreigners might appropriate it to emphasize global contributions, like dancing to alternative or electronic music, for example. Sharna Fabiano reserves the term *neotango* to refer to the practice of dancing to both alternative and electronic tango. In a 2006 interview published in the *Tangodanza* magazine she argues that this is not a rejection of tradition, but an effort to reinforce the link between old and new: "We are talking about the evolution of a popular art form (tango social dance), and this will always require experimentation and the addition of contemporary technology and human awareness. The important thing for me is to remember that we are not throwing away the old culture, we are not re-creating tango from scratch, we are connecting two eras, or maybe more than two" (quoted in van Kokswijk 2006). Though many acclaimed electronic tango bands have emerged from Argentina in recent years, including Tanghetto, Otros Aires, and Narcotango, the practice of dancing to non-tango music has been traced to Europe and the United States before it became popular in the *prácticas* of Buenos Aires. On my January 2005 trip, my American companion burned an alternative tango CD for a *porteño* friend who now organizes one of the city's largest *prácticas*, where many of these songs can still be heard each week. In my conversation with an electronic tango composer, he suggested that it is his band's acceptance abroad and among the local vanguard that eventually facilitated their entry into the *milonga* scene of Buenos Aires—an echo of tango's own journeys abroad and back, each time bringing greater legitimacy.

The extent to which tango is shaped by such global negotiation and exchange cannot be underestimated. Naveira, Salas, the other dancers attached to the Cochabamba group, and many of today's rising stars have spent significant time teaching abroad and to foreigners in Buenos Aires. Naveira admitted that teaching abroad has forced him to rethink things that once seemed natural, in order to clarify and simplify his explanations for a non-Argentine audience. Describing this experience as enlightening, he told me that his travels have had a profound impact on both his dance and his teaching.

Only after spending two years in Argentina could I begin to sketch out the myriad characters and events that together gave rise to the *nuevo* label: the Cochabamba investigation group, the entry of dancers from other disciplines, the increasing entry of younger dancers, the growth of new spaces, and finally, the growth of an interconnected global tango scene. Still, the significance of the term continues to confound. After describing it as a decidedly American trend revolving around new music, for instance, Ellen Mayer of Providence Tango observed that the trend may be on the decline, and with its passing, she confessed, she isn't sure how to define *nuevo*. Increasingly, young American dancers are distancing themselves from the label, highlighting "versatility" (citing fluency in a range of styles, embraces, approaches), speaking of "transcending" classification, or simply rejecting it. For instance, in 2008, on the Web site for their tango school, Homer and Cristina Ladas noted:

> Homer & Cristina prefer to not use the term "*nuevo*" in their approach to tango or in their class titles. Instead, they like to dance and teach a variety of connected, musical, dynamic, interesting, creative, liberating, etc., ideas / technique / movement. They both work towards the fusion of all tango concepts via the "one tango" philosophy in an attempt to reduce barriers that may inhibit themselves or other folks from really finding their own dance.

Meanwhile, some young Argentines appropriate the *nuevo* label to highlight the integration of old and new in their dance. Beyond attracting students, labeling one's dance is a means of demonstrating knowledge and establishing legitimacy. Framing *nuevo* a system of analysis, Andrés Amarilla highlights his participation in the Cochabamba investigation group in the description of his "Villa Urquiza with a Nuevo Twist" seminar. Defining *nuevo* as a tool that facilitates expansion of a traditional style, on his Web site, Amarilla and partner Meredith Klein trace their dance to the famed style of a *porteño barrio*, while opening the possibility of *nuevo* to more traditionally minded dancers (2008).

This approach smartly sidesteps the insufficiency of the label. Many dancers, Argentine and foreign alike, expressed something bordering on exasperation when confronted with the question of what *nuevo* means. Beyond the division and controversy the very word stirs up, several pointed out that difference, rather than similarity, seems to link the many dancers subsumed under the label. Whether "my tango," "contemporary tango," "one tango," or just "tango," even those connected with the label, or those who reluctantly employ it, note the somewhat arbitrary nature of such labels. Like the problematic *milonguero* label—an occasionally derogatory term whose currency has skyrocketed through the rather ingenious linking of authenticity, style of embrace, and feeling—such branding facilitates the dressing up, disguise, and selling of a spade:

> Get in a taxi and the driver has the same mind as the *milonguero*. Or go to the vegetable stand, it's the same. He's a guy from the neighborhood, not very cultured, sort of brute, old-fashioned. Okay, for tourists, because they don't know the common people . . . but if you know the people of Argentina, a *milonguero* is just a regular guy who happens to dance well. For the tourist, he's something sacred, but for me—I already know him, I don't have to seek him out. (τ)
>
> Gabriel Glagovsky, Argentine, tango professional and *práctica* organizer

So, is there a new tango? If we follow the advice of one famed *milonguero*, we'll have to wait another ten years or so to find out. At least if we're framing *nuevo* the latest in the tango's history of styles. For a style, according to Horacio, takes about forty years to solidify. Or perhaps Ellen Mayer's description of a declining trend is more apt. Then again, there is the system of analysis—the pedagogic revolution—cited by so many Argentines, whether they like the term or not. Perhaps it is all of these things, or none at all. Perhaps there is "only tango," as a recent Tango-L post implores.

In the end, the anthropologist in me finally settled on Naveira's summation: "What we have is a new situation in the world relative to tango. . . . I would guess that, from an anthropological point of view, this new situation is much more interesting than the tiny idea of a new style" (τ). By no means a solution, it opens up another can of worms entirely. Creating more questions than answers, suggesting more than it resolves, Naveira's observation is much like the dance itself.

But Naveira put me back on track, directing me to the politics underlying the debate, and situating this mini-world within a much larger context. For today's tango scene is a microcosm of the larger world, where global forces and local practices meet every day, yielding constant negotiations, ever-ending reshapings, and a decidedly less stable, more contested new world.

4

Manejame como un auto (Drive Me Like a Car)

Much of the romance of Old Spain still remains reincarnate in the lovely women of the Argentine. It is seldom that an Argentine woman is troubled about the rights of their sex, or any of the more virile notions that have stirred modern womanhood. For she seems to be content to live behind the veil of romance, and to accept as her due the admiration so lavishly bestowed upon her.

James A. Fitzpatrick, *Romantic Argentina* (1932)

Argentina and its tango are the third world other that provides a reflection of, and site to reflect upon, the dilemmas of gender relations in Western culture more generally.

Amy Kaminsky, *Argentina: Stories for a Nation* (2008)

The role of women? Minimum. They were like our tools to have fun. We cannot dance between ourselves, so we should call women. Yeah, that's the first thing that was really obvious in *nuevo*. Well, not *nuevo* but the thing we were doing—that it wasn't feminine. We were creating steps like kids, and we didn't ask the women for anything. We didn't care about their opinions. (ε)

Anonymous Argentine, tango professional, on the role of women in the 1990s investigation sessions that many cite as the breeding ground for *tango nuevo*

Some girls get fed up with following, and they want to dance like a man because they say it's more entertaining. But I say you don't have enough time in your lifetime to learn how to follow well. So I would recommend to these girls to really learn how to follow.

Carlos Gavito, quoted in Quiroga, *Tango Is a Shared Moment* (2001)

August 2006, Interview with a *Tanguero*

Barely slept. Awake at 6:00 a.m. in mild panic over impending departure from Buenos Aires, complete lack of funds, no clear sense of how I'll make enough money on return to the States to ever get myself back to Buenos Aires, forget about how and where I'll survive while I'm there . . . or maybe I'm just nervous about my interview with Xavier tonight. Now, after a day of doing nothing—lack of sleep after a night of dancing, too much nervous energy—I'm somehow still scrambling to get myself out the door on time. I've no time to buy pastry, a usual offering when I'm invited to conduct an interview in someone's home, and as an afterthought I grab the bottle of Malbec from the counter. I'm on the fence about this. Is it appropriate for a young female anthropologist to bring wine to her older male informant in his home? Especially if he's not too much older, according to Argentine standards at least. Moreover, is this too much?

Notions of machismo still color social life in ways I'm unaccustomed to, and despite heated protest, nearly every Argentine male I've interviewed (over a certain age) has insisted on "inviting" me (translation: paying for me) even though I've invited him (to the interview) in the first place . . . this notion of the invitation being confusing. "To invite" is one of those porteño *euphemisms that render mundane actions more delicate, further convincing me of the brute awkwardness of American English.* Te invito. *I invite you. So charming, almost British in its refinement, neatly sweeping the mildest hint of paternalism under the rug.*

In the end, it turns out I'd gotten all bent out of shape over nothing. The wine is a big hit with Xavier; his face lights up in surprise at the bottle and then elation at the label. He carries on about this particular year of this particular wine, how foreign investment in the nation's winemaking industry is revolutionizing production and bringing Argentina full-scale into the global market. I'm convinced, in fact, that this small gesture I'd obsessed and agonized over sets me up for what is one of my better interviews. I also feel myself more fully coming to accept the distinct nature of male-female relations in the birthplace of tango.

During our interview I ask Xavier about the changing role of the woman in tango. He responds that the roles of both men and women have changed, and then adds that I am not fooling him with my question. He knows what I am getting at: women's liberation, the purported connection between tango and machismo, tango as an example of male domination, and so on and so forth. But machismo is an attitude in life, he argues, not a problem of the dance, and furthermore an obsolete, irrelevant concern. Our interview concludes shortly thereafter. As he escorts me to the door, he stops me and confesses: "The truth, Carolyn, is that I'm a married man—and I can't hide it. But each time I see you, so beautiful, oh, what I would give to keep it from you!" I laugh in response, give him the customary kiss on the cheek and thank him again for his time. Walking away, on the crooked cobblestones of Villa Rivero, which is now dark and deserted save for a group of teenage boys on the corner, I feel safe in the knowledge that his glance trails me . . . and mildly conflicted in that feeling of safety.

Que lindos son tus ojos (What Beautiful Eyes You Have)

During our interview, Xavier confessed to being exasperated, at times even angry, when he first went abroad to teach and was asked time and again to explain why the man leads and the woman follows. Surely, he said, this most basic principle of tango, of social dance in general, is only natural. When I recounted our exchange to another expat, she was giddy and incredulous at once. "Oh my god, X *hit* on you!" she shouted. I shrugged her off: "That's just how male Argentine tango teachers say goodbye . . . isn't it?" While our North American upbringing taught us to find a bit of the ridiculous in such behavior, re-reading my journal I found similar instances, often portrayed as somehow essentially Argentine:

> This subject comes up again and again if you talk to foreigners. Women in general start judging that way of playing because we experience it as threatening, or sometimes without any respect, but for Argentineans it's a game. So asking a woman home is just their way of saying goodbye. And the other extreme—I have had experiences where if you don't ask a woman this question, [it] doesn't mean that she would follow you, but it's almost "Am I not worth this? I'm not attractive enough to deserve this invitation?" As much as you perceive with your American values, they perceive with their values. (ε)
>
> Matthias Kroug, German expat, scientist

Accustomed as I was to *porteños* at this point, I was unfazed by Xavier's comment, though it is amusing given his treatise on the irrelevance and inexistence of machismo mere moments earlier. If this isn't machismo, or at least some distant, watered-down relic of machismo, what exactly is it? It has a different shape than the catcalls and the famed Argentine *piropos* (artful compliments), at times as simple as a cheerful "*Que linda!*" (How pretty!), while at others a barely audible comment, muttered under a challenging glance by that lucky *porteño* who brushes close by on a crowded sidewalk.[1]

For the tango pilgrim who travels to Buenos Aires, the *piropo* is one of those local customs that immediately raises awareness of one's displacement from home. In the *porteño* tango world, sweet-talk on the dance floor has achieved the status of art form in the *piropo*, one-liners the likes of "What beautiful eyes you have" being on the tame end of the scale. A compliment bordering on pickup line, uttered without necessarily serious intentions or expectations, *piropos* are the *juego de jure* (authorized game) in many of the more traditional dance venues. With *piropos*, male dancers fulfill their partner's expectation of the *porteño* male, on the one hand conforming to the (admittedly clichéd) notion of what it means to be Latin, macho, a seductor, and on the other seeking to convince the *tanguera* of her singularity, to more fully extend the illusion of communion on a crowded dance floor. One wonders, of course, if he nurtures the slightest inkling of hope, if the *milonguero* is indeed defenseless in the presence of countless beautiful young women, many of whom hail from abroad, most in a desperate search for a "true tango moment" assumed to be achieved only in the dance's birthplace, in the arms of a real *porteño*, the older the better. More than simply generational, *piropos* are one of the many practices around which notions of style or community are constructed. As a game, *piropos* render the *milonga* a site for a theatrical enactment of traditional notions of masculinity and femininity, employed alternately to intimidate, entertain, define roles, fulfill the sexually charged promise of the dance's reputation—and test the boundaries of possibility.

However, a part of the steady growth of a younger community of dancers and the creation of new venues is an interest in approaching the dance and the larger social milieu in a more contemporary fashion, including relinquishing such postures as the *piropos*. Buenos Aires' "laid back" *práctica* scene offers relief from ritual theatrics deemed an annoyance, a hindrance to simply enjoying the dance itself:

> If you go to the *milongas*, you don't want to look at the *milongueros* if you don't want to be felt up, or if you don't want to be told how beautiful your eyes are, and "if only they were younger." And then they would mention that their last girlfriend was younger than you! There's this cropping up of *prácticas*, and a lot of people trying to get away from that—not necessarily the *milonguero* style but more so the *milonguero* attitude—*el juego de la seducción* [the seduction game], all of the old guys trying to seduce the girls . . . and the younger

> people are more interested in the dancing and having fun, and they're not analyzing it in this way that's so sexist, you know?
>
> Ginger, American expatriate, chef

Emphasizing, however, a distinction between age and style, Ginger pointed out that "even some of the younger guys will do that in the context of the *milonga*," thus framing the *milonga* as a site to play, to try out postures associated with a notion of *tanguero* identity informed by exaggerated representations of tango from the stage, screen, and visual media. It is also a form of apprenticeship in the *milongas* themselves. Of course, these exaggerated postures could also be the *milonguero*'s response to what he perceives as the foreign woman's expectations on her tango pilgrimage. Nonetheless, such reactions to this type of playing as sexist or macho (even if understood as play) are not uncommon among younger foreign *tangueras* like Ginger.

In this sense, *milongas* function as experiential containers, housing and imparting memories to those who will claim them. Drawing on the national obsession with remembrance, within sites constructed around and imbued with a sense of nostalgia, such posturing on the dance floor feeds from a sort of collective unconscious that is nourished at home and abroad through films, stage shows, images, and tango histories. Further, tango dancers insert themselves within a cultural tradition through a shared movement practice that doesn't merely reference but in fact pays homage to a worldview that emerged at a specific place in time. In manifesting such postures out of time, however, a degree of kitsch and caricature colors the behavior of the *milongueros*, their protégés, and the foreign dancers whose presence encourages their perpetuation.

According to Luciana Valle, who organizes the popular El Motivo *práctica*, the new social dance venues grew from a desire to escape an *onda* (vibe) approaching circus, and to create a scene accessible to dancers who had lives to attend to in the light of day:

> The night is weird. We were girls who lived in the daylight, we got up at 9:00 a.m. to go to yoga, so why I can't dance until 1:00 a.m., why I have to go to a place that is packed . . . have all that smoke, and be in a place where everybody is like . . . in a mise en scène. Why? (ε)

As noted, the *piropo* is part of *porteño* life off the dance floor as well. On the streets of Buenos Aires, the female form is fair game for male commentary.[2] For a woman in the Argentine capital, *piropos* quickly become one more element in an already-overloaded soundscape, blending in with the noise of too many *colectivos* (buses), and the incessant drone of the drilling, banging, and sawing that are slowly extending the reach of the city several stories higher, wider, or, for those with money, closer to a notion of "first world" comfort and amenities.[3] However, just as the foreign woman in Buenos Aires arms herself against such comments by cultivating a healthy balance of haughtiness and an acute ability to ignore, the *porteña* abroad acclimates herself to their absence. Rather than considered disrespectful or threatening, such comments are viewed ambivalently at worst. A young *porteña* who had relocated to Germany for several years confessed to exasperation over the lack of attention she received there. On her first day, she ran home five minutes after leaving the house, convinced she had made a catastrophic fashion blunder, for what other possible excuse could there be for the lack of male commentary? One of the many customs that allow the two sexes to revel in their separateness, *piropos* are generally perceived as harmless and, although unacknowledged, often secretly appreciated.[4]

Beyond the informality and anonymity of the streets, the *piropo* is also at home in the realm of the professional. In my own experience conducting research in the tango world, I grew accustomed to comments I would have deemed inappropriate, infantilizing, and sexist off of Argentine soil—like the tango instructor who told me he had "never met such a beautiful woman with so many problems" after asking about my research. Rather than a testament to my appearance, such flattery and flirtation are central to the business of tango itself.

It isn't just that these Argentine *tangueros* never learned to filter their thoughts, something Kaitlin Quistgaard (1999) attests to with humorous effect in describing the special attention she received from "fawning men in suits" (government officials and executives) as a foreign correspondent in Buenos Aires. In the *porteño* tango world, such posturing is expected, especially by foreign *tangueras*, who take *piropos* as confirmation of the cultural difference that makes the dance in its birthplace so enticing, regardless of how they might ultimately feel about their propriety. The *piropo* thus warrants analysis that looks beyond the message itself. As Matthias observed, foreign attitudes about such commentary reveal much about the recipient of the *piropo*, who "perceives with her values." If the foreign *tanguera* is unable to read such flattery as a game, she may be judged as unwilling to fully give herself to the experience of tango in

Buenos Aires, and there is a chance that she will miss out on more than just *piropos*.

Leading and Following: The Gendered Division of (Tango) Labor

> The dance portrays an encounter between the powerful and completely dominant male and the passive, docile, completely submissive female.
>
> Julie Taylor, "Tango: Ethos of Melancholy" (1987)

> Since my generation . . . women are also recognized as intellectual beings. We're able to see things differently; we bring different things to the table than men do, from a feminine point of view . . . without needing to be above them, but on the same level, in an equal relationship. I think this began about fifteen years ago. . . . About eight years ago I began to feel that I'd gotten to a place where people saw me as a human being, not just a woman. A human being, a thinking being. Not just a gender. (τ)
>
> Dana Frígoli, Argentine, tango professional and co-director, DNI Tango School

Pablo Veron's famous outburst in *The Tango Lesson*, exhorting Sally Potter to "follow, JUST follow!"—denying her any voice—mirrors Taylor's description of sexual domination in the physical enactment of the dance. In this passage, Taylor explores the contrast between the clichéd image of tango dance in the popular imagination, of male domination and female submission, and the message of many tango lyrics, in which men suffer at the hands of willful, cunning, heartless women. But the tango long ago evolved beyond this initial, chauvinistic signification. Juan Carlos Copes and María Nieves are often credited with placing the man and woman on equal footing. Yet even earlier, as Thompson notes, the female partners of the 1940s Club Nelson dancers "rebelled against men who bossed them around with peremptory hand motions" (2005: 257). Interestingly, dancers continue to make personal and generational claims to female autonomy and to equality in the embrace to this day.[5] Nonetheless, culture affects the way dancers conceive of, approach, and enact the roles of leading and following, and the modern implications of this (largely) gendered division of roles is anything but straightforward.

The title of this chapter comes from a friend's initiation into tango in Buenos Aires. In an effort to make him comfortable with the concept and practice of leading, his female teacher instructed him to "drive her like a car" as they walked through the space in a practice embrace. While this wording might seem a terrible step backward to some, the metaphor is not entirely uncommon among Argentine instructors. Indeed, one young couple noted that the idea of "driving" could propel anxious men into movement, *into* the woman's space, a difficult concept for many a beginner.

Translating the terminology of tango's partnership is not only a linguistic but a cultural endeavor. Foreign professionals and scholars have argued that the terms "lead" and "follow" are poor translations of the commonly heard *marcar* (to mark, to show the way) and *responder* (to respond), or *proponer y disponer* (to propose and to decide). During my time in Buenos Aires and in my interviews with Argentines, however, I found that *llevar* (lead) and *seguir* (follow) were just as often or more frequently used. Whether this reflects foreign influence—both from the early 1900s, when tango was codified and tamed by European dance masters who transformed the dance into a bourgeois commodity to be consumed by an international elite schooled in the heterosexist politics of leading and following (see Tobin 1998), and more recently, as Argentine professionals have incentive to learn the language and customs of foreign consumers—is an interesting question. One young *porteño* professional suggested that *llevar* and *seguir* were the preferred terms in verb form, and that *la marca* ("the mark") might be used more frequently in noun form.

Further, implicit in most instruction in Argentina is acceptance of gender division.[6] As Olga Besio told me, "I think it's very clear in tango that the man leads and the woman follows" (τ). Nonetheless, it stands in contrast to the generally more nuanced and egalitarian explications of the sexual and physical mechanics of the dance, commonly invoked by U.S. instructors.

Framing the dance as a conversation, an exchange based on the equal participation of each, many U.S. teachers present the woman as an autonomous figure through terminology like "active following." For instance, on his Web site, dance historian and Stanford professor Richard Powers (2010) speaks of "ultimate partnering," rejecting as outdated an approach to the roles of leader and follower that hails from an intense period of formalization in ballroom dance beginning in the 1930s:

> After centuries of ballroom emphasis on dancing for the pleasure of one's partner the 1930s saw the emergence of a particularly disagreeable phase of social dance, when the term "lead" came to mean "command" and "follow" meant "obey." . . . The main reason I don't like the term "following" is that it doesn't accurately describe the role. Women do not "follow," they interpret signals they're given,

> with a keen responsiveness that is not passive. . . . The follow role is mentally and physically active, like the flow state in sports.

Powers further describes the leader's role as "tracking," complicating a simplistic division between the two roles and pointing to the leader's responsibility to respond to the follower's cues as well:

> The best dancers now know that a part of great leading is following. (I prefer the term *tracking*—he leads a move, then tracks her movement and stays with her.) He is perceptive and responsive to her situation, as he watches where his partner is going, where her feet are, where her momentum is heading, which steps flow smoothly from her current step. He knows and he cares what is comfortable for her, what is pleasurable or fun. He dances for his partner's ability and comfort.

Despite his advanced approach to the concept of partnering, Powers nonetheless divides the roles according to gender. Reminiscent of Xavier's explanation in our interview, it is the man who "leads" or "tracks" and the woman who "follows" or "interprets." This division is not questioned.

This has interesting implications in the United States and in Europe, where instructors employ images, metaphors, and values from their various cultures to communicate the mechanics and meaning of the dance. The same dance can be imagined quite differently, and the relation of leader to follower can be played out and experienced distinctly. For example, in my interview with Sean, an American *tanguero*, he notes that a popular U.S. teacher explains the role of the follower through a postfeminist, American lens, encouraging a "masculine energy" in following. Arguing that such an approach would probably be considered inappropriate in Argentina, Sean distinguishes the intention with which he perceives Argentine and American women enact the role of follower:

> He'll tell followers that they need to step with a leader's energy, especially in the forward step; that they need to step as if they were leading, using his [the leader's] intention but with that kind of certainty, that masculine energy. This is something that I don't think you would hear in Argentina—they would never tell a woman to step like a man, you know? . . . I think the "active voice" of a follower in Argentina is more like what she can add in her own kind of monologue running on the side, and that the active voice of a follower say in the North-

> west [United States] is challenging or responding or provoking the dialogue between the two. It's not a sideline, it's essential to the conversation, and for me that's much more interesting.

According to this description, "active following" implies not only a subversion of gender, but a certain devaluation of femininity, where it is "masculine energy" that places the follower on equal footing in the embrace. The ambivalence expressed by foreign *tangueras* to traditions like the *piropo* and to the terms *lead* and *follow* may also be a reaction to such thinking, for despite the gains of feminism, empowerment and femininity have yet to be fully reconciled. Indeed, I believe, Argentine tango is a practice par excellence for confronting and negotiating what many foreign *tangueras* experience as profound contradictions.

Building on Powers's "tracking" and "interpreting," another U.S. teacher references on his Web site (Rabe 2009) Johanna Siegmann's 2000 *The Tao of Tango* to portray the interplay of masculine (yang) and feminine (yin) qualities in each of the roles. In an effort to overcome American resistance to the male-leader / female-follower dichotomy, he draws on Asian philosophy, separating and overlapping the masculine and feminine roles and energies under the guise of an ancient, exotic worldview. Interestingly, Argentine tango professional Rodolfo Dinzel used the same image to free the tango from its image of strict heterosexuality, muddying or dissolving gender distinctions: "At times the idea of the two sexes is lost. . . . My experience of the dance lies beyond the identity of the person I'm dancing with" (τ).

Indeed, some foreign dancers employed the yin-yang image to frame the tango as a place where dancers are free to embrace a separation of the sexes now often discounted:

> The primary thing for me is that you've got the connection of the male-female, masculine-feminine energy, which for me can create synergy and it's fantastic for people to get through their prejudices.
>
> Sarah Bonnar, Australia, tango instructor

> In Europe we always look for the equality, while here it's more obvious that the man and the woman have different roles. . . . You could say there's the feminine and masculine qualities that meet each other and do something together. It sounds maybe philosophical but I think every experience where opposites in a way unite is something

> we strive for. And it's for me one explanation why this dance fascinates people all over the world. (ε)
>
> Matthias Kroug, German expatriate, scientist

In *Tango: Un baile bien porteño* (Tango: A Very Porteño Dance; 2006) German native and *tanguera* Nicole Nau-Klapwijk describes a similar quest for balance in her life, attained through her discovery of tango in Argentina, an activity and culture that together teach her to be a woman and to allow herself partnership with a man. A common theme in my conversations with foreigners is the idea of the tango as a realm within which sexual difference is accepted and celebrated. A dancer and choreographer from the United States, Michele Kadison, described how tango has released her from assumptions about her dynamic, external, almost masculine body, freeing her to explore another dimension of her being through movement:

> I was always a toughass—whatever the role was that did the most jumps and turns, that was me. So when I came to tango all of a sudden I could really explore my truly feminine side. . . . Tango is unraveling all of these neurological pathways to my muscular system to get me to be soft and listening and acquiescent, and really appreciate the goddess side of being female.

Foreign dancers also contrasted the experience of tango in Buenos Aires to that in their home community, where notions of gender equality pervade nearly all aspects of life. For example, Nancy underscored the experience of femininity in Buenos Aires, while she described her first year of tango in the United States as a nearly genderless experience: "I didn't feel the dance at all, which means I wasn't in touch with my femininity. It was just, 'I'm a person and I'm dancing with this person and we're creating something,' and it was creative, but I didn't feel feminine" (American expatriate, actress).

Embracing distinctions between the sexes is not simply a concept connected to the idea of place—Argentina, Buenos Aires. It is perpetuated through representations and descriptions of the dance, and these ideas seep into the skin through touch, in the face of images, and in response to evocative, image-producing words.[7] As Foster (1988) points out in her study of modern dance performances, reception of these events begins long before the actual dancing. Potential audience members consider advertisements and ticket prices, and once the audience has arrived, the formality and arrangement of the space, program design, titles, and program notes all influence the audience's evaluation of a show. What's more, this evaluation is fed by prior experience, by the memories and feelings evoked by words, images, and physical design.

Similarly, promotional images, advertisements, and tourism materials target the reader's senses and inspire the imagination much like tango stage shows and films. Such materials and media have traditionally reinforced romantic notions of the essential "Argentine-ness" of the dance, represented through a passionate, heterosexual embrace and references to late-nineteenth- to early-twentieth-century *porteño* society symbols and characters, such as the *farol* (gas lamp), the *conventillo* (tenement house), the port slum of La Boca, the *compadrito* (hoodlum) with his fedora and knife, the *maleva* (bad girl) in high heels and fishnets.[8]

While the tango has evolved beyond its bordello, slum, and tenement house origins, this narrative—of its dangerous, lower-class origins and its connection to a licentious heterosexual embrace—lingers. It is carried in movement vocabulary passed down through generations, lifted from historic images, and transferred from the stage performer's theatrical reenactment to the classroom. Like Browning's (1995) "survivals" in samba—gestural references to a colonial or precolonial past—the plethora of tango movements developed since the dance's inception are a window onto its past.[9] The Argentine professionals who brought the dance abroad through stage shows, training locals and planting the seeds of global tango communities as they traveled, carried these narratives as memories, cultural heritage embodied. Further, these narratives play out in classroom exercises, whether to mock and discount as clichéd or to elicit heightened performances from students through romantic and theatrical anecdotes that get at one particular aspect of the dance's history (where tango equals passion and drama), often at the expense of any other.[10] Thus, this facet of the tango is deeply embedded in the global imagination as *the* image of tango.

Outside Argentina, the tango is a safe space to explore the separation of masculine and feminine because it is "other," "exotic," and "Latin." Indeed, part of the dance's appeal for the nonnative may be its perceived "dangerousness," which is subverted and cleansed through its very performance. It is safe, for example, for foreign *tangueras/os* to dress and dance suggestively, for there remains a degree of cultural appropriation or a sense that one is playing a character. This performance of a more traditional gender identity often involves a sense of theater, for example, donning fishnet stockings and a slit skirt or a fedora and scarf. The "costume" allows the dancer to avoid the contradiction of the assumptions about gender and equality that one encounters in the dance and those that one lives by in all other facets of one's life. Others simply find dancing "in costume" or "in character" freeing, a way to break barriers of inhibition.

Further, behaviors prohibited by notions of propriety enter a state of limbo or experimentation when abroad, when thrown into contact with a culture or subculture where a separation of the genders and their roles is quite firmly embraced, and the notion of equal rights does not yield an erasure of male-female difference. This is by no means to suggest that feminism is not alive and well in Argentina, but rather to point out that the struggle many foreign women face in reconciling feminism and femininity is not equally problematic for their Argentine counterparts. So it is that tough, independent, foreign *tangueras* often find themselves accumulating corsets and stiletto heels in Buenos Aires, and dreaming of a *tanda* in the arms of a *viejo milonguero.*

While the tango embrace sanctions a performance of gender that many non-Argentines describe as freeing in contrast to that experienced in their everyday lives, others frame it in a negative light. In contrast with tango's humble origins and general association with lower-class *porteños* (despite a lengthy period of widespread popular appeal), tango communities around the globe are decidedly middle- and upper-class enclaves, where the majority of practitioners are degree-holding members of the professional class, and thus generally educated, successful, and financially stable. In particular, foreign women spoke to the initial distance they perceived between their assertive, independent, egalitarian selves and the tango self who "surrenders," "follows," and "listens."

Distinguishing between the relaxed codes of the emerging *nuevo* or *práctica* scene and the codes of the more traditional *milongas* in Buenos Aires, some dancers highlighted an emptiness in the theatrics of the latter:

> You have to get dressed up in fishnet stockings and a short skirt to dance tango . . . no, more of that stuff we don't need. You know, more of that fakery and all that stuff on the surface. The world is already enough about that and it's not helping. You know, the facelifts and the lies and the bullshit.
>
> Sarah Bonnar, Australia, tango professional

Underscoring the difference she experienced on her first visit to Buenos Aires, Pia, a painter from Sweden, noted an emphasis on appearance in the more traditional *milongas*, where women are especially subject to all manner of inspection and discrimination, and one's ability is often the least important factor in securing dances:

> Just sitting here and thinking maybe my dress is not nice enough. . . . And all of these beautiful girls. That's another thing I don't like about Buenos Aires. The macho culture and the idea that you have to be beautiful to dance, and if you're not beautiful you're not worth anything. And there's no old women in the *milongas*—if they're not so beautiful they can just sit at home. (ε)

As these two young foreign women perceive it, the culture in some of the traditional *milongas* not only is superficial but also places disproportionate demands upon men and women.

Savigliano (2003) describes the *milonga* as a site where such external factors dissolve, where the dance comes first. For her, no matter how young, old, short, tall, fat, thin, or in whatever manner aesthetically endowed or challenged the participant, it is skill that determines whether and how much one will dance (153–55). This is still the case in many venues, and among certain dancers, in most venues. But the sentiments expressed by Sarah and Pia also ring true. It is important to reiterate that Argentine tango stands out among dance forms for its acceptance of the aging body. In a realm that generally celebrates youth, tango is considered an appropriate activity for people of all ages; there are plenty of traditional *milongas* where one will encounter a largely mature crowd.

At the same time, however, there is a parallel *milonga* circuit that has grown with the support of the city's ever-expanding tango tourism, where the absence of older women is striking. As tango communities have developed around the world and Buenos Aires has situated itself as the center of the global industry, these *milongas* have become sites for the city's growing class of tango professionals to promote themselves. This shift toward the *milonga* as both marketplace and spectacle, as opposed to merely social gathering, places even greater demand upon women to look good, as does the growth of "exhibitions," or short performances by professional couples at the *milongas*. These exhibitions, marked by a general shift toward more elaborate, showy choreography, in particular for the woman, suggest that professional tango favors a young and agile female body (often capable of executing balletic and acrobatic movements), while the man may be of any age.

These famed *confiterías* (tearooms), dance halls, and social clubs are attended by a mix of foreigners and Argentines, the percentage of each shifting throughout the year according to foreign holidays, *porteño* festivals, and international demands on Argentine teachers. The clichéd yet defining image of this particular *milonga* scene is the famed *milongueros'* table, where the old-timers hold court, drinking champagne, watching the floor with an alternating mix of amusement and disdain, and occasionally rising to grace one of the beautiful young *milonguitas* with a song or, if she is lucky, an entire *tanda*. The young women wait patiently on the sidelines, maybe stopping at the table to say hello, but never to stay and certainly never to invite the revered male *bailarines* to dance.[11]

The cultivation of fantasy that this particular *milonga* circuit perpetuates is inspired by both historic anecdotes and images that favor the dance's male forebears, traditionalist arguments that link age to authenticity, and global desires to experience the "authentic." The further they decline, the greater the *milongueros* are celebrated and rewarded with the adulation of the young and beautiful, while the young and beautiful act out an exaggerated notion of femininity inaccessible to them in the light of day—or at home in another country.

My conversations with foreign men did not reveal a parallel desire to encounter the tango in the arms of elder *porteñas*, though this likely reflects the absence of any relic of inspiration in the social scene or the larger imaginary created in films, media images, lyrics, and promotional materials. (On the other hand, perhaps these foreign men wouldn't divulge such a desire to me for the simple fact that I don't fit that profile.) Or perhaps the greater risks of leading temper these fantasies, for it takes a bit of nerve, or at least a healthy dose of confidence, for a foreign man to invite an experienced *porteña* onto the dance floor.

At the same time, this subworld serves as a window onto the values embraced in *porteño* society, where "true beauty" does not preclude surgical intervention, in turn encouraged and heightened by global desires. The United States currently ranks highest in the number of cosmetic procedures, and Argentina in eleventh place, according to a 2011 survey by the International Society of Aesthetic Plastic Surgery,[12] but the growth of "destination" cosmetic and medical industries suggests the intensifying triangular relationship of economics, aesthetics, and health. While economic inequities are surely driving the commodification of medical care, they may also be encouraging aesthetic surgery among locals in the postcolonial sites where many middle-class, "first world" clients go for such

1. Mural of tango composers, Club Villa Malcolm. Conception and research: Eduardo Gálvez; Art: Lina Boselli; Production: Lina Boselli, Gimena Drughieri, Eduardo Gálvez, and Laura Parras.

2. *Nada nuevo* (Nothing New). Barrio Norte, Buenos Aires. Photo by author.

3. Dance Philadelphia *milonga*. Photo by Lesley Mitchell.

4. Four *bandoneons*. Orquesta Típica El Afronte, Plaza Dorrego, Buenos Aires. Photo by Paloma Baytelman.

5. A modern close embrace. Kara Wenham and Javier Antar, www.todaviatango.com. Photo by Pablo Rincon, www.pablorincon.com.ar.

6. A *colgada.* Claudio Dario Cortejarena and Yanina Quiñones in Caminito (Tango Walkway), La Boca, Buenos Aires. In a *colgada* (from the verb *colgar*, "to hang"), the follower moves off-axis in a direction away from the leader, who supports the follower. Photo by author.

7. Milonga La Calesita. Photo by Carlos Vizzotto.

8. Comme il Faut—*Los mejores zapatos para bailar tango* (The best shoes to tango). Used with permission.

9. A *volcada*. Ariadna Naveira and Fernando Sanchez, at Nora's Tango Week, 2009. Photo by Jerry Jew. In a *volcada* (from the verb *volcar,* "to tip over, upset, spill"), the follower moves off-axis in a direction toward the leader, who supports the follower.

10. *Un tango en el agua* (A tango in the water). 1912. Archivo General de la Nación, Dto. Doc. Fotográficos.

11. *Tango criollo* (Creole tango). From *Caras y caretas*, January 31, 1903. Archivo General de la Nación, Dto. Doc. Fotográficos.

12. *Disociación* (Torsion). José Halfon and Virginia Cutillo, from *El tango en la piel* (Tango on the Skin). Body Art by Alfredo Genovese.

13. *Tango centenario* (Centennial Tango). Fourth Centennial of the founding of the city of Buenos Aires. Avenida Costanera, Buenos Aires, 1936. Archivo General de la Nación, Dto. Doc. Fotográficos.

14. A *milonga* at Salon Canning. Photo by B. Jönsson.

15. An alternative embrace. Moira Castellano and Pablo Inza, 2006. Photo by Gabriel Cano, www.gabicano.com/tango.

16. Andrés Amarilla and Meredith Klein, www.philadelphiatangoschool.com. Photo by Zebra Visual.

17. A *práctica* at Club Villa Malcolm. Photo by Carlos Vizzotto.

18. An alternative embrace. *El de ojos tiernos* (The guy with the sweet eyes). Tango postcard. Club de Tango, Editorial Inca.

procedures, unable to afford such luxuries at home. As with tango tourism, since the 2001 economic crisis and devaluation of the peso, a medical tourism market has burgeoned in Buenos Aires.

The importance accorded physical appearance in the tango world is reinforced in the city's tango guides. These glossy, full-color, magazine-style pamphlets include, in addition to the predictable information on classes, *milongas*, shoe and clothing outlets, tourist excursions, interviews with dancers, and photos of *milongas*, ads for aesthetic-surgery clinics (Palumbo 2006; *Tango Map Guide* 2006). Speaking about the connection between tango and the city's booming aesthetic surgery industry, a native *tanguera* roots the precedence accorded physical appearance in tango within the larger *porteño* culture:

> If you like to dance tango, you're going to like to look good. . . . Buenos Aires was a city and it still is a city where everybody really takes care of themselves. The ladies like to be elegant. They really want to look the best that they can. . . . The beauty and cosmetic clinics are all full, and the prices are much better than in the United States. So I think it is one of the reasons that a lot of people come here right now—because of the exchange. (ε)
>
> Celia, Argentine, doctor

Despite this cross-promotion of tango and aesthetic surgery, there is no question that the cult of good appearance exists outside of the tango world as well. Moreover, many tango venues *do* offer older women refuge from a media-saturated culture that favors youth and beauty above all else and that arguably places higher demands and pressure on women in this respect. There are plenty of traditional *milongas* where older women are evaluated for qualities other than their appearance, and in tango communities around the world, older women are accorded license to express their sexuality in ways that are generally at odds with society's expectations of women over a certain age.[13] Nonetheless, the pairing of beautiful young women with older *milongueros* speaks to the fact that men still wield greater power in the tango world, and to the sexist ageism women face, both in the tango world and at large.

In the *nuevo* or *práctica* scene, dancers claim less pressure to conform to ideals of gender and appearance. In the *prácticas*, dance sneakers and bell-bottoms, t-shirts and tattoos are accepted, *tangueras/os* dance as many or as few songs with each partner as they choose, and, dispensing with the *cabeceo*, dancers may walk right up to a prospective partner of their choice, making the invitation unmistakably clear (if not potentially coercive, as declining the invitation is equally clear and public). Further, women are (theoretically) free to invite men, and same-sex partnering is more widely accepted than in the traditional *milongas*, though outside of the specifically sanctioned "gay" spaces, same-sex partnering is usually a practice technique or a last resort.

About a month into my two-year stay in Buenos Aires, I was lamenting to a *porteña* friend the difficulty in getting dances in both the traditional venues and the younger *práctica* scene. Reassuring me that it's hard for everyone, she then asked her husband, a native and longtime dancer, for advice. He offered the following:

> She should wear a shorter skirt. The top could be tighter too. Wear more make-up—on the eyes, and darker lipstick, and tell her to put her hair up, too. And she doesn't need to be nice to anybody. Tell her to watch the girls near the bar in Canning. The women don't make friends in the *milonga*. She needs to act like a total bitch.

Interestingly, this advice was meant to serve me in the *práctica* as well as the *milonga*, belying the claims that gender norms and dress matter less in these sites. Conversations with foreign women confirmed that while the formality in dress expected in the *milongas* dissolves in the *prácticas*,[14] showing skin always helps, suggesting that the aesthetic values and rules of looking good are simply different here.

Many women also noted an inability to invite men to dance. An unremarkable occurrence in the United States, the freedom to initiate the invitation clearly divides the "traditional" from the "*nuevo*" or younger scene in Buenos Aires; however, to do so is still out of the ordinary, marking the woman as masculine and forward:

> Knowing how desperately I need to dance has made me ask people. . . . In Buenos Aires, sometimes I feel like I need to stick to the social norms; sometimes I feel like that guy is really traditional, this is a traditional *milonga*, this particular guy I can tell will not want to be asked by a woman to dance. But many times if I need to dance, I will go find somebody to dance. . . . In tango, you have to be tough or you'll sit a lot, which I cannot abide.
>
> Laura Pellegrino, American expat, tango professional, and musician

"Women Who Lead" and Tango Queer

Many dancers argue that learning the other role helps them better understand their partners' position and feedback, thus allowing them to refine their overall dance. With the entrance of increasing numbers of younger practitioners to the dance and the creation of social and practice spaces in which increased experimentation is encouraged, the division of roles according to gender has relaxed in tango communities the world over. Increasingly, more women are learning to lead. At times a practical solution to a shortage of men, just as often it reflects an interest in more fully understanding the mechanics of the dance. And, increasingly—although chiefly outside Buenos Aires—women are leading in social settings, dancing with other women in *milongas*. The gender balance in classes and *milongas* outside Buenos Aires may discourage the reverse among men, less often at a loss for a partner. Still, the man who wishes to follow is offered comfort in the generally accepted notion that knowledge of the other role will assist him in execution of his, as well as tango lore and historic images that trace the dance's origins and development to male-male practice (Benarós 1999; Collier et al. 1995; Salessi 1997; Savigliano 1995; Thompson 2005; Tobin 1998). Indeed, some older Argentine males have argued that this tradition of male-male practice produces sensitive and understanding leaders precisely because they have first learned to follow, and they question the potential for equality in the embrace with the loss of that tradition today.

Though male-male partnering was crucial to tango's development and the spectacle of two *compadritos* dancing on a street corner is a fixture of the tango stage show, this practice is consistently attributed to the demographics of early-twentieth-century Buenos Aires, when men greatly outnumbered women. Such same-sex partnering is regularly defined as "practice" and distinguished from "dancing," both in tango histories and in *porteño* tango classes and *prácticas*. Interestingly, several scholars have drawn attention to tango's homosexual and gender transgressive roots, noting public discourse surrounding male transvestite prostitutes in the brothels that gave birth to the tango, as well as shifting gender roles in early-twentieth-century Buenos Aires, exemplified by "masculine" women entering the public domain (whether prostitutes, artists including early tango singers, or working-class women) and the "feminine" tango pimp, a vain character who depended upon a woman to support him (Saikin 2004; Salessi 1997; Savigliano 1995; Tobin 1998). While Tobin (1998) frames the pairing of elder male dancers with *nenas* (chicks) in 1990s *milonga* exhibitions as "homosocial desire," evidenced in the *milongueros'* verbal exchanges of praise in response to their displays of young women, the *porteño* tango scene has more openly embraced its transgressive roots in recent years.

After La Marshall, Buenos Aires' first and most popular *milonga* gay, opened in 2002, a handful of gay-friendly venues emerged. Among the more successful is Tango Queer, which, like La Marshall, has already relocated at least three times to accommodate growing crowds. Tango Queer is open to all regardless of sexual orientation, and it was founded on the desire to create a space where all feel free to dance the role of their choice. In weekly classes, students learn both to lead and to follow, switching roles throughout the ninety-minute lesson. And sex is not the best indicator of a dancer's role in the post-lesson *milonga,* where the exchange of lead and follow, often during a single song, is a common sight.

Beyond the weekly class and *milonga*, Tango Queer has a decidedly political bent. Founder Mariana Docampo advocates tango as a platform to explore questions of inclusion and exclusion, and the relationship between gender and power. Because of its historically macho profile, Docampo believes tango is the ideal context for such exploration. Through events such as scholarly conferences and the annual international Queer Tango Festival, Tango Queer links dancers, researchers, writers, and artists interested in the role of gender in tango and the fields of gender and queer studies.

I was struck, however, by the absence of women leading and men following in Buenos Aires' *práctica* scene outside of these specifically advertised gay spaces. On those rare occasions when women dance together outside the classroom, it is likely that one (if not both) is from abroad, while men simply don't appear to dance together except at the gay-friendly venues like La Marshall and Tango Queer and more private practice sessions.

One night at El Motivo, I danced a few songs with a female friend who is a skilled leader. As I exited the floor, a young *porteño* acquaintance, a beginner, demanded, "But why are you dancing with a woman, Carolina?" My response, "She dances *really* well," was met with a barely audible "*Sí, me parece*" (Yeah, it seems so) as he skulked away. And in Buenos Aires' more "traditional" venues, same-sex partnering can elicit outright hostility.

December 2005, Confitería Ideal

John and Nancy, friends from New York, are visiting Buenos Aires for the first time. Nervous about navigating the scene on their own, they've taken me out to dinner in exchange for an escort to Confitería Ideal. A famed tango institution, Ideal is classic porteño *faded elegance, engendering a sense of nostalgia even in those who never knew its better days. Behind the decaying façade is an imposing, wraparound marble staircase, at the top of which the dancer finds a massive tile floor lined with marble pillars, surrounded by café tables and chairs on three sides, a bandstand and bar on the fourth; the room is topped by high ceilings, chandeliers, and ornate, gilded touches to complete the picture. Sally Potter secured Ideal's place in the global tango imagination: in* The Tango Lesson, *this is where she takes her first café and* medialunas *(croissants); where Gustavo Naveira, Fabian Salas, and Olga Besio escort her to her first* milonga; *where now famed instructor and studio owner Carlos Copello introduces her to the eyes-closed-tango-moment ecstasy that followers yearn for. (Not bad for an Englishwoman with less than a year of tango under her belt.)*

Color Tango, among the city's most renowned tango quintets, is playing. A follower who can hold her own, Nancy has also been leading for a couple of years. She is a new face in Buenos Aires. She entered the milonga *with a male companion, and she sits beside him and dances with him: all signals that she is "with" that man and thus off-limits, unavailable. Popular to the point of being an icon, Ideal functions as both a sort of "tango museum" for tourists and a beloved site for serious* tangueros *who appreciate the romance of the place and the live music offerings. Because it draws these different populations to the same events, Ideal is a place where traditional* milonga *codes are respected one moment and tossed aside the next. Twenty-year-olds struggle with the subtleties of the* cabeceo, *while retirees cockily cross the floor and walk straight up to a table to invite a woman to dance. After a couple of* tandas *with her husband and a lot of sitting, Nancy invites me to dance. A glance at the floor reveals a mix of average dancers young and old, and a fair number of tourists with little to no knowledge of the dance and even less knowledge of floorcraft, so I accept. We struggle through the first song, but midway through the second I begin to settle into her embrace. Closing my eyes, I'm still aware of the softer suggestion I generally feel from female leaders, and less concerned with my surroundings, when suddenly I feel someone invading our space. I open my eyes to find an elderly gentleman in a suit, tie, and fedora, closing in on us, walking right up to us.*

Smirking under his hat, he claps in our faces and mutters, "Que bueno, que bueno, que bueno" *(How nice, how nice, how nice), his voice dripping with condescension and disgust.*

* * *

While it is essentially required that today's female tango professionals understand the lead, this capacity is not as prized in Buenos Aires as it is in the United States and Europe. When I broached the topic with local professionals, for example, they noted the context of the larger *porteño* culture, framing the *milonga* and the *práctica* as spaces in which to "have fun," where "fun" is a male-female encounter:

> It's a social thing—why I don't dance with girls in the *milonga*. When I go out to a *milonga* or a *práctica*, the dance is no longer about investigating. I investigate in Gallo Ciego [where I teach]. When I go to dance in the *milonga* it's an outing, it's a social encounter. I don't know, I'm going out to have fun and dance, and if I'm going to have fun and dance, I want to have fun with a boy. (τ)
>
> Silvina, Argentine, tango professional

Simultaneously, foreign women described Buenos Aires as a sort of "follower's candy store," where the unimaginably large pool of male dancers makes leading unnecessary or even uninteresting:

> In the U.S. tons of women are leading, but here there's not many women leading really. There's women who know how to lead but women don't lead socially. You know for me, I was leading more than I was following in the U.S. and I've led . . . I don't know if I've led two songs in the past six months. I have no interest right now. I feel like leading for women also has a feeling of last resort, like "I want to dance tango and there's no one to follow, okay I'll lead." You know if you get to follow, for a lot of people it doesn't seem to be that important.
>
> Deborah, American expat, tango professional

Inherent in Deborah's comment is acceptance of the division of dance roles according to gender, and further, an acknowledgment that women lead more out of necessity than desire. As Silvina notes, for a woman to lead falls under the realm of "investigation"—understanding the dance in a more complete fashion, in order to transfer that knowledge to students in the classroom. While one could argue that in some tango communities elsewhere women more often lead because women enact a different notion of what it is to be female in those societies, many foreign *tangueras* describe their entry into leading as a way to keep the tango interesting when there aren't enough skilled men to follow, or as a necessary step toward professionalization, rather than some sort of expression of feminist ideals. In my own experiences trying to lead at Tango Queer, I discovered my internal resistance to this role. Much as the feminist in me might hate to admit it, I discovered that, in partner dance at least, I am a natural follower.

May 2006, Tango Queer

El Laberinto, a small bar and restaurant on Avenida Bolivar in San Telmo. The class and práctica *attract more women than men, though I notice male faces I've seen before at La Marshall. The bulk of the students appear to be young lesbians, plus a few gay men, and a handful of hetero men and women interested in developing their following and leading skills, respectively. While my following still needs a lot of work, I decide it's time to at least try leading, if for no other reason than to have a stronger grasp on the dance conceptually, in the hopes that this will help me to convey it more clearly in writing.*

The general level in the class is fairly low. The atmosphere is informal; students move back and forth from their tables to the floor, stopping to engage in conversation, eat, or drink when the urge hits them during the class. Seeing that I have some miles on my tango shoes, the instructor, Mariana, pairs me with a woman from Germany who's been dancing for six years. She started leading only last week, but it's clear she has a knack for it. I, on the other hand, am a minor disaster. I manage well enough as we walk the length of the room. But each time we switch roles at the end and I take the role of leader, grasping my partner's left shoulder blade in my right palm and extending her right hand out into space with my left, I'm suppressing the nervous laughter bubbling up inside me. If I'm not convinced of this, how will she be? I silently apologize to every leader to whom I've given the least bit of attitude in the past.

The hardest step is the ocho*—the follower executes a consecutive forward- or backward-moving step that creates a figure eight along the floor in response to a pivot in the hips initiated primarily by torsion in the leader's upper body. We practice out of the embrace, the leader holding arms straight out to the side to locate the internal twist that should indicate the lead and* *to avoid brutely steering the follower side to side with the hands. Each time Mariana demonstrates the lead, she asks me to follow her. I feel the lesbians, La Marshall dancers, and everyone else watching with a mixture of admiration and envy. The ease and confidence I bring to my role as follower disappears, however, when it is my turn to lead: I struggle to convince my partner to move through space in the curving path I imagine before me, desperately trying to mimic Mariana's commanding yet fluid brand of invitation. When I finally manage to relax the tension I send through my arms—my body's immediate response to my mind's instruction to "lead," my slight frame eases back into its softer, listening, follower's state.*

My attempt at leading follows this pattern—tension, relaxation, followed by a glimmer of restrained strength emanating out from my chest that just doesn't seem to last. "Menos manteca *(Less butter), Carolina!" I hear Mariana yelling again and again, she and my partner laughing in an effort to hide their growing impatience. However, the stronger (but not forceful), masculine (but still female), "less buttery" leader inside me is nowhere to be found.*

A *Nuevo* Machismo?

> I think it's very clear in tango that the man leads and the woman follows. But that doesn't mean that the woman is passive, nor does it mean that the man is the boss, that he commands the woman. Because the tango is a dialogue, it's a conversation—one proposes the topic, and the other continues the conversation, and the content and the form of the dialogue is constructed according to the manner of each. . . . The man who dances tango well dances smoothly, clearly, piecing together the dialogue one step at a time. And this isn't a new idea. If you look at the old dancers, and the true *milongueros*, the really good *milongueros* don't have that arrogant attitude in their dance. On the contrary, the man who dances like that doesn't know how to dance. (τ)
>
> Olga Besio, Argentine, tango professional

En route to a *milonga* one night, I got into a discussion about the role of the woman in tango with Jorge, an Argentine expatriate living in the United States. Jorge argued that what makes traditional tango are the pauses, and that it is the woman who signals and makes these pauses happen. He contrasted this to *nuevo*, where, he maintained, the man manipulates the woman through complicated, acrobatic figures that grant her no voice in what is happening; he suggested that the woman exerts much greater control in traditional tango. Dancers who identify with *nuevo* may counter that this is a misconception, that the tango currently being danced by young people is based on a new manner of thinking about the dance, and with that an expansion in vocabulary. But calling it "acrobatics" reduces contemporary tango to one element—and not a necessary one by any means—that ignores the conceptual and pedagogic revolution at its heart. Still, such manipulation—or manhandling, as Jorge suggested—and acrobatics do have their place in contemporary tango, complicating the claims that *nuevo* accepts and celebrates female autonomy.

In responses to my questions about changes in the woman's role in *nuevo* or contemporary tango, I encountered a few recurring themes having to do with movement vocabulary. First, many dancers noted that the woman dances on her own axis, rather than leaning or depending on the man. Also common is the idea that the dance's increasingly complex vocabulary requires a more skilled and active follower. Many dancers also argued that the follower has more freedom, citing flexibility in the embrace that may open and close and, as noted previously, *disociación*, or torsion, the spine spiraling, the torso breaking from the hips, creating a more circular and less rigid dance. Many pointed also to the introduction of movements "off-axis," where one or both partners lean into or away from one another, as a recent development necessitating both a more skilled follower and a more sensitive leader.[15]

Many of these dancers argued that women are just as free to introduce pauses in contemporary tango as they are in traditional tango. With the opening and loosening of the embrace, the follower is free to comment on the lead with her entire body, thus increasing her role in defining the dance. The possibilities within the embrace have expanded greatly, a development I attribute directly to the increasing entry of dancers from such disciplines as modern dance; classical ballet; contact improvisation; martial arts; and partner dance, including salsa, zouk, swing, and rock 'n' roll; for these dancers, professional and social, have made deliberate efforts to expand the vocabulary of the dance through the integration of non-tango elements. The contributions of those who bring experience in other disciplines have allowed the tango to stretch beyond the bounds of the embrace. Now the woman does not remain rigidly upright or constantly pegged to the leader. Her legs, torso, and hips are relaxed and free to explore the space away from her partner, and the timing with which her limbs fly, explore, and rebound through space may slow down or speed up the lead, thus shaping the conversation. While the *milonguero* or "close" style of embrace may encourage the follower to give weight to the leader, the contemporary emphasis on the follower maintaining her own axis encourages the follower to exercise greater control over her movement.[16]

Many young dancers from Buenos Aires and abroad connected the emancipation of the follower to the evolution of the dance begun in the 1990s. Further, as Luciana Valle suggested, changes in the gender politics of the dance reflect larger social shifts that have empowered women in other aspects of their lives:

> The tango changed a lot; it evolved a lot and the last big change in the past ten years is that of the woman; the big change is in the role of the woman. . . . The woman has a much more active role but not in the sense of stealing the lead, not active in leading, but active in dancing, because the woman is more active in life. Women carried on with men differently and they lived life differently; today women are much more active in general, they're much more free in general, and so we dance differently. If you look at tango fifty years ago, the big difference you'll see will be in the woman. (ε)

However, many dancers pointed, instead, to an earlier revolution in conceptualization and instruction, and of the democratization of information in the classroom. As explained in Chapter 2, Naveira and Salas, rather than demonstrating entire figures for reproduction, broke the dance down to its simplest elements—front, side, and back step—providing both leader and follower the basics with which to deconstruct, improvise, and re-create their own dance. As a result of this approach, female teachers now command the classroom on their own.

Graciela Gonzalez, for example, was considered revolutionary when she began teaching classes in women's technique in the 1980s, but such classes geared toward and instructed by women are now quite popular. They generally address walking, balance, or the aesthetic contribution of the woman through adornments or embellishments. Female instructors noted that to move beyond women's technique classes and to broaden their professional possibilities, they have to take responsibility for understanding the mechanics of both lead and follow. As Cecilia Gonzalez pointed out, "Until we'd studied enough to know what happens in the dance in its totality, and not only how to follow the man, there wasn't work for women alone. But having studied a bit more profoundly now we're able to travel and work on our own" (τ). Moreover, such knowledge provides one security in a market where women are viewed as plentiful and more easily replaced than men:

> You need to teach, to be the one speaking in order to have an independent reputation. Your dancing isn't enough. And like we've all said a million times there are more women who can dance at the level that they could partner with any of the top dancers than there are those top dancers, so the women are quite interchangeable.
>
> Deborah, American expatriate, tango professional

While the advances acknowledged above are noteworthy, resistance to women leading, and women in leadership positions, remains among male *tangueros*. Perhaps that resistance reflects anxiety, or fear that their territory will be infringed upon. In one illuminating interview, for example, a young professional first rejected the notion that a woman can hold her own in an advanced tango class, then suggested that even if a woman can lead at the level of a male teacher, such behavior is an attempt to deny her gender, something that makes him uncomfortable:

> Female instructors can't teach advanced classes, aside from a women's technique class, okay, but they can't demonstrate sequences that are long or difficult, because they can't lead them. I don't know of any girl . . . there are some that lead well, but I don't know of any who is at the level of a man. And if she is I don't like it. It's ugly; I don't like how it looks. Because it's a woman acting like a man, maybe she can do it, lead the sequence, but I don't like the way it looks; it turns me off. (τ)
>
> Anonymous Argentine, tango professional

And in a conversation with me, Dana Frígoli recalled being ignored by male students when she and partner Pablo Villarraza began setting choreography on other companies. She could have transmitted the same information, just as clearly or even better, she told me, but the male dancers had to hear it from another man or they simply wouldn't listen.

While the image of the dance as conversation might be the ideal, the fact remains that it is the leader who retains responsibility for initiating. With the role of lead comes the job of choreographing on the spot. The epigraph opening this chapter referred to women as "tools to have fun," yet the reverse may also be true. For instance, I once heard a very traditional *tanguera* refer to men as "danceable objects." Both male and female dancers are capable of manipulating or using their partners for entirely self-serving purposes. However, men's generally greater size and strength do allow unfortunate practices: I have both witnessed and heard of manhandling of the follower among dancers of all ages. For instance, one night at an investigation session, I observed three young Argentine men trying to execute a complicated figure with two foreign women. Tossing the women back and forth like dolls, they shouted over them in Spanish, talking much too quickly for the women to understand as they discussed the mechanics of the step. Only when they determined what the followers needed to do (without asking their input) did the men speak either in English or more slowly and clearly in Spanish. This pattern continued for most of the night. While there was arguably a problem of language and translation, and perhaps a difference in skill levels, this scene illustrates a fundamental asymmetry: the follower is largely at the mercy of the leader.

* * *

Promotional images are often no less ambiguous in depicting gender relations. Entrepreneurs on equal footing with their male counterparts, female dancers are heavy hitters in today's tango industry. Nonetheless, many tango ads suggest a more complicated story, walking a fine line between celebrating and exploiting the female form, and unabashedly linking the tango to sex through nudity and even references to domination. In these ads, women may be the dominators and the protected, "tools to have fun" and acrobatic innovators, anonymous seductresses and savvy businesswomen, proudly flaunting and quite strategically trading on their feminine assets.

The nude male form appears less often in promotional materials, although a handful of ads in recent years point to a potential shift in this regard, most notably the billboards and DVD cover image for the stage show *Bocca Tango*, which reveal nearly all of Julio Bocca. Bocca is famed for his long career as a ballet dancer, not as a *tanguero*, and the nude or partially nude male form has a long history in ballet. While shirtless men have appeared in a few tango ads of late, the message in this case tends to celebrate male strength or even prowess. In general, in contrast to the ambivalence suggested by many representations of the *tanguera*'s body, these images of men reinforce the role of the male as protector or protagonist.

July 2006, A Taxicab en Route to the *Milonga*

Our driver sings us tangos and engages Nadav in a discussion of porteñas, *or as he calls them,* "la otra carne blanca de la Argentina" *(Argentina's other white meat). So sensual, curves in all the right places,* "seductoras" *(seductresses). Nadav, an Israeli student abroad, eats it up, a knowing laugh in response to every description of what they agree is an innately Argentine power to seduce. This goes on for a while before Nadav realizes perhaps this isn't the conversation to be carrying on when a lady is in the car, moreover, one he'd been working pretty hard on the dance floor not ten minutes earlier. The cabbie catches my eye in the mirror and asks how good my Spanish is.* "Entiendo bien" *(I understand quite well), I reply. I've managed, in fact, to follow every word. When I tell him I'm an anthropologist, and that I'm doing some investigating of my own, I watch his eyes widen in the mirror. Turning round, he flashes Nadav a big smile and in a tone at once of warning and congratulation exclaims,* "Que brava, esa chica!" *(She's wild, this one!)*

El tango del futuro (The Tango of the Future)

Tango and machismo have become so intertwined in the global imagination that some may mistake that connection as being somehow causal. But machismo is not an element of the dance itself, and this linking of the two ignores the fact that the essence of the dance depends upon communication, a social interaction. The threat of machismo lies in the practices of individuals themselves and in the relationship they must establish within the embrace: "And that's where the fear is—you have to talk to the guy you dance with. So when that other is from another culture, the perception is 'it's that *porteño* machismo!' The question of culture exists in that connection with the other, not in the dance itself" (τ; Gustavo Naveira, Argentine, tango professional). As Naveira reminded me, this relationship is fraught with the potential for misunderstanding, especially in Buenos Aires, where the two dancers are often communicating across languages, cultures, and generations.

The notion that meaning is dependent on context is hardly revolutionary, but I would take this idea further to suggest that place in its larger sense—including its history, mythology, and the traces it imparts upon people and things—affects our actions, interpretation of, and response to behaviors. Following Jackson's (1996) notion of intersubjectivity, I suggest that activities that engage the self and others offer participants an opportunity to confront and explore difference. In tango, this experience of being with others is heightened by the physically intimate, nonverbal nature of the dance itself. The differences that separate—language, culture, worldview—are subsumed in the moment of the dance, and this ability to have a dialogue through tango may facilitate communication outside of the embrace. In short, tango may have something to teach about accepting difference, allowing (even enjoying) contradiction, honoring the existence of self and other.

Deeper than the glamour of romance and exoticism, playfulness—the capacity to receive and work with what one is given, to advance and retreat, to perceive exactly when it is one's turn—is the way to the heart of tango, which is the moment of blending, with another, into an almost seamless whole. And the skills and attitudes that serve the dancer on this quest spill over into the social context. While a questioning of rigid social codes is inherent in the philosophy of *nuevo,* new trends are subject to more intense scrutiny in the dance's birthplace. The future of the dance lies in the ability of practitioners young and old, local and global, to transcend the romance and exoticism of the tango's often consuming macho imaginary, and to embrace the future.

5

¿Droga o terapia? (Drug or Therapy?)

Now you see people discovering tango because they embrace, they leave behind the telephone, the machines, and they listen to a music that doesn't assault them. . . . You find something else in the tango . . . you feel the warmth of another human being in the embrace. (τ)

Juan Carlos Copes, Argentine, tango professional

I physically need this dance. . . . I haven't been depressed since I started tango, not for real. I have days, but I haven't been in that place in the two-and-a-half years I've been dancing tango.

Anonymous, tango dancer

June 2006, Estudio Dinzel

Racing out the door (pre-noon activities being early after a night of milongueando*), I stop at the* panadería *(bakery) and exchange my 2-peso bill for a* medialuna *(croissant) and the* monedas *(change) that will get me on the 128 to Villa Crespo. For about a month now, I've made the trek to Rodolfo Dinzel's studio once or twice a week for the* "tango teoría" *(tango theory) sessions. Though prized among dancers because you can come and go as you please—there is a patio open for chatting and sipping* maté *(an herbal tea) and a dance space open for practice at almost any time—there are also a handful of regularly scheduled classes, among them different levels of dance technique, physical training for tango, history and music classes, and my favorite, tango theory. These are Socratic-like sessions where Dinzel holds court in the corner of the room, cigarette in hand and a nearly ever-present cloud of smoke overhead, save for those moments when the* maté *gourd finishes its path round the circle of students who hang on his every word, and, replenishing the* yerba's *(herb's) liquid from a plastic thermos, he takes a sip from the* bombilla *(straw) and passes this most Argentine of beverages along, beginning the ritual cycle again. At the studio, you* *can always count on a few things:* maté, *tango music in the air, a group of dancers from around the world, and love for Dinzel. For not only is he charismatic, but the adoration is both infectious and expected, and the dancer who doesn't demonstrate that love through daily attendance is subject to an unspoken yet palpable suspicion from the "Dinzelitos," as I've heard them called more than once. Lucky for me, I fall quite easily. Though I don't attend with enough regularity to make everyone happy, I achieve at least partial acceptance through my obvious affection for Dinzel.*

These sessions are for me a different sort of tango therapy, one that exists entirely outside of the physical practice of the dance. In a sense they resemble so many of the conversations I engage in with fellow dancers—the ups, downs, and mysteries of tango. But they are at once more organized, usually starting with a question planted by Dinzel for discussion, and more chaotic, with ardent debate from all sides expressed through a combination of words and movement. While often originating in a theoretical discussion of the mechanics and structure of the dance, the ninety-minute session invariably turns into either a philosophical free-for-all or a self-help session, guided by Dinzel's inquisitive mind and probing nature, and fueled by the tireless passion with which we all seek to investigate, live, conquer the tango.

Today, someone asks whether the idea of gender ever disappears in our practice of the dance. The response from one young woman from France sticks with me. Speaking of one of the first milongas *she'd ever attended, on the outskirts of Paris, she describes a place where people are truly seeing, listening, and understanding one another—free of the prejudices and judgments humans are so prone to; a place where superficial differences and categories like race and gender seem to dissolve. Transcending the bounds of the couple, what she describes is a communion that embraces the very place itself, and although only momentary, makes it one of limitless possibility.*

My skepticism, my silent critique—nearly always on hand these days—are suddenly nowhere to be found. The room falls silent, for what else can we say?

This is why we are here.

* * *

A recent study at McGill University highlights the healing capacities of Argentine tango, noting that elderly participants demonstrate improved balance, posture, motor coordination, and cognitive performance after a ten-week tango course.[1] Researchers at the Washington University School of Medicine report heightened benefits among patients suffering from

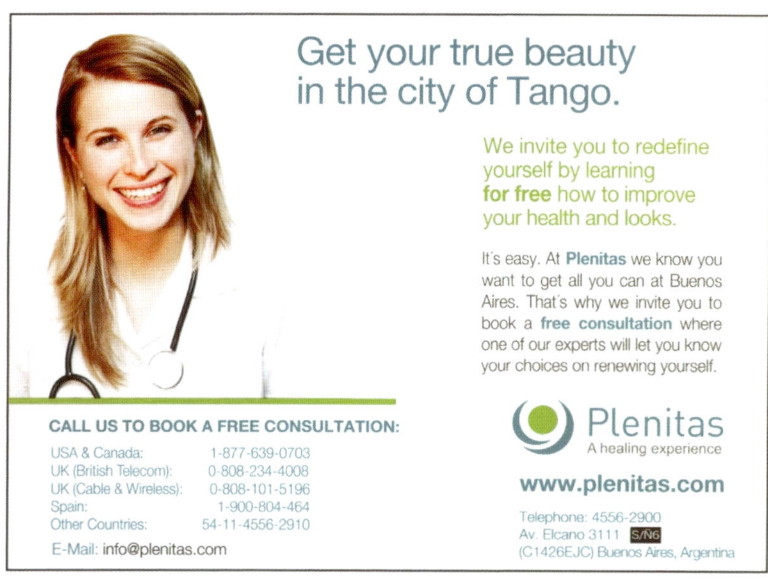

19. Plenitas. Promotional image, *Tango Map Guide*, August/September 2007.

20. "El Flaco Dany" (Daniel Garcia) for Fabio Shoes.

21. Compadritos. *Nuestro tango* (Our Tango), El Querandí Tanguería.

22. Tango Queer. Photo by Karina Maccioli.

23. Confitería Ideal. Photo by Lesley Mitchell.

24. *Mar y tango* (Sea and Tango). Dana Frígoli and Pablo Villarraza, DNI Tango Academy. Promotional image, 2007.

25. *Tango Zen: Walking Dance Meditation* (2004) by Chan Park. Photo by Angelike Bardehle.

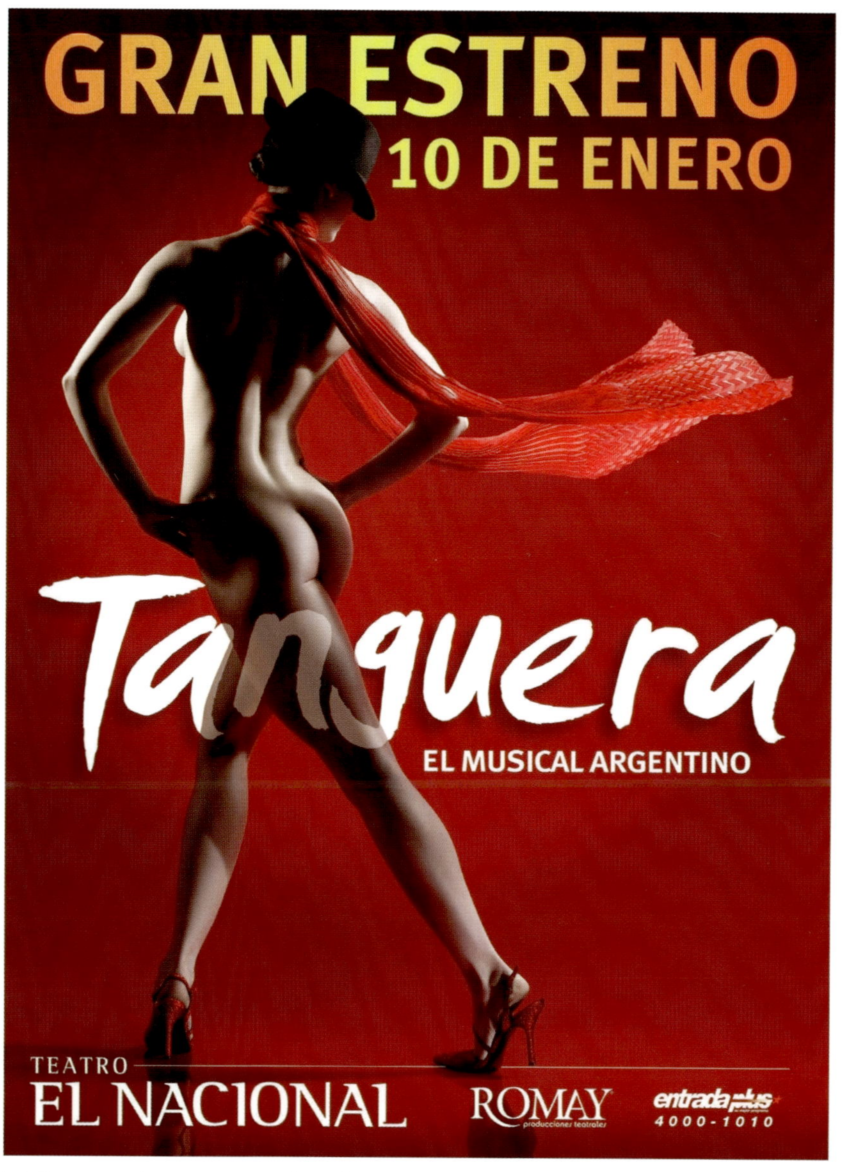

26. *Tanguera*, the tango musical produced by Diego Romay. Promotional image, 2007.

27. "Práctica X: A Classic in Buenos Aires. A space dedicated to contemporary tango. An open *práctica* in a relaxed atmosphere, with good music, where we investigate movement and exchange ideas to develop the tango." Promotional flyer, 2011.

28. *Esquina tango* (Tango Corner), San Telmo, Buenos Aires. Carlos Gardel and Alfredo Le Pera. (Artist unknown.) Photo by author.

29. Tango mural by Guillermo Perez Bravo. Restaurant y Parilla Matias, Boedo, Buenos Aires. Photo by author.

30. The *Compadrito* and His *Maleva.* My parents in Caminito (Tango Walkway), La Boca, Buenos Aires. Photo by author.

31. Tango TaxiDancers Agency magazine advertisement.

32. María Nieves and Juan Carlos Copes. From *Quien Me Quita Lo Bailado: Juan Carlos Copes: Una Vida de Tango*, by permission of the author.

33. "La Moderna: San Telmo's Most Traditional Pizza, Like Argentina's Tango." Photo by author.

34. The Immigrant. *Nuestro tango* (Our Tango), El Querandí Tanguería.

35. Melina Brufman and Claudio González. *Episodios cifrados en el tango* (Tango Encoded Episodes), www.tangopulenta.com. Photo by Mario Albarracin.

36. Orquesta Típica El Afronte. Milonga Bendita / Milonga Maldita. Photographer unknown.

37. Fernando Sanchez and Ariadna Naveira. Nora's Tango Week, 2009. Photo by Jerry Jew.

38. PRAKTIKA8-MILONGA10. Photo by Dolores Gambino.

39. Festival Estilo Parque Patricios. *Left to right*: Julio Bassan, Federico Naveira, David Palo, Frank Rossi, and Hernan Leone. Promotional flyer, 2010. Photo by Dolores Gambino.

40. Cecilia García and Serkan Gokcesu. Photo by Bengt Jönsson.

41. A *milonga* at the Philadelphia Argentine Tango School. Instructors Damian Lobato and Sarah Sookyung Chung in foreground. Photo by Angie Youkyung Chung / Yellow Sky Photography.

Parkinson's Disease who took part in a thirteen-week Argentine tango course in comparison to the gains of those enrolled in a more traditional exercise regimen (Hackney, Kantorovich, and Earhart 2007). For years, psychologists, psychiatrists, and medical doctors in Buenos Aires have been running "tango therapy" programs for patients suffering from psychological disorders as well as terminal illnesses, including cancer and AIDS. At the Miami Lighthouse for the Blind in Florida, the Shimmy Club has been organizing tango classes for blind and visually impaired adolescents since 2007, alongside a sister program for elderly students in Buenos Aires.

Ten years as a *tanguera*, and I can no longer keep track of all the conversations I have with fellow dancers about the catharsis achieved through the practice of tango, which, when at its best, is claimed to heal on any number of levels: social, physical, psychological, spiritual. Then again, I've surely engaged in just as many gripe sessions (to put it delicately), spent just as much time sitting around waiting for a good dance (or trying to recover from a bad one), silently lamenting the frustrations of tango. And what of all those dancers I met in Buenos Aires, who spoke of the need to free the tango from its cultural context in order to fully realize its healing capacities, citing machismo, competition, and an atmosphere approaching the theater of the absurd as impediments to the dance's true benefits? Meanwhile, there are the critics of *tango nuevo*, who attack contemporary trends based on a purported connection between therapeutic potential and style, arguing that catharsis is the by-product not just of any old tango, but of the *true* tango.

What of this connection between the way one dances and the comfort to be found therein? Should our comfort and pleasure be subject to the evaluation of others? Be dictated by supposed experts? Just what is it about modern life that necessitates all this therapy? And what is it about tango that fills this need—despite general agreement among practitioners that it offers such an uneasy path to pleasure? Moreover, would the freedom described by the French *tanguera* above be accessible to the average Argentine? Does it not, like the luxury of therapy, depend on a certain "first world" privilege?

Tango: Beauty and Misery

> People don't realize the anguish that goes into this dance, how trying it is, how ego demolishing it can be in a lot of ways. It's probably the only dance that can reduce

> you to a sliver of nothingness and at the same time transport you to the ultimate ecstasy . . . and we like that torture because it helps us feel alive.
>
> Michele Kadison, American expat, choreographer and writer

If I had a penny for all the people—friends, family, colleagues, *tangueros*—who rolled their eyes, who laughed, winked, and smiled knowingly when I told them about my book project. Rather than take their pennies, I would challenge them to spend a year in my shoes, dancing tango in Buenos Aires. No pun intended. For Michele captures perfectly the ever-changing and occasionally devastating nature of this dance. (I have to confess, I nearly jumped across the table and hugged her when she produced this elegant reduction of what I knew would be a chapter topic.) Argentine tango is not a dance for the easily discouraged or the weak of heart. While the dance itself requires a fair amount of practice and dedication, its improvisational nature renders the experience of tango new every time, offering limitless possibilities in terms of study and growth, and absolute uncertainty as to what may happen next—"next" being the next night, next *milonga*, next partner, next *tanda*, next song, next minute.

Tango dancers often employ one of two metaphors when describing the dance and its allure: tango as therapy and tango as addiction. Like the chicken and the egg, putting one first is no easy task. Rather, they seem to operate in a cyclical fashion, and each cycle can be as short-lived as a single tango. The fix achieved by a great dance, satisfaction can fade by the time the dancer reaches her or his chair, and the prowl begins anew so as to reduce down time between one "up" and the next. Addiction to the therapy, if you will. But wrapped up in all this talk of the bliss or other benefits of tango is another narrative of damage and pain. Beyond the physical difficulties of the dance, *tangueros* locate such suffering in the postures and attitudes that are rewarded and thus prevail in the social scene, and in the ever-present potential for disappointment, rejection, or failure.

Though dancers across the board cite "connection" as one of the primary goals of social tango, it is also acknowledged that the larger setting contributes significantly to this experience. Couples may practice alone or dance alongside others in a class, but tango dancers of all ages and stylistic preferences speak of the heightened sensation of connection on a crowded dance floor, where you move in communion with your partner, the music, and the surrounding couples. At the same time, it is exactly the social setting and its codes of behavior that complicate the pursuit of connection, bliss, catharsis, communion, experience, or whatever it is one hopes to find in the tango embrace. Further, while the *prácticas* are generally described as "laid back," sites where the rules of the *milongas* are more relaxed, my time in Buenos Aires convinced me that the lamented aspects of social tango—surveillance, display, exhibitionism, anticipation, waiting, self-doubt, pressure to perform, potential for rejection—are in equal supply in both settings.

Many traditionalists reject *nuevo* (or the tango as it is danced by young dancers in the *práctica* scene) for what they term its "inauthenticity," a state that disallows not only connection to one's partner, but healing as well, for there is great comfort to be found in the state of authenticity, when one is dancing the "true tango." According to this logic, connection and catharsis derive from any number of factors related to style (itself a loaded term), including the distance separating partners in the embrace, the music danced to, the clothing worn, the manner in which the invitation to dance is negotiated, the quantity of time spent on the dance floor, and more. Add to this the potent influence of place on the desires and attitudes of dancers—the pull toward tradition one may feel in Buenos Aires, for instance, and the contradictions this incurs when things like machismo are permitted under the guise of authenticity—and disentangling the relationship between style, culture, generation, and catharsis in tango becomes complicated.

Modern Malaise: Anguish as Resistance

> Uncertainty excites me. Who knows what's going to happen?
>
> Björk, "Possibly Maybe" (1995/2007)

In an age of unparalleled global connection, the very means facilitating these ties provide new ways to remove the self from direct engagement with others. As our lives become more deadline driven and goal oriented, it seems there is less place for nonutilitarian, face-to-face interaction.[2] Compounding the increasing demands on our time, modern technological innovations that are designed and sold under the guise of connection often effect that contact in isolation. In a world where success and identity are largely constructed and manifested through consumption, the value of that consumption is ever changing. With capitalism's ability to place nearly every luxury within reach over time, things once coveted often lose their allure, and the pleasure and satisfaction attached to attainment wane with their increased accessibility, until such objects are rendered mundane, unrewarding necessities.

One possible response to this condition includes the pursuit of physical contact and immediacy, of the comfort and reassurance of community and place, of activities that engage the body, mind, and spirit. In the face of the dull and deadening safety of things, experience can be a profound form of resistance. Following this logic, *tangueros* often speak of the dance as an experience that stands out from their normal, everyday activities, and they frame that experience in terms of power. Transcending the value of currency, the dance is life-changing, therapeutic, confidence-building, and its pure and healing potency is realized through a negation of the sexually charged image that lies on its surface: "I can see that it's a really fantastic form that could have a lot of power in the world to change people's lives. To me tango is not sex; to me tango is like a heart chakra connection rather than a sexual chakra connection" (Sarah Bonnar, Australian, tango professional).

Moreover, many contend that the superficial qualities that help or hinder one in the world—wealth, beauty, influence, connections—don't factor as much in the embrace. Savigliano (2003) describes the *milongas* as a parallel universe that comes to life when the world goes to sleep; in this otherworldly realm, daytime measures of success are tossed right side up, and one's dance is a fleeting act of vengeance on such unforgiving criteria. Seen from this angle, one's dance is a passport to protagonism, the tango a path toward freedom, if only until the sun comes up.

But what of the labor involved in that journey? As Michele Kadison's comment suggests, tango places the dancer in a sort of existential limbo, subject to the whim of circumstance, where each new dance is equally likely to incur pleasure or pain. In the face of such odds, the commitment of the dancer lies in the desire for experience of any kind, whether good or bad, because "it helps us feel alive." Such comments are common among dancers from abroad, and to a lesser extent, among Argentines. I make a distinction here for a couple of reasons. The majority of the foreign dancers I met in Buenos Aires hail from urban settings in the United States, Europe, Russia, Japan, South Korea, and Australia. Many of these dancers cited the lack of connection in their fast-paced lives as one of the primary reasons for taking up partner dance. Further, those who have experienced the dance in Buenos Aires tend to link the connection found within the dance to the connection they experience—and cite as much more accessible, quotidian, and essential to the culture—within *porteño* society at large.

While the malaise of modern times certainly affects *porteños*, their city being one of the largest and most cosmopolitan in Latin America, I can't deny the sense that life does move at a kinder pace in Buenos Aires. Whether it is the pace that encourages contact or the cultural emphasis on contact that encourages the slower pace, there is precedence accorded face-to-face interactions, a comfort with physical contact, and a resistance to expediency that, when combined, can surprise the visitor from abroad. Add to this the simple fact that tango remains somehow "Argentine," even though it may go in and out of fashion there, and even though its roots and development may be traced to other cultures, to circulation, and to globalization. For Argentines in general, and *porteños* more specifically, the tango is not exotic. Although the percentage of *porteños* who dance tango today is quite small, and it is unlikely to ever recapture its Golden Era mass appeal, opportunities to take up the tango as social diversion in Buenos Aires are unlimited. Whatever natives might feel about tango, it remains an undeniable local referent. While foreigners cited the *falta de conexión* (lack of connection) more frequently in explaining their entry into tango, the remedy of connection—in the dance itself but also as a relic of its Argentine-ness—has been rather artfully co-opted and marketed by Argentine professionals. In turn, this notion has been hungrily consumed and reinforced in a manner at times approaching fundamentalism among non-Argentines.

The potential for remedy in this connection is perhaps all the more compelling for the very fact that you can't count on it. As the heartbreaking lyrics of Björk's "Possibly Maybe" suggest, there is a long fall from the eager heights of anticipation, when in the first moments of a relationship, we imagine all that could be, to the uncompromising lows of disappointment, realization of the imperfect promise of fantasy. Likewise, tango encourages but doesn't always reward fantasy. Rather, as one American *tanguera* described her time in Buenos Aires, the dance demands surrender and acceptance: "Like everything related to tango it's been heaven and it's been hell. . . . It's just weird how you can't count on dance relationships; they're constantly changing and you just have to be happy when it's working and accept when it's not" (Eleanor, American, grant writer).

This element of insecurity is perhaps the only unchanging aspect of tango. Like the Heraclitean notion that "nothing is permanent but change," a fellow dancer's claim that "the tango is and always has been new" (τ; Laurent Hutin, French, tango professional) describes precisely the element of uncertainty that holds so many practitioners in its grip. Though one possible outcome is suffering and pain, the flip side to that is surprise, pleasure, even ecstasy. That this uncertainty is invited by touching someone with whom we might never communicate otherwise is part of what makes tango so radical. As Manning suggests in *Politics of Touch* (2007), tango requires that we reach beyond ourselves, creating new worlds through physical contact. Add to this the promise of novelty assured by improvisation, the power of the body to remember, and the human propensity for fantasy, and you have a practice that seduces not only through its mystery but also through its possibility, both real and imagined, nourished by the physical residue it leaves behind. To enter the embrace is, in a sense, to stand atop a precipice. With each new dance the *tanguera/o* has the opportunity to jump off, to plunge into the possibility-laden space of groundlessness, to reap the rewards, and to suffer the pain, of experience.[3]

Tango Here Now

A play on Baba Ram Dass's quintessential 1970s mantra, "Tango Here Now" greets me when I open the copy of *Tango Zen* (Park 2004) lent by a friend. Translation: the tango demands presence, in this time, in this place. As Rodolfo Dinzel described the tango in our interview, its practice offers a unique possibility for communion, where that communion arises from a shared present: "It's a meeting between a man and a woman, or between two people, who together produce one of the most wonderful things a human being can experience—communion. Communion to halt the future, life, existence, time and space, without pre-arranging it in any sense" (τ). To reach this place, the dancer is effectively required to be *in the moment*. Beyond the physical space of the *milonga*, where the demands of everyday life are left at the door, at the heart of the dance is a space created through the combined energy of two people, the shape and potency of which rests on the ability of each to live that moment: to step outside one's own existence, future and past, to open oneself to the realm of connection to another, to dance a brief existence where the normally rigid dimensions of time and space are suddenly experienced as malleable or transformed. Often referred to as "tango trance," many dancers described this altered state as one of clarity, peace, euphoria, bliss, or transport.

The metaphor of the dance as a meditation in movement, an activity that transports the willing and able participant to another dimension entirely, already quite familiar to me before arriving in Argentina, came up repeatedly in interviews and conversations with practitioners of all ages and outlooks:

> A good dance might be that you lose track of time and where you are, and it's just the moment, almost like meditation.
>
> Nancy, American expat, actress

> Something happened to me that I'd never experienced with other dances. I'd danced all that time, holding onto another person, embracing another person, another person in a crowd of other people, and my mind had traveled. I'd encountered a journey . . . fascinating, no? (τ)
>
> Rodolfo Dinzel

> The tango bliss is when you are completely transported. . . . It's like sailing and there is good wind, and you're in a perfect position on the boat and you're just going and you have that feel of lightness. (ε)
>
> Laura Digilio, Italian/U.S. resident, scientist

> I'm no longer thinking when I dance. When I'm dancing, I'm dancing. It's a state of meditation; I'm in another world. . . . And it's important that the tango permit that—that it transport the dancer to another dimension. (τ)
>
> Gabriel Glagovsky, Argentine, tango professional and *práctica* organizer

Descriptions of the trance, bliss, and meditation experienced in tango sound much like the state of flow outlined by psychologist Mihaly Csikszentmihalyi. A state approaching unconsciousness, flow occurs when the performer loses sense of him- or herself and the effort involved in the execution of an act, the bounds between self and environment dissolve, and the distinctions between past, present, and future are consumed by the moment. A testament to the body's capacity to incorporate and express knowledge, portraits of flow tend to highlight the brain's or, more correctly, the conscious thought process's potential to derail or inhibit such a state. Countless artists and athletes have described a similar transcendence of the mind during physical activity, both in the creative process and in the act of performance.

Beyond the dance itself, many *tangueros* also pointed to the social atmosphere in describing their experience of trance. In a fascinating work on music and healing in Africa, Friedson (1996) argues that the act of making music together erases the distance between people and, in turn, creates the conditions necessary for healing. Similarly, many tango dancers argued that trance is dependent on the presence of others—that it arises from the act of moving with another to music amid a crowd of others moving in partnership to that same music: "Even though while I'm dancing everybody else disappears—but if that were the case then I would be as happy dancing in my apartment with my favorite partner, but it's absolutely not the same as dancing in the *milonga*. It's the combined social energy that comes with it" (ε; Sridhar Hannenhalli, Indian/U.S. resident, scientist, and tango professional).

This blissful transportation creates a sense of communion that may be traced in a series of successive circles around the dancer—beginning with one's partner, extending to the surrounding dancers on the floor, to the observing dancers, and to the larger room, which in Buenos Aires may include the organizer, waitstaff, disc jockey, and orchestra. "Dancing and trancing" in social tango venues thus engenders a certain degree of camaraderie among attendees, in many cases fostering relationships that are continued off the floor and outside the event, while in others giving rise to fleeting bonds that may evaporate with the *tanda*'s end, only to be reconstituted should the stars align the next time the two dancers embrace.

In his observation, Gabriel Glagovsky suggested that the possibility of trance is important in tango. I agree, and I would add that this goal, increasingly coveted among social dancers, is promoted simultaneously through discourse and imagery that is decidedly placeless. At the level of image, the tango trance displaces the camera's focus from the surface—the overly dramatic and passionate clash of the sexes suggested in the photos on countless postcards and stage-show advertisements—to the more personal, internal realm accessed through the embrace. This is most effectively evinced through closed eyes, a look of peaceful transcendence, a half-smile at most, and a tight embrace that evokes love and caring rather than sex and passion. In contrast, the body in its whole is manipulated in the traditional tango image. Intertwined footwork and fishnet-clad legs are favored elements, as are the colors red and black, a fedora and *pañuelo* (scarf) for the man, situation on a street corner of a historic tango *barrio*, and, most importantly, expressions of sexed-up passion that are ultimately directed out, intended for an audience.

Such images locate the passion and drama of the dance in largely external elements, both specific references to the dance's history and origins and vague gestures to the underlying Latin-ness that gives Argentine tango its exotic and erotic face. In redirecting the camera up, to the embrace and to the placeless expressions of the dancers, the state of tango trance is free of such cultural baggage, which is arguably superficial and reductionist.

The photographs framing the text of *Tango Zen* (Park 2004), for example, are a perfect illustration of the tango trance image: a series of waist-up shots of couples dancing, nearly all with eyes closed, their expressions evoking a sensation along the lines of meditative calm. For the non-Argentine practitioner, the appeal of tango trance lies, at least in part, in its freedom from physical and cultural bounds. At a very basic level, claim to authenticity accompanies cultural membership. As outdated as this notion may seem, the full extent of cultural ownership eludes even the most skilled, experienced, and dedicated of dancers from abroad.[4] The tango trance permits access to authenticity at a more internal and, thus, culturally democratic level.

The discourse of tango trance is similar in terms of the emotions and feelings it evokes: an internal journey, transportation, entry into another realm. Deborah, an American expat and tango professional, suggested that the language of trance positions the dancer moving away from, rather than into, the activity itself: "It's almost like going beyond the dance rather than going into the dance. That's how that language [of tango trance] sounds to me. Using the dance to get to another place, like meditation or something." Moreover, the state of meditation lies beyond culture. Though grounded in an Asian philosophical tradition, the achievement of a zen state denotes a transcendence of one's worldly, material, even cultural surroundings. *Tango Zen* (Park 2004) exemplifies this point quite nicely. In essence a collection of quotes, arranged in mini-chapters and framed by a paragraph or two from the author, much of the text is neither tango- nor zen-specific, its inspirational nuggets drawn from sources around the world.

Interestingly, I found a similar focus in the promotional materials of many "*nuevo*" dancers and events: the evocation of a placeless feeling through text and visuals that highlight a sense of freedom to play, experiment, and create in the embrace. With time, however, this distinction between traditional and *nuevo* became less clear. By my second year in Buenos Aires, a handful of young *porteños* who proudly employ the *nuevo* label are making place and tradition central to their marketing campaigns. However, they manipulate these themes in innovative ways. For instance, on their Web site, Andrés Amarilla and Meredith Klein (2008) evoke experimentation through images of wide *volcadas,* back *ganchos,* and inverted embraces. Though they situate these moves in recognizably *porteño* sites, the sites—a Subte (Buenos Aires subway) station and the *Floralis Generica* sculpture flanking the city's law school—are a far cry from the usual suspects favored in tango postcards. Another young couple put a decidedly retro twist on their *nuevo tango* flyer: a black-and-white silhouette of the couple in a close embrace, he in a smoking jacket, she in an elegant knee-length dress, her hair swept up in homage to 1950s chic. More recently, Gustavo Naveira and Giselle Anne blend old and new to promote an upcoming festival: their close embrace, their lunging rock step, and Gustavo's pinstriped suit all communicate *milonguero,* while Giselle's backless dress and the festival's location (the United States) are arguably "new."

Many Argentines highlighted the role of the music above all else in describing a great dance, often identifying the music as an underlying force that literally enters into and moves through the self. This force, as they described it, generates an experience that arises from within:

> At times it's like I give myself over to the music, and it does what it wants with me; these aren't everyday experiences. . . . In certain moments of inspiration, the music creates what it will through me. (τ)
>
> Claudio, Argentine, tango professional

> When I was still a beginner . . . the music got so deep inside me that it brought me to tears. I felt something here inside me that later, with time, I learned to disguise. I felt a beautiful anguish—with the music and the woman I held in my arms—I'd have tears rolling down my cheeks. (τ)
>
> Juan Carlos Copes, Argentine, tango professional

More than a means to an end beyond the dance, *porteño* descriptions often highlight a sense of descending into the music and the lyrics—a bittersweet reveling in melancholy—as opposed to a blissful release, hovering above the self and transcending the lyrics. My point here is not to suggest that non-Argentines are somehow inherently less concerned with or moved by the music, but to acknowledge that the journey to transport via the music and the lyrics of tango is of necessity a longer one for the non-Argentine. It demands a sophisticated level of fluency: in addition to becoming familiar with the musical structure and tradition of tango, to fully appreciate the music, the non-Spanish-speaking foreigner must learn a new language and a dialect of that language, *lunfardo*, and then learn to decipher each as sung in primarily early-twentieth-century recordings.

A friend and *porteño* expat once chastised me for my bad habit of giggling whenever I make a mistake, suggesting it revealed a shallow engagement with the music. He argued that I wouldn't laugh if I were responding to the meaning of the lyrics, not only their sound: "I'm not only thinking about the music, I think about the words. Very often I dance to the words and not to the music. . . . You need to pay attention to the words, to the lyrics, and if you pay attention to the lyrics then you see that loss is the real theme. . . . So that's why you don't laugh when you're dancing tango, if you're lamenting loss you don't laugh" (ε; Gerardo, Argentine/U.S. resident, scientist and software engineer). It is only many years later that I can begin to appreciate his frustration. Hearing and dancing the music week after week, listening at home, studying the lyrics, reading up on the history—all of these helped, and I'd entered the tango with a background in Spanish. But it was not until I had spent a full year in Buenos Aires—hearing *lunfardo* from *tangueros*, cab drivers, and shopkeepers; walking the streets and breathing the air in some of the places made famous through alternately maudlin and poetic lyrics—that the full impact of the music began to resonate through me in the act of dancing.

While I might once have argued that the themes of loss, nostalgia, love, and betrayal make themselves heard in the very sound of the tango voice, I would now counter that the ability to make out the particular stories giving shape to these sentiments in the act of dancing opens the door to a more layered, heightened, blissful experience in the embrace. As another expat *tanguera* puts it, understanding the lyrics transports one beyond the sentimentality of romance and into a more specific landscape of feeling: "As I am learning the lyrics of tango, I am understanding what it means to really feel tango, rather than just enjoying the beautiful music. My *milonguero* boyfriend says tango without lyrics is romantic; but tango with lyrics is a feeling" (Kenyon 2000).

Tango as Mirror

> It's such a mirror, for me. . . . To dance tango just shows you everything. Really, I think it's the best therapy. You recognize so many things. (ε)
>
> Karina, Swiss expat, lawyer

It is often said there's no hiding in tango. A sort of silent confessional in movement, much can be revealed in the three and a half minutes of a typical tango dance. Whether in the arms of a complete stranger, lover, or friend, the dance demands an openness and exchange from both parties; the result is a dialogue described by many as "yielding truth." As the saying goes, the body does not lie. Hold back in the last nerve of your baby toe and the most sensitive of partners will know something is amiss. Indeed, a decade into my own practice of tango, and I still on occasion find my body mysteriously gripped by nerves.

The one time I had the opportunity to dance with Naveira, he exposed my worst flaw in a matter of seconds. Helping my partner with a step during class, he grabbed me to demonstrate, nearly knocking the wind out of me with his embrace. But rather than begin with the figure we'd been practicing, he mixed up the order and threw in a few new steps. Caught off guard by the force of his embrace, the unexpected steps, and the anxiety of dancing with this tango great, I tripped up. He stopped, grasped my shoulders, and stared for a second before demanding, "But, *what* are you doing?" I had to admit I had absolutely no idea. He then politely reminded me that I must be willing to surrender, to give up control, to accept the fact that I can't know what's going to happen, and to allow myself to listen, to wait for his lead, so as not to fall apart whenever something unexpected happens.

Discussing the couple who share life and dance, Luiza Paes noted that the tango can be therapeutic, but then reminded me that therapy may just as easily precipitate rupture as closeness. Moreover, the surrounding dancers influence the pair's negotiations, their presence transforming a rather intimate exchange into a quite public display:

> The dance doesn't lie. . . . It's therapeutic in this sense because at times it's very painful, but therapy can be quite painful as well. . . . In the moment of the dance, everything is there—the couple is no longer alone in bed with no one else around, but out there where everybody sees them, their relationship on display, so it's very reveal-

> ing. I see it as very therapeutic in that sense. Trying to dance together on the floor can bring a couple closer together or drive them apart. (τ)
>
> Luiza Paes, Brazilian expat, tango professional

The possibility of rupture aside, the dance can also be painful in its potential for disappointment. Julie Taylor (1998) hits on the paradox of Argentine tango: while the image of the dance is one of ultimate sexual tension and the lyrics are chock full of themes like lost love, betrayal, and nostalgia, the embrace, she observes, "can establish the most intimate of links or none at all" (65). After ten years of dancing and interviews with nearly a hundred social dancers and professionals, I have to agree. In conversations with the uninitiated, I often struggle when trying to gauge how much truth to reveal. Better just to give them the fantasy? It certainly involves less effort and entails less discomfort than bursting the bubble of danger, sex, and drama that surrounds the very utterance of the word *tango*. There is simply no getting around the fact that the tango can be a quite lackluster experience, with moments pedestrian, boring, and even unpleasant. It may "take two to tango," but the pursuit of connection in this partner activity often transcends the notion of "another." Rather, by way of an activity that depends on the presence of another, the dancer is actually confronted with her- or himself.

Descriptions of tango as a medium for self-realization, its study entailing a myth-like journey of self-discovery, arose in countless interviews:

> It starts out as being "Oh, tango, Buenos Aires, high heels!" It's a big fantasy. . . . But you can really use it as a therapeutic tool to learn about everything that has to do with relationships, and not just relationships with another person but the relationship of you with you. You know—where are your fears? What are you afraid to do? What are you afraid to relinquish?
>
> Michele Kadison, American expat, choreographer and writer

> The only time I feel myself is when I'm dancing tango . . . when I'm dancing tango that's me, that's just me, nothing else. (ε)
>
> Sridhar Hannenhalli, Indian/U.S. resident, scientist, and tango professional

Such descriptions recall my formative years in dance, fifteen years within the same studio walls, the resounding refrain "Dance to your heart across the room!" eventually leading me to the knowledge that movement, not the incongruous beauties and violences of the faith I was raised in, is my religion. These intimate confessions also bring to mind tales of transformation: of the reticent outcasts who learn to be with others through movement; of the awkward loners reborn as masters and seductors; of the terminally ill patients who put aside the fatalism of prognosis to embrace the present.

Just as often, though, I found myself on the receiving end of stories and the protagonist in experiences that challenge simplistic portraits of the healing, transformation, and positive self-realization engendered through the dance. More than the humility required to learn a new discipline, and the particular difficulties that such intimacy with another can present, the themes of pain and suffering arose time and again in conversations and interviews, cited as by-products of the very modus operandi of the scene. Common to the tango therapy programs mentioned in this chapter's opening is their self-containment within therapeutic institutions. I suggest that it is precisely this distance from the larger social and cultural context that clears the path to healing in these settings. As Michele Kadison argued in our interview, the dance possesses tremendous therapeutic potential, but the act of harnessing that potential is complicated by the postures and attitudes at play in the social setting. Commenting on both the *milonga* and *práctica* scenes, she noted:

> I think the potential for tango is enormous as a way for people to learn about their limitations, their expectations, not just limitations physically . . . but emotional limitations. But it has to get completely away from ego. And that's absolutely doable; you just have to take it out of the environment because the environment asks for ego. It's all about the prettiest girl, the thinnest girl, the girl with the great ass or the big tits, the guy with this or that. . . . You know, it's all nonsense in the end because, really, if you close your eyes, none of that matters. Our best dances are the dances when we close our eyes and we're dancing with somebody who's not at all our ideal but who knows how to transport us and allows us to be who we really are.

The preservation of alternately charming and outdated codes, a certain degree of pageantry, a healthy dose of machismo, and an undercurrent of violence combine to create their own set of challenges in the *milongas* of Buenos Aires. The result is a hierarchy that is inscribed by and upon the tango bodies that perform these sites into being: "The appearances, the protocol, the hierarchy, the who's dancing with who, which ones are sitting at the big tables close to the floor and which ones are sitting in the back where they can't see anyone, are you local or are you from out of the country, where do you sit in this great hierarchy of the *milonga*?" (Korey Ireland, American, tango professional).

The social pain of the *milongas*, and of the *milongas porteñas* in particular, was a recurring theme in conversations with foreign women. Whether the young female who grows tired of come-ons or the more mature female whose dance skills don't trump youth and beauty, foreign women highlighted the need to have a thicker skin when in Buenos Aires: "The culture there is very difficult, unless you're a superstar or under thirty and beautiful. I don't know what I would gain by going there and suffering through that. I know some people there, but I don't think it would make much difference" (Ellen Mayer, American, tango professional and director of Providence Tango).

Time and again the *prácticas porteñas* were described to me as more laid back and relaxed than the *milongas*, a place for practice, where young dancers can play and experiment, and more importantly, make mistakes away from the judgmental eyes of elders. In promotional materials, modifiers like "free," "investigation," "experimentation," and "alternative" abound. Nonetheless, many informants lamented their tribe-like atmosphere, a tendency toward hierarchy and elitism, an emphasis on performance and display, a competitive culture where one's abilities may be trumped by another's appearance, where one's partner and friend today may be a star and teacher tomorrow, where relationships are forged not only upon skill and "*conexión*" (connection) but also around a precarious exchange economy of prestige, sex, money, and social connections.

La Corcha (The Cork): Money, Tribe, Surveillance, Sex, and Violence Float to the Surface

July 2006, Club Sunderland

It is my birthday, and I've invited a group of friends to Sunderland, the famed social club lying on the northeastern edge of the city in the barrio *of Villa Urquiza. Over the past few years, Sunderland has become the place to see and be seen—attendance a testament to one's understanding of and respect for the dance form and its history, evidence that you've seen "the real thing." Cedric, an architect in town from the States, confirms this when I invite him. His Argentine instructors in New York waxed nostalgic about this* barrio *and the style of tango that arose there, insisting he make the trek out during his brief stay. The* milonga *is held in the back room, a basketball-court-turned-dance-floor that fills to capacity every Saturday with a mix of neighborhood couples, the occasional table of foreigners, and a handful of luminaries. Among them tonight is El Morocho Esteban, an older* milonguero *whose dance skills assure him a crowd of young female admirers wherever he goes. Once inside, I find a banquet-sized table full of friends, my name on a card at the center. Midway through the evening my birthday is announced and the whole gym sings to me. It is one of those magical nights when every dance is good, when the cheap champagne could almost pass for Veuve, when I feel I am where I should be, my love affair with the city and its dance reignited.*

Two revered older locals, teachers of the Villa Urquiza style, are performing. Also performing is a very young, very talented female dancer. Sixteen, they say, she is the most aggressively sexual high schooler I've ever seen, the attacking rotation of her walk and suggestiveness of her adornments at once alarming and fascinating in someone so young. When the older professionals enter the floor, a friend leans over and whispers, "This is the real thing." But at their age, the dance is little more than a mix of sweet musicality and the lightness that comes to those who've danced the tango for decades. Meanwhile, I can't get my mind off the near-incestuous advertising campaign recently launched by a new tango team, a brother and his (underage) sister. As I marvel at the unabashed sexuality of the young girl who danced tonight, the shock of these images still with me, my thoughts turn to the growing ranks of young female professionals, and the options before them in this world, where sex and passion are often the path of least resistance. And what of the rumors of physical abuse and sexual predation? They circulate far too much, to my mind, to be nothing more than talk.

The crowd breaks into wild applause, but my head is spinning at this world, the unassuming charm of it poised to crumble at the least provocation.

* * *

During the *milonga* shutdown of January 2005, the desperation to dance wherever we might find music, a floor, and a few other dancers before the police turned up created a magical sense of camaraderie and openness among the young *porteños* and foreigners clued into the *práctica* scene. When I returned to Argentina nine months later, those events had grown in size and organization. Many of the people I befriended in these once underground settings now had professional aspirations. My third time in Buenos Aires, I was no longer a novelty. In short, I quickly grew accustomed to sitting . . . a lot. When I talked to a friend from the States a few months into my two-year stay, her complaints—that it is so hard to get an invitation to dance, that she can't even count on her friends in that regard—seemed impossibly naïve, even laughable. She compared it to the salsa scene, where, she reported, everybody dances with everybody else, regardless of level. Not so in tango. Especially in Buenos Aires, where you'd be hard-pressed to find a dancer with no agenda. For the tango pilgrimage has truly become a rite of passage, the fantasy of living and breathing the tango all the more plausible in the wake of the country's economic crisis, the devalued peso encouraging more visitors to stay longer.

While these visitors have given rise to an industry that extends beyond the social dance venues and academies to encompass clothing and footwear, *cena* (dinner) shows (see the next chapter), specialty hotels and pensions, and most recently, "taxi dancers" for hire, it is no secret that the real money is to be found abroad: "There's a difference between the euro and the peso, or the dollar and the peso, and if you make money in Europe the difference is enormous. If I make 1,000 euros in Europe, that's $3,700 here, a little more than three times more, so to work abroad you can live a little better back home" (τ; Raul Masciocchi, Argentine, tango professional).

Teaching group classes in Buenos Aires will not put food on the table. Likewise, *milongas* are not money-making events. *Prácticas* even less so. *Cena* shows are now a dime a dozen. More than one informant lamented the instability and poor pay for the tango performer in Buenos Aires. A violinist argued that the dinner-show venues pay musicians and dancers poorly because tourists generally know so little about the product they demand. Even Juan Carlos Copes, internationally renowned star of stage and screen, attested to this: "There's no profession here; I have to leave the country to make money, to make a living. I was on Broadway for the third time from 1999 to 2000; what I earned there in two months was enough for nearly an entire year here. Here I've seen projects that pay for one day, you pick up your check and 'Ciao, get lost'" (τ).

As Masciocchi and Copes attested, the *porteño* looking to make a living in tango will do well to befriend a foreign dancer who might help organize a series of workshops or classes in their home community overseas. Teaching private lessons to foreigners in Buenos Aires is the next best thing, and often a doorway to future teaching gigs abroad. Taxi-dancing, or offering oneself as an escort for classes, *prácticas*, or *milongas*, is quickly becoming an industry unto itself, though it is arguably the least prestigious means of making money in tango. Thus, it is in the entirely bodily negotiations—in the *milongas*, the *prácticas*, and the classroom—that the stakes are highest. For the *porteño* dancer, the promise is not only economic reward, but the prestige that comes with travel and teaching abroad. While for the foreign dancer, body and pocketbook become a dangerously intertwined bargaining chip, realization of one's tango fantasy dependent upon investment, and a certain degree of gambling with both.

As the generous exchange rate stimulates greater investment on the part of foreigners—not just of time and money, but of pride, sweat, and tears—this yields an often palpable sense of expectation for a return on all that one has invested. Over the course of two years, I was surprised at the number of dancers, both local and foreign, who confessed professional aspirations. Even more surprising was the number of "green" locals who told me they are teachers. Simply put, it seems everybody wants something from the tango. (Of course, a moment's reflection reminds me that I do as well. Sure, I want something different—history, stories, scandals, experiences—but I was mining the scene just like everyone else.)

The result is a high-pressure environment, where a quasi-religious culture of devotion is manifested through consumption, consumption referring not only to the purchase of the tango experience and all its attendant accessories (shoes, clothing, music, books, and more) but also to the very state of being consumed. For the pressure to be consumed is quite palpable, fed by the frenzied devotion of the dance's global pilgrims, and the inexhaustible roster of tango offerings in Buenos Aires.[5] Commenting on the fanaticism of the scene, Ingrid, a dancer from Copenhagen, described the particular stresses that arise in a practice where one's progress depends so wholly upon others:

> There's a lot of very fanatic people. . . . People are talking all the time about teachers and where to take classes. . . . Especially now, there are a lot of foreigners who come here only to take tango. They only study, they only take tango classes and go to *milongas*. . . . In other dance I can go to class and I can just be concerned with my own progress and no one else cares. But in tango it's important that I find a good partner and it's important for the partner that I

> dance okay. You're so dependent on other people and I think that affects the whole society. Everyone wants to dance with good dancers and is searching for that, and is stressing about becoming better themselves so that they can dance with good dancers. It's very stressful. (ε)

Further, this desire for improvement, for a return on one's investment, heightens the pressure to perform. Grounding this pressure in a larger atmosphere of surveillance, another young woman from Europe described the impossible task of negotiating invitations—where each acceptance, each refusal, every tiny evidence of happiness or discontent is silently recorded by others:

> And you have the pressure that you have to show that you are good so they ask you for a dance, so it's really difficult. And the stress that someone asks you where you already know he's not a good dancer, so I cannot show what I can do . . . it's already like you go with a face like not really happy to dance and they think "Oh, she is not fun." Or they know if you dance with people who are not good that there is a reason. It's very hard to go out. It's very stressful. (ε)
>
> Karina, Swiss, lawyer

In my interview with Juan Carlos Copes, he described the tango as a *corcha*, or a cork in the water, to explain its resurgence in the Argentine cultural landscape. It may have died down for a while, he argued, but it will always rise to the surface. This image is also useful in thinking about the presence of hierarchy, elitism, surveillance, pressure, and violence in the *práctica* scene. Certainly not strangers to tango in Buenos Aires or abroad (countless dancers speak of ability as an underlying source of friction in U.S. communities), many dancers still remarked with surprise at the rigidity of the hierarchy, the overwhelming pressure, and a pervading climate of surveillance in the *práctica* scene. While not intended as hand-holding lovefests, the descriptions provided by *práctica* founders and the language of their marketing materials suggest an openness that seems to be fading fast.

A male friend from Germany lamented that these events have outgrown their original purpose: they are no longer sites for practice, where one feels comfortable experimenting, but rather places where you'd better show up ready to perform. Korey Ireland, a professional dancer from the States, noted that while the etiquette may be different, the hierarchy is equally present in both the *prácticas* and the *milongas*: "You don't have the same protocol but I do think you have a pretty clear awareness of hierarchy or of status, in that scene. There are people who won't dance with me at El Motivo who will dance with me at Canning." (Popular sites among both foreigners and locals, El Motivo is a *práctica* and Canning is a *milonga*.) In my interview with Nancy, an actress from the United States, she admitted to feeling unwelcome in the classes of many of the rising young teachers housed under the *nuevo* label. Speaking in particular of the *prácticas*, she described a stifling atmosphere where an upper echelon of dancers maintain a strict hold on their position through a combination of distance, judgment, and surveillance:

> Some *prácticas* you have to be ready to go to. If I don't feel like I'm on my game I don't want to go, because I find that people are sitting there to watch you and judge you—I feel like I'm being judged. The cliquishness . . . I feel that there's an upper level that wants to always be the upper level and aren't as willing to share, and it is like that in many communities.

Echoing Nancy's description, an organizer of one of the city's popular *milongas* attested to the elitism of the *práctica* scene and the unapproachability of some of the rising young tango stars when she told me she is often mistaken for the host at others' events:

> They want to be in a position of importance and they remove themselves from reality. I go to [an event] and people come up and ask me:
>
> "*Che*, can you lower the air conditioner?"
>
> "I don't organize here."
>
> "Oh. Who's in charge?"
>
> "Well, they are."
>
> What happens is I arrive and I greet people. In this special place—for superstars, super-connoisseurs of the secret technique . . . *Por favor*! (τ)
>
> Mariela, Argentine, tango professional and *milonga* organizer

Over drinks one night, a French journalist and housemate of a young Finnish dancer questioned my absence from their recent house party: "I thought you were part of the mafia," she joked. A newcomer to the dance, she admitted to finding the *práctica* scene adolescent, cliquey, too serious for its own good. She said she prefers dancing in tacky neighborhood social clubs with "bad older dancers," arguing that these people, the bad dancers, are the ones that will keep the tango alive. Rather than mediocrity, I believe she was making a case for popularity, for a social dance of the people, in lieu of an elitist scene that consumes its own.

For there are vestiges of a "mafia" in the local *práctica* scene. Rumors circulated of one young professional threatening another to get out of the business. The crime seemed to be one of bypassing the local hierarchy and outpricing his competition, who were beginning to feel the pinch. I also caught wind of organizers conspiring to put a handle on the scene's growth and keep a hold on their share of the pie by establishing some sort of professional criteria for organizing *prácticas*. Interestingly, such efforts are perhaps more at home in tango communities outside Argentina than in Buenos Aires. The sheer multitude of *milongas*, and the many public confessions that they are not lucrative events, suggests there is not much ground for competition. Outside Argentina, the size of tango communities necessarily limits the number of teachers, organizers, and events that can coexist. Competition among rising *porteño* professionals, however, reflects all that is at stake for these young dancers. With the growth of tango communities the world over, a once small-scale alternative social scene has transformed into a highly professionalized, international industry. Moreover, the Argentines' arbitrary positioning within the global economy impacts the overall energy of the scene and shapes each exchange. While skill, youth, and appearance are generally highly valued attributes, money and power come into play as well. The foreign organizer can offer much to the aspiring Argentine professional, as can the foreign dancer with money to burn on private lessons. Just as the foreign dancer may negotiate his or her position with any combination of skill, cash, and sex, the Argentine may draw on any combination of skills, sex, and prestige to negotiate his or her future.

Addiction: *Tango Droga*

I danced every *tanda* for five hours without pause. When I attempted to leave, a taller man standing in the lobby wearing a black shirt and pinstriped trousers gave me the nod. The music was irresistible so I accepted. His embrace was gentle, his interpretation playful, his musicality exceptional. Heaven. He told me he lives and breathes tango. We danced at least three more *tandas*, and I was loath to leave, but I hadn't eaten all day and after five and a half hours of nonstop dancing, my feet hurt. He asked me if I like *adornos*, women's embellishments. I told him I needed

> to learn them. He gave me his business card. I asked him how much he charged for a private lesson. Fifteen US dollars. He told me: "*Tango es una droga. Yo soy traficante.*" (Tango is a drug. I am the dealer.)
>
> We're on for Monday.
>
> Lara Triback, American, musician and teacher, "Oldies But Goodies" (e-mail journal)

Testaments to the addictive power of Argentine tango are anything but scarce. One finds evidence of the spell it casts in writings and interviews left behind by the dance's forebears, in the packs of dancers who chase the tango across state and country lines, in the "otherworld" that comes to life when the "real" world of Buenos Aires goes to sleep. From the time I began dancing tango, I have been treated to innumerable accounts of the dance as a drug or an addiction, most invoking its cathartic or blissful properties. As Ellen Mayer described it in our interview, this particular brand of "high" leaves its followers insatiable for more: "Well, it's the catharsis that creates the addiction, isn't it? . . . It really is frenzied. . . . You know, some animals just don't ever stop eating. Some will stop when they get full, but then . . . there are some animals that will just eat; they don't have that mechanism. I think tango dancers are like that. They don't know how to stop."

A few gems from the open-contribution list on the TangoPulse Web site, "You Know You're a Tango Junkie When . . . ," highlight the eccentric behaviors of the tango addict, from the harmless quirks to the more rash expressions of devotion:

> You walk backwards to the refrigerator.
>
> You keep a pair of dance shoes in your car.
>
> Your mind visualizes and calibrates square-footage in terms of open dance space.
>
> You have developed a healthy fear of foot injuries.
>
> Before traveling, you check out the net for tango events in that area.
>
> You are considering the purchase of clothing not commonly seen in public.
>
> You cross state lines to tango.
>
> You are willing to spend twice as much time driving to a *milonga* as you actually dance.
>
> You are unable to schedule major surgery without compromising tango commitments.
>
> You have crossed an ocean just to dance with a favorite partner.

> You've put your house on the market to support your tango habit.
>
> Wong (2009)

Meanwhile, Alex Krebs's online survey, "How Addicted Are You?" (now defunct but accessed in 2008), provided the dancer a point system to measure addiction, ranking behaviors from the most rudimentary and appropriate to the more radical and highly valued for their extremism. For example, spending money on tango when in debt to friends earns you two points. Crying while dancing, listening to tango music, or just thinking about tango is viewed positively, each instance worth two points. Depression, on the other hand, is more complicated: absence of depression earns a two-point deduction (perhaps evidence of heartlessness?); a period of depression lasting between one day and two weeks earns points; but depression sustained longer than two weeks is the sign of an overdue hiatus, and depression beyond four weeks is warning of a more serious problem.

As the global tango community continues to grow, the nature of addiction has evolved as well. In successive visits to Argentina, I reconnected with friends and acquaintances from abroad, the allure of the dance and its birthplace a very powerful combination. For the foreigner, addiction to the dance is often intertwined with an enchantment with another way of life: "I really fear when I leave here, not being able to dance every day, having a normal life where I'm so busy that I'm not going to be able to do it every day, I wonder, how will I feel after having it be such a part of my life?" (Nancy, American expat, actress). By no means necessarily *porteño*, many are immersed in a sort of mini–United Nations of tango—an international circuit centered within the larger *porteño* tango scene and Argentine capital—where the cast of characters is constantly changing. This is a world where the distinctions between "host" and "guest" are fuzzy, where the opportunity to live and breathe the dance night and day is supported and shaped by the very presence and investment of other outsiders. Labeling this an expat or tourist existence is insufficient, for more than likely the dancer from abroad will encounter a degree of "staged authenticity," or experiences that are created specifically for tourist consumption, alongside others that can best be described as sincere. And they will surely experience situations where the influence of outsiders is undeniable, though equating foreign influence with lack of authenticity is shortsighted at best, ignorant at worst. But the differential in purchasing power sets the foreigner apart from the start, enabling the construction of a lifestyle not wholly accessible at home, and a manner of financial/consumption therapy, out of reach to the average Argentine in Argentina:

> A lot of people use it as a great vacation because, honestly, you'll get whatever you're looking for. If you're looking for sex, if you're looking for shoes, if you're looking for food, if you're looking for sleepless nights, or if you're looking just to make some nice connections, or if you're looking to be part of some kind of mystique—it's whatever you want there, it's all there ready for you.
>
> Homer Ladas, American, tango professional

Moreover, consumption is an increasingly encouraged and legitimized expression of addiction, the wealth of offerings to be consumed—from classes to shoes to clothing to *cena* shows to books and music—resulting from the growing numbers of tango visitors each year, and the incomparable prices in the wake of the crisis.[6] For the local, addiction may be inspired, or at the very least legitimized, by the earning potential represented by the tango.[7]

Cecilia Gonzalez, an Argentine professional, suggested the growing emphasis on consumption reflects an addiction to consumption rather than to the dance itself: "There are people who come and buy everything they can related to tango, but if it wasn't tango it would be something else. It's an addiction to shopping, not to tango. And there are others addicted to taking classes, but it's not really the class. It's not the tango, it's not the product—it's the person" (τ). Her comment gets to the heart of the same issue raised in debates over style and authenticity: just what is the dance and how is it achieved? Is it something that can be taught, learned through the consumption of classes and accessories, or is it the more intangible representation of a fading way of life, a skill to be acquired and honed over a lifetime, ultimately personal, mysterious, impenetrable? It also engages the "less is more" argument that reappears every now and again on Tango-L, according to which a true tango lover will sit all night if need be. Such arguments tend to connect the desperation for experience or "mileage" on the dance floor with the consumption of external accessories including clothing and shoes, and the execution of particular moves and embellishments, in turn evidence of the consumption of classes. In essence, this line of thought frames certain manifestations of addiction as inauthentic and representative of the novice, and links these to stereotypical portraits of the tourist, as in a 2007 Tango-L post:

How to Spot the Tourists in Buenos Aires' *milongas*:
They wear black t-shirts and cargo pants.
They accept verbal invitations at their table.
They ask men to dance.
They begin dancing as soon as the music starts.
They expect or try to dance every *tanda*.
They dance consecutive *tandas* with the same man.
They add embellishments to excess.
They prefer quantity over quality of partners.
They will suffer through a *tanda* just to be dancing.
They arrive early and leave within a short time if they haven't danced.
They don't feel the music or know the orchestras.
They don't learn or follow the rules of the *milonga*.
They attend CITA[8] and go to the *milongas* to show off their new moves.

Within this argument is the notion of labor at the heart of tango, and moreover, the idea that tango is more than just dance but also music and social encounter. The seasoned *milonguera/o* cultivates an ability to wait, for the sweetness of the dance is heightened by that wait. And rather than an escapist transcendence, the *milonga* is for delving into and reveling in the depths of the music, both on and off the floor. In *El abrazo del tango* (The Tango Embrace), Mafalda Trotta's wonderful 2006 documentary on the *milongas* of Buenos Aires, the late, great Gavito and "*milonga* king" El Flaco Dany define a *milonguero* as one who lives for dancing until the sun comes up. This experience is often centered on the table, at the bar, or the perimeter of the dance hall, in the somewhat superficial socializing that fills the void between moments of inspiration. In essence, this tango is about quality, where that quality is entirely antithetical to quantity.

In contrast to this, manifestations of addiction in the *práctica* or *nuevo* scene often revolve around the accumulation of experience. A reflection of generation, this is also indicative of the increasing emphasis on consumption and thus return on one's investment. A necessity for the novice dancer, the emphasis on experience also reflects the lighter philosophy of the *práctica* scene, where experimentation and mistakes are (theoretically) encouraged. Further, addiction via accumulation demonstrates the distinct focus of social tango events abroad and in Argentina, and the impact of the growing foreign presence on the local scene. Though the sense of community is arguably quite stronger outside Buenos Aires—smaller size and less circulation of members being two main reasons—events in the United States, for example, are generally centered on the dance. In contrast, the *milongas* and some of the *prácticas* of Buenos Aires take place in venues that offer food, drink, and table seating, encouraging more of a back and forth between dance and social encounter.

Community or Industry?

The combination of addiction and high expectations can yield an atmosphere of superficiality and competition. In particular in Buenos Aires, where the desire to make good on one's investment is so strong, friendships and relationships built off the floor are put to the test time and again by the tango *droga*. Tango dancers are adept at carrying on conversation while scanning the room and quickly become accustomed to being dropped midsentence in favor of an invitation. A deft behavioral analysis of the professional networker, Barbara Ehrenreich's portrait of "prowling alone" is reminiscent of the social patterns in tango that threaten to undermine connection and community off the floor:

> It feels "fake" because we know it involves the deflection of our natural human sociability to an ulterior end. . . . The networker is always, so to speak, looking over the shoulder of the person she engages in conversation, toward whatever concrete advantage can be gleaned from the interaction. . . . No matter how crowded the room, the networker prowls alone, scavenging to meet his or her individual needs.
>
> *Bait and Switch: The (Futile) Pursuit of the American Dream* (2005): 62

Still, countless dancers cited the importance of the relationships they have found in tango. Ellen Mayer noted that her pursuit of the dance has been driven largely by a desire to create community: "I think I realized right away that the focus of tango for me was not going to be about my dancing, it was going to be more about what I could build and provide. So I think the community factor . . . I've had some really fantastic experiences with people in the down time." Others cited a back and forth in their tango lives, from an obsession with the dance, where a moment's sitting is experienced as nearly intolerable, to an appreciation of all that exists in between, where important friendships are developed and these relationships thrive beyond the *milonga* walls. The importance of cultivating relationships is also cited by more experienced dancers, who noted that over time and with progression, one's pool of partners, or at least those with whom one can expect a great dance, lessens. Still others, the more enlightened (or resigned), proclaimed a zen-like transcendence over expectation, where their practice has evolved to the point of simply enjoying each dance for what it will offer.

Dancers from Argentina and abroad pointed to the recent explosion in tango academies in Buenos Aires as evidence of the dance's transformation into profitable industry. Aside from classes, many offer clothing, footwear, books, music, posters, and other tango paraphernalia. And more recently, several offer intensive package tours that combine daily instruction, hotel accommodations, *milonga* escorts, city tours, *cena* shows, and jaunts to gaucho towns for *asado* and *chacarera*. More than supply and demand, these schools are strategically fostering a sense of family and community in a scene that has grown to the point of being unmanageable and intimidating for many foreigners. These institutions also make tango addiction more legitimate. Displaced from the seedy underworld of the *milongas*, chasing the tango by day is the decidedly academic counterpart to nightly travails through a much darker abyss. Indeed, a friend whose five-week tango vacation in Buenos Aires stretched out into nearly three years as she transformed her passion into vocation told me this extended period was her graduate school.

In a 2007 Tango-L post, a foreign *tanguera* notes that it took more effort to find the tango back in the early 1990s but that outsiders were often embraced as rarities:

> When I was introduced to tango, there was no Internet discussion group. Tango wasn't being force-fed in classes and festivals. People who wanted tango had to search for it. A typical *milonga* in the *centro* might have a European or two, now and then—maybe even an Asian or North American. It was an odd enough experience that when a host discovered someone from out of town, introductions would be made during the announcements.

Nowadays, the visitor need not work so hard to locate the tango, but the wealth of options can be overwhelming, and the presence of so many foreigners is often cited as disheartening. Thus, many dancers find comfort in the family atmosphere of a handful of schools and studios. And as the number of tango schools grows, courtship of potential members takes on greater importance, often mirroring the complex seduction at the heart of the dance itself:

June 2006, Estudio Agustín

Milonga *class ends and Agustín rises to his feet with a dramatic pause. His eyes locked on mine, he announces we're going to the other room to dance. It has been cold and gray all morning, there's no heat in this place, I am past frozen. The last thing I want to do is dance. I protest that I don't have my shoes, and he just laughs, asking whether I'm actually turning him down. (Apparently he doesn't take no for an answer.) So I smile, accept my fate, and follow. He holds his arms open for an embrace, his gaze boring right through me. Did he tell the others not to follow? Normally everyone spills into the practice room after class, but today it is just the two of us. Walking into his embrace, I realize I'm not just cold, I am literally undone by the intensity of his attention. I'm very nervous.*

He whispers into my ear "Donde queres, dale, te sigo" (Wherever you want, just go, I'll follow you). He's no dummy, Agustín. I've done little to hide my ambivalence about the whole "leader-follower" thing, and now he's using it against me. My lead elementary at best, we rock back and forth in an embrace for a moment. And then he moves in for the kill. Grabbing my arms, he moves his cheek from mine so that we are face to face, so that I can't get away from those eyes. "Where have you been?" he demands. "Why don't you come more often?" more urgently, his eyes never once leaving mine. I laugh and tell him that "Todo el mundo" *(All the world) is here in his studio every day.* "Eres tan bella" *(You're so beautiful), he tells me, "Don't you know that you're the one I wait for every day?" We dance two songs like this. A different sort of exchange. His* piropos *for my nervous laughter. My commitment for his attention. Negotiating my devotion.*

Back in the classroom, the studio regulars are all winks and knowing smiles. He pats the chair next to his and I assume that most coveted of spots, watching in awe as one after another dancer drops in—for a kiss, a hello, a quick question, a new exercise—and he masterfully doles out just enough to satisfy each, all the while maintaining his one-on-one with me, keeping me right by his side. A maestro *in every sense of the word. An entirely new kind of seduction.*

Or is it? This is tango after all—the realm of the piropo, *a dance of suggestion, the illusion of tension, at its best when possibility remains just that. Besides, Agustín is old enough to be my father, and he loves his wife.*

In the end, I remain a casual presence at the studio. I see what keeps the others there, but I'm loath to limit myself to just one among the many tango camps here. I do, however, pin him down for an interview that day. And it is a good one.

* * *

While the spread of tango communities around the world can be traced to the global traffic in culture—growing out of spectacularly packaged stage shows that reduce a tradition to exotic product for export—their survival, growth, and connection to one another reflect an involvement that transcends mere thirst for cultural consumption. Tourist attraction, industry, social activity, passion, addiction, and philosophy of life, tango thrives in Buenos Aires through the intersection of global and local desires, where meaning is created in situated, interactive practices. What's more, this desire for contact and experience can be a powerful form of resistance to the increasingly isolated nature of modern life. Although it is hailed as a means of healing, addiction, and suffering, I believe that the real power of the tango lies in its ability to confront the dancer with some brand of truth. Whether fleeting, uncomfortable, or transcendent, such truths are perhaps even more compelling as once stable and comforting notions like culture become every day more fluid and shifting.

A Kinder Dragon?

January 2008, *La Rubia Golpeada*

I am house-sitting in idyllic New Canaan, Connecticut, desperately trying to get some writing done. A picture-perfect town where the American dream seems alive and well, it is perhaps the farthest I have felt from Buenos Aires since my return two months ago. I've nearly completed a chapter, a tour through my ever-changing feelings about tango, when I receive an e-mail entitled "the beat-up blonde" from a friend in Buenos Aires. Following a long string of forwards, I finally reach the original message, a desperate plea in capital letters, followed by pictures of a young blonde, her right arm in a cast and her left coated with bruises. The most recent performance partner of a very famous, very successful tango professional, she is—according to the message at least—his most recent victim. The author begs recipients to share these pictures with the global tango community, to stop giving him work, to make a collective statement that such abuse will not be tolerated.

I have been loving tango since returning to the States. I am new to the scene in Boston, there are a handful of fabulous leaders, and I get to dance with all of them. After Buenos Aires, the absence of "attitude" is refreshing. Perhaps they are impressed by my time there. Perhaps this boosts my confidence and improves my dancing. Perhaps this will all change. There is no constant in tango.

But this e-mail strikes a chord. It leads me down familiar paths, where again I marvel at my dedication to an art form with such violent undertones. To my mind, the seduction of this dance lies not in love, sex, passion, even authenticity or exoticism, but rather in its endless contradictions and challenges. With each achievement, it seems I am rewarded with a new hurdle. With each dance, I may come face to face with one or another uncomfortable truth. Tango is seductive because it is not easy, it is never the same, it does not last, and, at its heart, it resists—the passage of time, the sanitizing effects of globalization, the modernizing efforts of its young devotees and savvy entrepreneurs. There is much to object to, to find offense in, to ridicule or reject. Perhaps for that reason, those moments of ecstasy and bliss are felt all the more pure and beautiful, and often despite myself keep me coming back for more.

6

Locating the Tango

Tango is a contradiction in terms: even though tango is a transnational crossing of cultures, for many, tango remains a stable signifier of Argentine national identity. As a result of this paradox, many aficionados of tango resist all transnational implications where tango is concerned, insisting instead that tango is the unique reference of the symbolic identity and territory of Argentine culture.

Erin Manning, *Politics of Touch* (2007)

It seems to me that the tango is attractive, and it has a place in the world. And this place that it occupies in the world, it's not as a representative of Argentina. It holds this place on its own, as a form of dance that is very useful and very necessary and very good for our modern way of life, in all parts of the world. To put it another way, it's entirely likely that there are people in another country who dance tango, who not only don't know that the tango is from Argentina, but aren't even interested in where tango is from. (τ)

Gustavo Naveira, Argentine, tango professional

[Where does the tango exist?] In my heart, my mind, in a bar, Avenida Corrientes, the obelisk, Buenos Aires, in a meeting with friends, the couple. You have to be born here to feel the tango, or marry a *porteño* and live it through your children. (τ)

Mariano Olman, Argentine, tango professional

February 2008, Tango Café, Boston

He drags my left foot to the side so that it rests, weightless yet present, on his right. The last notes of the music hang in the air, and I catch them, leaning my right shoulder in as I shift legs, slowly tracing my right foot up his calf until my knee bends beyond a full passé. *As I exhale, it drops; he subtly shifts my weight and opens his left shoulder, inviting me to lunge ever so slightly into my right leg, to lean directly into his chest, my right arm curving in an upward arc in his left, as we each gaze diagonally downward to my left, poking fun and reveling in this clichéd tango pose.*

The music is over, but he holds me for a second before releasing all but the tiniest grasp on my right hand. I smile, unwilling to jinx the moment with talk. He looks at me thoughtfully, then says something I've heard more than once recently: "Nobody here dances like you."

Funny, I don't quite know what to make of it. Has Buenos Aires changed my dance that much? When I think back over my time there, it's often easier to dwell on the negative: the sitting, the waiting, the wanting. The lows were as deep as the highs were, well, high. Especially during that first year, when I yo-yoed like an overeater on a fad diet. Of course, there was plenty of watching and a fair share of lessons, and eventually, some great dancing. After two years, it seems something has finally sunk in. Then again, reducing my dance to the dance itself neglects all that I absorbed in Argentina.

I'd come to the tango as a dancer; even the anthropologist in me remained primarily focused on the tango as dance. But two years in Buenos Aires changed that. Over time, the memories of a life became enmeshed within the stories of the songs, so that the places they recount bring back the sites as I lived them. Now, as Manzi's horses move toward Centenera y Tabaré,[1] *I am inches from Tata Cedrón in Bar Turon, and then I, too, am descending into Pompeya, by way of Boedo and Parque Patricios, where the roads slope gently south; where the trees flower blue and Saturdays are* tranquilo *(quiet); where teenage boys hunch over cars—the likes of which I haven't seen in twenty years—and soup up engines for date night; where little girls float on handlebars and* abuelos *(grandfathers) man bicycles in suspenders. Balloons ascend to the sky from tires, and I walk hand-in-hand with a strange painter who can't hold still but constantly shifts, squeezes, and looks to make sure my hand is still there; who plays musical chairs each time we cross the street so that I am not on the side of traffic; who tells me of a childhood in the* campo *(countryside), a house with no bathroom, a blind father gunned down, a mother committed, a loving grandmother who sneaks books by moonlight, Sabato's bench in Parque Lezama, and so much more.*

Back in the States, I find myself transformed. At the milonga, *I turn people down. I groan when Rodriguez is followed by inane, undanceable, alternative fare. I cut off chatty leaders with the same ultimatum:* "Bailamos o hablamos?" *(Are we dancing or are we talking?) I marvel that so many dancers do not know the music.*

No, I didn't breed any offspring at the other end of the world. I fell victim to the romance of the place itself, and to the romance of place as recounted in the tango as music. I had lived a life in tango. Like Martha Graham be-

fore me, tango had "entered the rhythm of my blood" (1991: 176); like Helen Stevenson, I had dropped my accent, become part of the landscape (2000: 56). I was porteña, *and my life was a tango.*

The Reality of Romance

Esta ciudad no se si existe, si es así . . .
¡O algún poeta la ha inventado para mí!
(This city, I don't know if it exists, if it really is like this . . .
Or whether some poet has invented it for me!)

Siempre se vuelve a Buenos Aires (You Always Return to Buenos Aires),
lyrics by Eladia Blázquez, music by Astor Piazzolla (1989)

Dismiss me from the falsehood and impossibility of history, and deliver me over to the reality of romance. . . . Nothing is more uncertain, more contradictory, more unsatisfactory than the evidence of facts.

William Godwin, quoted in Jill Lepore, "Just the Facts, Ma'am" (2008)

Midway through my time in Argentina, I meet Carla, an Argentine folklorist, who like many of her generation now resides outside her home country, at Las Violetas, the most beautiful café in all of Buenos Aires. Recently restored to its old grandeur, Las Violetas boasts imported marble floors, stained-glass windows, golden chandeliers, and an afternoon tea that seals the visitor's transportation to Buenos Aires' storied past. It even holds a place in tango history: Pascual Contursi and José Martinez are said to have paid off debts owed the establishment by signing over the rights to the composition "Ivette" in 1920.[2]

Carla raves over my accent and tells me I am "already *porteña*" as I wolf down a *mil hojas* (Napoleon pastry) and she elegantly sips a *café con leche* (coffee with milk). She asks why I love the city so much. I respond that it is the most intense place I have ever been. She agrees and we commiserate. The noise, the pollution, the crowds, even the weather: all are such that on a bad day, life can feel impossible. On the other hand, life moves at a kinder pace, friends and family come first, mothers and daughters walk the streets arm in arm, strangers touch unapologetically, corner cafés are filled with patrons of all ages at 1:00 a.m., the need for sleep is sublimated in favor of other activities, conversation and connection abound, and even the animals seem somehow happier. Carla speaks about the energy fields lying beneath the city, tells me they are rumored to be especially potent, that conspiracy theories have linked the country's cyclical crises to this phenomenon.

Back in Philadelphia, I have a similar conversation with my Spanish teacher, a *yanqui* with a perfect Argentine accent. Even as a child, she felt drawn to Argentina, but she never understood why until years later, when she met her *porteño* husband in a Philadelphia nightclub. The energy of Buenos Aires is so powerful, she tells me, yet it also fills her with comfort; a sense of *déjà vu* convinces her that she lived a former life there. When *porteños* and Americans alike ask me what it is that keeps me in Buenos Aires, my most succinct answer is "*Hay más vida*" (There's more life). The Argentines smile and nod approvingly while my family shake their heads and pursue their interrogation with growing impatience, demanding, "But what does that mean?"

In my conversations with other dancers, the pull of this place is likewise revealed. Andrew Burt, a young American *tanguero*, described his transformation after a year in Buenos Aires. Once host of an alternative tango event in the United States, he is now fanatical in his pursuit of traditional music. Determined to tailor his dance to each particular orchestra, he is also developing a roster of preferred partners for dancing to each of these orchestras, much like a real *milonguero*. Pia, the painter from Sweden, likened Buenos Aires to mecca, in terms of both saturation and romance. Not only does one have more options, but there is "the romantic dream of these old *milongas*" that draws Pia and other foreigners to the birthplace of tango. Claudio, a young Argentine recently back from Europe, summed up the appeal of tango in Buenos Aires in terms of *clima* (vibe):

> I've been to *milongas* in Germany, and I like it, I love it, but after a while I want to scream a little. . . . If only there were a little more noise, a bit more feeling of tango. You know what I mean? Here, there's more atmosphere. Over there you can't smoke. Here you can do whatever you want. You can smoke, you can drink, you can go to the bathroom, you can beat the shit out of somebody . . . and this all creates a different ambience. (τ)

A product of the place itself, the *clima* in the *milongas* of Buenos Aires suggests that more than song, dance, or poetry, tango is a way of life. Moreover, its existence is not confined to the *milongas*; rather, it lives in the streets, among the people, in the way they speak and interact with one another. As locals and foreigners pointed out, one can learn to dance tango almost anywhere nowadays, but a trip to Buenos Aires offers much more to the student of tango than the dance itself. In the mecca of tango, its presence is felt, and thus, it may be absorbed, in the most mundane of activities:

> You can learn tango in any academy in any part of the world, but as a language, as it is expressed—if you really want to see the essence of that language—it lives in Argentina. Go to any *milonga* and it lives there. And you'll see it, and you'll understand something. Take a taxi and listen to the way the driver talks, or stop in a newspaper stand and listen to how the vendor speaks, or stop at the vegetable stand. . . . It's in the way of speaking, of standing, of being. Everything. (τ)
>
> Gabriel Glagovsky, Argentine, tango professional and *práctica* organizer

> It's something I live through, I smell, I feel . . . and I feel that the idea of tango, that level of interaction was not only present in the *milonga* scene. For me, tango in Buenos Aires was also present outside—how people live their lives, how people interacted in the cafés or in the subways, or how you take a ride in the taxi and the way you communicate with the taxi driver. For me there's snippets of tango there.
>
> Cristina Ladas, American, tango professional

The streets of Buenos Aires present a barrage of images that attest to the very contested status of tango in its birthplace. From ordinary to kitschy, quasi-religious to artistic, these public representations—varied as they are given their number—generally share one important trait: they tend to situate the dance, music, and poetry of tango firmly within the past. Such imagery underscores the distance implied by authenticity. Like Russian philosopher Mikhail Bakhtin's (1986) *chronotope,* in which events exist in the intersection of a specific space and time, tango is grounded in a historical place, where its global roots combined to create a decidedly "Argentine" cultural heritage. Dancers can evoke this era through the clothing they wear or the music they explore, and they can even travel to Buenos Aires, but they can never truly revisit the *place in time* from which the tango emerged. Recognition of this rupture, I believe, is at the heart of local and foreign efforts to preserve the "true tango," and it reveals the particular potency of place, for the simple fact that it is still accessible, altered as it may be, in a way that time is not.

This distance is reinforced in the visual images and tourist experiences that so often limit tango to stereotype. Selling patrimony via caricature, the face of the dance remains in characters and scenes that evoke its history: El Zorzal Criollo (famed singer Carlos Gardel); Golden Era composers; rough-and-tumble European immigrants; pimps and prostitutes in *prostíbulos* (brothels); *compadrito* (hoodlum) knife fights on street corners; neighborhood-sweethearts-turned-champagne-dancing-girls. In Caminito, the tango walkway in the *barrio* of La Boca, cardboard cutouts invite tourists to embody this past, while in San Telmo, "traditional" pizza is likened to "traditional" tango, as danced by *compadritos* and played by *gauchos* at the turn of the twentieth century.

At the same time, the growth of tango communities around the world and the increasingly global character of the *porteño* scene speak to its universal appeal. Dancers from Argentina and abroad highlighted the tango's very transcendence of culture. The stories of the lyrics, though situated in a decidedly *porteño* landscape, resonate beyond those borders in the entirely human themes of love, loss, nostalgia, and displacement. The product of the meeting of lower-class groups in late-nineteenth-century Río de la Plata society is now pursued by largely middle- and upper-middle-class dancers around the world, their members linked by a desire for contact, connection, and experience:

> Beyond Argentina, the tango brings with it something of the essence of humanity. It's a very human need—the need for contact, the need to move, to touch, to feel the music . . . so, through this phenomenon, we begin to see the things we have in common, what we share as human beings. This also helps us to see that, above all else, the essence of tango is global—it's not only local; it goes beyond that. (τ)
>
> Luisa Paes, Brazilian expat, tango professional

> Tango was an immigrant music in my own country, so it does not have a nationality, its only passport is feeling, and everybody has feelings.
>
> Carlos Gavito, quoted in Quiroga (2001)

> The content is universal—it's all about love and loss and nostalgia, for a place, and maybe Buenos Aires is not our *barrio*, you know? We didn't grow up here and lose our love here, and we're not going to die here, but we all know what that home is; it's a reference for everyone.
>
> Naomi, American, tango professional

Meanwhile, the *porteño* tango community—every day more an industry—thrives thanks to the constant influx of foreign bodies and currency. What's more, the evolution of the dance and its codes cannot be traced to any single place. Rather, this is increasingly the result of transnational interaction, borrowing and fusion, facilitated by media technology, and fueled by the goals of innovation and authenticity.

All of which raises the question, how to locate the tango? Where does the reality of romance intersect with contemporary voices that urge the dance and music beyond a static reenactment of the past? What do aesthetic movements toward fusion and freedom from the bounds of culture mean for traditions? Does tango, a historically Argentine tradition, belong more to some than to others? In an era of globalization, how do we account for the enduring significance of place?

Culture in the Veins

> The baby was between her legs and he wasn't walking yet. She was manipulating his feet in the way that their dancers manipulate their feet. When this child grew older he would not yet have to learn the dance. He would already know it. It would have become a part of his memory and entered the rhythm of his blood.
>
> Martha Graham, *Blood Memory* (1991)

The growth of the taxi-dancer industry speaks to the "reality of romance" in the birthplace of tango. *Los taxi*, Argentines who serve as dance partners for classes and social dance events in exchange for money, capitalize on the notion that culture carries a passport. Like Martha Graham's observation of the passage of dance from mother to child, and author Geraldine Brooks's assertion that young Egyptian girls have an aptitude for belly dance, the idea being that culture is "learned" by members in an altogether more organic fashion than implied by the verb. Along the lines of the acquisition so many older *tangueros* speak of, these descriptions conjure notions of culture as biology that the anthropologist in me had been trained to reject:

> My own quest to become a wonderful dancer wasn't going so well. Egyptian girls acquired the ability to dance as naturally as the ability to walk, watching their mothers, sisters and aunts. At my friend Sayed's house, the three-year-old could already do fluid hip drops and scissor steps. Sayed's sisters tried their best with me, but it was

hard for them to teach something that they had never actually learned.

Geraldine Brooks, *Nine Parts of Desire* (1995)

While the taxi industry feeds from traditionalist arguments that link culture and place, it also speaks back to minimalist arguments—generally voiced by traditionalists—that belittle the accumulation of tango experience, and that position quality and quantity in an adverse relationship. As the growing presence of foreign dancers makes the *porteño* tango scene overwhelming and decidedly less Argentine, the hiring or "purchase" of a native partner is a means of ensuring a return on one's investment, in terms of both actual dance experience and authenticity. Underscoring the economics of tango study in Buenos Aires, the Tango TaxiDancers advertisement authorizes a circumvention of traditional codes, reassuring frustrated dancers that purchase of the tango experience is preferable to sitting or *planchar* (wallflowering).

Yet the taxi-dance profession is not the domain of Argentines alone. I was surprised to learn that a fellow American expat was paying a European to practice with her. New to the dance and overwhelmed by the scene, she claimed that she found a compelling combination of comfort, trust, and value with her foreign partner. A friend of a friend, he had been dedicating himself to nothing but tango since his arrival in Buenos Aires over a year ago, and his rates were dirt cheap to boot. For my American friend, it was a no-brainer. My initial shock aside, I had to admit she had a point. An American paying a European social dancer to teach her tango in the dance's birthplace speaks to the identity crisis that has long plagued the country, its capital, and its national dance.

Borges famously labeled his country "imported," while foreign correspondent Miranda France characterizes *porteños* "victims of a dreadful accident of history" (1999: 54–55), their unfair displacement from Europe yielding a society built on things from without, from material goods to food to ideas. Likewise, displacement and circulation are constant themes in the tango world. Savigliano (1995) draws attention to the confluence of *porteño* and national identity in tango when she notes that Argentines abroad take up the dance as a "shield against the dissolution of identity," regardless of whether they hail from the port city or not (4–5).

Studies of contemporary art have noted the lessening of community identity when a cultural product begins to circulate within the global market.[3] Although tango arose on the port city's streets and is located most specifically in the cafés, clubs, and salons of Buenos Aires—and is thus a strong symbol of *porteño* culture for Argentines—outside the country the dance often stands as a signifier of the nation. Among Argentines, dancing tango and listening to tango music are activities that open the self to imagine an identity grounded in the larger nation. What's more, the power of such activities may actually be rendered more palpable "out of place," where the tango themes of migration, the lost *barrio,* and nostalgia[4] play upon diasporic sensibilities.[5]

Miguel Di Genova, singer and songwriter of the electronic tango band Otros Aires, located the tango, like the city of its birth, in the dispersal of its devotees around the world, just as many Argentine natives are themselves dispersed outside their homeland:

> When I think of the word, I immediately think of Buenos Aires, but I chose the name "Otros Aires," because Buenos Aires is scattered in many places. Many people from here leave, and then there are the foreigners who come and take something of the culture with them when they leave—like you, perhaps . . . because Buenos Aires is like New York was in its moment, like Barcelona is now—it's a mix of cultures. So that mix of cultures and races and people from all these countries is in many places. The tango can be in any place. (τ)

What's more, the passage of information through secondhand routes and media technology complicates efforts to get at origins. Chatting with a *porteño* musician at a *práctica* one night, American composer and dancer Korey Ireland was shocked to hear his own music playing at the exact moment he was asked to describe it, as it had never been officially released in Argentina: "A funny example—I was in Gaby's *práctica* last year. I was talking with Carlos [Libedinsky, composer and member of electronic tango band Narcotango]—he was at the *práctica* and we were chatting about music and he was asking 'Well what kind of stuff do you write?' And as soon as I started to answer I hear one of my pieces being played at the *práctica*. Now, okay, this has never been available or sold or distributed here." Oddly enough, there's a good chance this track found its way to that *práctica* playlist thanks to the alternative music CD my American friend burned for the event's future host when we met him in January 2005.

At that time, several Argentines remarked on the growing presence of foreigners, some expressing concern that these "guests" might eventually outnumber their "hosts." This trend has only continued since then, to the point that some now question Argentine claims to the dance based on an unspoken link between culture and skill:

> I see foreigners who dance better than many Argentines, in terms of technique and sensitivity. Sometimes I dance more with foreigners than with Argentines. They live the tango more unconsciously. In the tango world—of dancers of a certain level in Argentina—since they're already tied to a style, or they want to imitate someone, they don't dance freely. Meanwhile, a foreigner arrives and she's fascinated, in another world, and she dances with that emotion on the tips of her toes. (τ)
>
> Gabriel Glagovsky, Argentine, tango professional and *práctica* organizer

This "fascination," as Gabriel terms it, while in part a product of the romance of Buenos Aires, is also transforming the *porteño* tango scene. What was a community is now an industry—its local and foreign practitioners positioned in an unequal relationship through the larger global economy. Claims of ownership may evolve for the simple fact that some may be able to invest more than others, as one native *tanguera* suggested:

> I believe in a few more years, the European and the American people will dance better than the Argentines. . . . Because people in the United States take the time, take lessons, practice, and take initiative to improve a whole lot, even if in the beginning the music is different and it takes a lot for some people to get the rhythm because it's completely different, but people dedicate more time. And here, I go to the *milongas* and I feel bored because I feel that the men dance always the same—even if you dance with a few different men, to me it's just very simple. (ε)
>
> Celia, Argentine, doctor

The implications of this evolution are manifold. On the one hand, the growing global community creates a market for the consumption of a decidedly Argentine commodity, facilitating the professionalization of tango among native Argentines, in particular among young people who do not find enough opportunities at home. Like their foreign counterparts, most have only recently become "fascinated" by a dance that long seemed impossibly outdated: "Tourism gave an injection—of money, of people, of consumption. . . . Young [Argentines] see that it's possible to dance professionally, where they couldn't before. Everybody who danced did it as an activity, a hobby. But tango opens the door and suddenly they can go professional very quickly, so many people are doing it" (τ; Gabriel Glagovsky). Meanwhile, the tradition of acquisition, the informal passing down of tango through family, friends, and neighbors, has largely died out.

While more and more young *porteños* are learning to dance in a classroom setting, foreigners far surpass locals in the consumption of classes. The director of one of the city's largest academies told me that 95 percent of their students are from abroad, and that the industry is constructed with this audience in mind. Several dancers spoke to the impossibility of surviving from the tango in Buenos Aires, noting that only travel and teaching abroad can keep one afloat:

> It's not easy surviving from tango here. Very few can really do it. And I don't survive—if I didn't travel, it would be very difficult.
>
> Kara Wenham, American expat, tango professional

> There's no profession here. I have to leave the country to make money, to survive. (τ)
>
> Juan Carlos Copes, Argentine, tango professional

And as more and more tourists and expats descend upon the city, this drives local pricing up, and access to certain schools, professors, even *milongas* becomes unequal.[6] While nearly all the Argentine professionals I spoke with acknowledge dependence on the global community for their livelihood, one young *porteño* highlighted the ambivalence he perceives among local professionals toward foreign incursion for purposes other than study: "People are afraid of other professors coming from abroad. I tell you this because I have a festival with foreign professors and [local] professionals approached me and told me not to invite them" (τ; Norberto "El Pulpo" Esbrez, Argentine, tango professional).

In an era of disappearing boundaries, media and the imagination are ever more central to identity construction. Today's global community is linked across time and space, this distance collapsed through technology and the ease of travel, for those who can afford it. In this world, where foreigners are constantly descending upon Buenos Aires, and Argentines eagerly seek work abroad, local membership is a fluid and ever-changing category. Tango films, instructional and performance videos, and video-sharing Web sites like YouTube facilitate global fan bases and virtual participation in locally situated *milongas*, exhibitions, festivals, and classes. Such mediated performances hold the potential to de-center the tango industry from its birthplace, especially when combined with the complex politics of a post-crisis, post-9/11 world. For example, when tango instructors in the United States admire a European couple on YouTube and organize their visit to give a series of workshops, they promote that pair in lieu of an Argentine couple, whose influence in the United States is already threatened given increasingly strict immigration policies for Argentines trying to enter the country today.[7]

In my conversation with Lisa Battan, a tango dancer and immigration lawyer in the United States, she noted that entering the United States became much more difficult for Argentines after the crisis, when the country was removed from the U.S. visa waiver list. In particular, following the crisis, the American consulate was unlikely to grant a visa to the Argentine who had never traveled abroad before, was unmarried, did not have significant savings, and did not own property, for fear that dancer would not return home. Since 1997, Battan has managed the visa applications for more than 200 tango dancers to work in the United States, a process that became arduous following September 11, 2001, and even more so following revisions to the artist visa process in 2008. Since then, Argentines looking to work in the United States have had to provide a written contract for every event on their itinerary, placing enormous pressure on local organizers, many of whom engage in tango as a hobby or a form of community service and most of whom do not make money by hosting guest teachers for a week of workshops.

And as tango continues to expand around the globe, the rise of new tango sites may challenge the allure of authenticity with something altogether different—tango in the city where "East meets West" at the Istanbul tango festival, for instance. A double-edged sword of sorts, globalization drives the growth of the global tango scene while also dispersing its center and potentially threatening its soul.

Tango as Souvenir

Argentina. ¿Que historia queres vivir? (Argentina. What story do you want to live?)

Tourism Campaign, Buenos Aires (2006)

During the *milonga* shutdown of January 2005, when young dancers took to the streets after police raided a *práctica*, television crews covering the event zoomed in on the dancers from abroad, perhaps more compelled by the story of tourist demand for an Argentine commodity, or perhaps finding more value in local patrimony through this foreign validation ("*Por las clausuras*," 2005). Since the 2001 financial crisis, tango has become a highly marketable, and marketed, symbol in Argentina. The rising popularity of *tango nuevo* presents an interesting challenge to Argentine policies promoting tango as cultural patrimony, grounded in notions of place and tradition. As tourism takes on an increasingly important role in the country's economy, the ability to sell Argentina through tango images, performances, and experiences inherently limits the nature of that tango, tying it to recognizable, stereotypical, and quite often outdated representations. In an interview, for example, a staff member of the Buenos Aires Ministry of Culture highlighted government-funded efforts to recuperate the tango as cultural patrimony. There is the 2×4 tango radio station, now dedicated solely to tango music for over ten years; the Orquesta de Tango de la Ciudad (City Tango Orchestra), now more than twenty-five years old; the Orquesta Escuela de Tango school for tango musicians; the (now defunct) Academia de Estilos de Tango Argentino (ACETA) training program for young dancers; the (now defunct) tangodata Web site, which was a virtual port of entry to the wealth of tango offerings in the city, including interviews with dancers and musicians, links to tango events abroad, and more; the Buenos Aires Tango Festival, the local festival celebrating its fourteenth year in 2012; and the Metropolitano competition in Buenos Aires' *milongas* and the Mundial world tango championship, both celebrating their tenth anniversary in 2012.

The Ministry of Culture has also made efforts beyond mere preservation to support the development of new trends and to build new audiences. For example, electronic tango bands featured prominently in the 2005 Buenos Aires Tango Festival. However, my informant lamented that openness to expansion is easier abroad. Outside Argentina, fusion and innovation are less inhibited by the weight of history. What's more, as tradition itself becomes a commodity, in the birthplace of tango it is easier to package and sell the tango as "souvenir," the most obvious example being the city's impressively ever-growing roster of *cena* shows (also see Chapter 4). Dinner shows that pair wine and steak with passion and sex, these spectacles are strikingly similar in their selective presentation of tango as *porteño* history. Focusing largely on early 1900s Buenos Aires, we are taken from the arrival of the poor European immigrants on the shores of the Río de la Plata to the *compadritos* fighting and dancing on street corners, to the brothels, the champagne and glamour of the post-European-approval tango craze circa 1920, to the tango as song of the 1950s, culminating in an acrobatic performance to Piazzolla as representation of the present.

Efforts to expand the story told through tango on the stage do exist. The annual Cambalache festival, featuring the work of international artists who blend tango and theater, is a fast-growing and prestigious event among Buenos Aires' young *tangueros*. Melina Brufman and Claudio González's stunning integration of tango, modern dance, and theater, Dana Frígoli and Pablo Villarraza's DNI company productions, and the theatrical exhibitions of many young dancers in social tango venues, are just a few examples of boundary-breaking efforts that depart from the *cena* show standard. Nonetheless, these performances are generally presented within the tango community, so they do not receive the reception (or the material rewards) enjoyed by the tango houses catering to tourists.

Government-funded tango efforts are largely preservation oriented. ACETA was founded with a mission to preserve and pass on the dance styles of a number of established *milongueros* and couples. While in operation, it was a tango training camp for approximately twenty couples ages thirty-five and under, with at least two years of dance experience, where, three days a week, seven months a year, the goal was to literally copy what they saw, in order to preserve a style or approach to the dance that would otherwise soon die out. The Orquesta Escuela de Tango operates according to similar objectives: the preservation of the sound and style of Golden Era orchestras that are no more.[8] In two years in Buenos Aires, the only electronic tango I heard on the 2×4 radio station was a thirty-second promo clip (advertising the station, oddly enough). And the rules and regulations governing both the city and global salon tango championships are quite rigid, prohibiting the rupture of the embrace, *ganchos* (leg hooks), and any movements above the knee line (see Appendix II for the complete Mundial evaluation criteria). While government-funded heritage programs arguably commodify culture in their efforts to reproduce local citizens, they also contribute to debates over authenticity in rendering certain versions or interpretations of customs and practices "official."[9]

But tourism is too easy a target for the ills wrought by globalization. As Shepherd (2002) rightly points out, critiques of tourism tend to equate cultural commodification with spiritual death, to ignore the fact that today's innovations may be tomorrow's traditions, and to portray native cultures as unrealistically pure, innocent, and helpless in the face of Western forces. Whatever truths lie in these critiques, tourism also stimulates interest in traditions and provides resources for keeping them alive. Shepherd also highlights the irony of Western desires, which often *lessen* in response to the development that invites tourism or facilitates the presence of foreign visitors in the first place. In the global tango scene, many dancers alternately demand the maintenance of "authenticity" in the birthplace of tango, only to lament the inevitable cultural commodification this demand incurs.

For the desire to preserve is not the domain of Argentines alone, but very much a concern of non-Argentines in the international tango community, the more extreme among them insisting on local ownership with a vehemence approaching ideology. For instance, a 2007 Tango-L post advocates a "look but don't touch" policy for non-Argentines in the *milongas* of Buenos Aires: "But Buenos Aires is a unique place. It is a sanctuary. And any invasion dilutes purity. To safe [*sic*] the atmosphere and customs at the Buenos Aires *milongas* should be the goal of all consciousness [*sic*] tango people. It is like a museum for me. What should civilized people do with museums?" Another warns Americans that it is their place to "watch and learn," essentially prohibiting foreigners from the very Argentine tradition of playful improvisation and innovation that has defined much of the dance's history:

> To really appreciate tango, you need to approach tango for [what] it, as a part of Argentine culture, has to offer. You need to try to understand tango on tango's terms, not fit it into your own cultural preconceptions, modifying it until you fill [*sic*] comfortable with it within the dimensions of your own cultural frame of reference. Of course, not being Argentine, we can never understand tango as an Argentine. However, Americans need to watch and listen more and be objective in seeing what this part of Argentine culture can offer us and what we can learn from it and how we can grow from this knowledge, rather than claiming artistic creativity in adapting tango until it is no longer recognizable as Argentine.
>
> Tango-L post, 2007

Another Tango-L subscriber, writing in 2006, suggests the solution is to separate "US American" from "Argentine" tango, arguing that foreign contributions and adaptations render tango as it is practiced in the United States another beast entirely.

Chambers's 1994 work on cosmopolitanism provides a helpful framework for critically examining the desire to preserve a culture that is not one's own. Attacks on *tango nuevo* and "foreign pollution" of the "sanctity" of Buenos Aires' *milongas*, though arguably arising out of love and respect for tango, suggest a certain degree of arrogance when coming from nonnative practitioners. On the one hand, these global devotees demand an authentic tango—that authenticity arising from the very fact that it belongs to another culture. At the same time, they take it upon themselves to define what kinds of manifestations are and are not "Argentine." As Chambers labels them, such "imperious gestures" reflect, for one, the particularly modern, Western desire that other cultures (more "primitive," less "developed," more "traditional," or somehow more "authentic") remain as such for our own enjoyment, often precisely because we have not. They also betray, suggests Chambers, a sense of entitlement and hypocrisy; for these outsiders demand authenticity and assume the privilege of defining what that means, yet, according to their own logic, it is not theirs to define. Thus, those who demand that tango remain "pure" and untouched may be, in the process of enjoying it, contributing to its "sullying" through their very presence in the "museum of tango." Further, such efforts to freeze culture in time not only deny the history and agency of the people to whom it belongs but also preclude discussion of the entirely more complex, global dynamics of today's world.

The Comfort of Authenticity: A Politics of Place

> I think it's very rare to feel the kind of connection, sigh "Oh, what a beautiful moment" watching a couple at El Motivo. There'll be intensity, there'll be excitement and drama, sometimes connected to the music, not always. But you won't see this transformative bliss, this rapturous expression. . . . It just doesn't seem to be part of this style, it's not the main concern. The main concern I think is the physical possibilities of the dance, not so much the emotional possibilities of the dance.
>
> Korey Ireland, American, tango professional

While narratives of the healing power of tango tend to revolve around descriptions of trance, connection, and self-realization, another line of discourse, about "authenticity," intersects it. Both, I believe, are connected to issues of culture and style. While *nuevo*, or contemporary tango, is attacked simultaneously for an emphasis on analysis, a flexible and open embrace, fusion with other movement disciplines, and an overall bent toward rule breaking and experimentation, many detractors also highlight its "inauthenticity" as one more impediment to catharsis. Though the narrative of trance is arguably compelling to foreigners for the very transcendence of place and culture it implies, the possibility of trance is said to come from the style of tango so often referenced in its promotion—the *milonguero* or close embrace style of dance—which, in turn, is connected to place. In a decade of dancing tango, I have observed a very impassioned debate in the U.S. tango scene. One camp argues that the potential for connection, emotion, and feeling in the dance rests upon the style or approach to its enactment—"style" often meant as the manner in which the couple hold onto one another—while those on the other side contend that there is no necessary correlation between style (of dance or embrace) and feeling. The same chest-to-chest embrace that is thought to facilitate the state of trance is also the foundation upon which the *milonguero* or close embrace style of tango has been constructed and marketed.

This particular style has been packaged and sold by Argentine tango professionals who, propagating the notion that a chest-to-chest connection is the authentic approach to the dance, contend that the crowded *milongas* of Buenos Aires do not accommodate a more open frame. Argentine instructor Susana Miller has arguably been the most successful in marketing a close-embrace approach to the dance under the title of *estilo milonguero* (*milonguero* style). Through successive tours in the United States, Miller has built a mini-empire around the notion of "dancing on a dime," a philosophy very much at home in her club, El Beso, a charming *porteño* dance hall that houses one of the city's tiniest floors. As stated on her Web site (accessed in 2010), a true *milonguero* needs no more than the ground beneath him to navigate the tight quarters of the dance hall, and the result of this "closed tango" is trance, a state of conscious transportation:

> The steps are the means for circulating round the space, which is very tight; it is a closed tango. . . . A *milonguero* can dance on four tiles, one tile, or even in place, maintaining both the rhythm and contact with his partner with incredible precision, in a combination of muscular/sensitive relaxation and control. The man offers the woman his feeling for the music, and she sticks with him like the shirt on his back. The style is one of great energy, the couples are in trance, in a sort of conscious space beyond. (τ)

Miller herself roots her approach in an effort to export technique appropriate for the social dance floor, as opposed—or as she states, as a complement—to the more external, acrobatic, and exaggerated version seen in countless touring stage productions since 1983's *Tango Argentino.* All the same, many promoters and adherents of *estilo milonguero* have advanced the notion that the embrace, feeling, and authenticity are intricately bound. In turn, this notion has been hungrily devoured outside Argentina, inspiring the construction of stylistic divisions that may exceed *porteño* conceptions of such categories. As Anabella Diaz-Hojman, a young Argentine, noted, "We all dance tango, each dancer with his or her own style, vibe, particularity . . . but the minute you step off Argentine soil, everyone wants to know which tango you dance" (τ). Meanwhile, the Web site of an American dancer (accessed in 2010) demonstrates how the embrace-authenticity ideology can be a shrewd marketing strategy for foreign professionals: "All classes emphasize authentic Argentine tango, danced in close embrace as they dance in Argentina" (Donnay).

Nonetheless, countless Argentines rejected the notion that proximity between the partners is an appropriate means of gauging authenticity. For instance, Olga Besio argued that the feeling of tango rests more in the relationship between the couple than in a measuring of the physical distance that separates them: "You might see a couple dancing on stage with a bit more distance, and it might give the sensation of tango, or not. On the other hand, you might see a couple dancing super close in the *milonga* and say to yourself 'This isn't tango—they're together, but he's looking away and she's thinking about something else'" (τ). Despite the label's endurance—a glance through any of Buenos Aires' tango magazines will yield many instructors offering *milonguero* or *apilado*[10] classes—many *porteños* argue that the style of close embrace is a well-marketed construction. In an interview, Rodolfo Dinzel called it a passing trend that appeared in the mid-1990s and has "already disappeared." The point of contention seems to be one of misrepresentation. Simply put, many dancers, *porteño* and foreign alike, find fault with the idea that the tango danced in the city's *milongas* is primarily danced chest to chest, arguing that a bit more space, or an embrace that breathes when the opportunity arises, is the common image. Brooke Burdett, an expat who first visited Buenos Aires in 1996 only to relocate permanently, attested to this, as well as to the confusion that reigns around the title itself when I asked her what *milonguero* means:

> [W]hen I started here in 1996 there was salon style and this whole idea of "*milonguero* style" was becoming popular. . . . People were dancing chest to chest, but there weren't very many people doing that from what I could see, you know. The predominant style was not pasted against each other. Even the really outstanding *milongueros* who danced in neighborhoods closer to downtown—Tete, Eduardo Arquimbau, Tomi O'Connell, El Tano—they all danced chest to chest, but each very differently, and none of them would call what they were doing "*milonguero* style." From what I could see in the *milongas* that I went to, people danced with a little bit more space between them. . . . And all of the dancers, a lot of the old dancers from the neighborhoods, out here in Villa Urquiza, they'd dance with a tiny bit of space between them.

It is worth noting that foreign demand has played a part in the growth of close embrace. The pressure to identify with a style in the United States is a point that arose in many interviews. Grounded in a rejection of stage tango and a desire for more socially appropriate techniques, the growth of labels has had the unfortunate effect of encouraging a certain amount of fracture and division in the U.S. scene, while simultaneously driving the marketability of styles among Argentine professionals, as the industry thrives upon what foreigners are interested and willing to invest in. While one *porteño* professional confessed to finding the language and approach of close embrace "fundamentalist," Korey Ireland described how such stylistic divisions are manipulated outside Argentina: "For a few years I think I would have considered myself a *milonguero* dancer. And back in North America where that ends up drawing these kinds of party lines, I think there was a time when I was sort of pushing the propaganda of close embrace."

The "propaganda of close embrace," when employed for such purposes, seeks to create a hierarchy of tango experience, where certain ways of enacting and speaking of one's enactment of the dance are, at the very least, presented as more authentic than others. The emphasis on authenticity outside Argentina is undoubtedly grounded in passion and respect for the art form; however, it may also arise from the foreign dancer's displacement from the source, discomfort with the notion of appropriation, and the impact of the homogenizing forces of globalization. In an interview, Deborah, an American expat and tango professional, suggested that the desire for truth is perhaps stronger among practitioners for whom the practice of tango is a cultural appropriation:

> There is something inauthentic about structuring your life around something that's from someone else's culture. It's also important. . . . It's wonderful that I can become a shaman today or I can become a Chinese herbalist, or I can find a tradition or a way of interacting or practicing with people, teaching, whatever—that really makes sense to me, and that I'm not confined to the culture that I was born in. . . . But maybe because of that conflict people are so eager to claim truth.

This conflict, as Deborah labeled it, is further compounded by the modern drive to consume authenticity before it disappears altogether. Averill (1995) suggests that, for those of us who benefit most from globalization, the flip side is a sense of "transcendental homelessness" that drives us to seek comfort in the form of place. Finding solace in the authenticity we feel abroad, which we may no longer feel at home, we often desire that exotic locales and peoples remain as such for our own enjoyment and cultural rejuvenation.

It bears noting that such freedom—to "try on" other cultural traditions—is not equally accessible to all. An emphasis on authenticity might be a means of assuaging both the sense of guilt attached to appropriation and the self-conscious knowledge that such freedom (to appropriate) is a luxury. This approach to our modern world feeds global inequities by alternately primitivizing and romanticizing (generally) formerly colonized cultures, and more importantly, by denying their right to develop, modernize, and change, under the seemingly benevolent but rather paternalistic guise of cultural preservation. As cultural patrimony policies politicize and commodify memory and nostalgia, these policies may encourage archaic behaviors in Buenos Aires' tango scene; in turn, these behaviors and the culture sanctioning them give credence to foreign constructions of "the authentic." From this angle, the efforts of young *tangueros* to refashion the dance in a more cosmopolitan light can be seen as a form of resistance—both to local forces that would relegate tango to the status of kitsch in the name of economics and to global desires to consume some sort of authentic experience.

For *tangueros* outside Argentina, there is great reassurance in the notion that they are dancing the same dance as the *milongueros* of yore, that they are not getting hoodwinked or trained to regurgitate patterns that will not serve them on the social dance floor, that they are carrying on rather than destroying or contaminating a great tradition, that they could go to Buenos Aires and blend in with locals at the *milongas*. That the ethos at the heart of *estilo milonguero* is (theoretically) justified by the size and shape of *porteño* clubs is all the more comforting.

It would be unfair to lay all the blame for discord on the rise of close embrace, and irresponsible to label all close embrace enthusiasts propagandists or fundamentalists. Still, attacks on the authenticity of *nuevo* often highlight its "absence of feeling"—alternately arising from the physical distance separating the couple, the expression on their faces, and their movement vocabulary—and appear to be grounded in the same sort of style = feeling = authenticity ideology that underlies many descriptions of *milonguero*, as a recent Tango-L post exemplifies:

> But Does It Make You Cry?
>
> When I look at *nuevo* tango dancers, I've noticed they never seemed to look at each other, just at the floor or each other's feet, connected only by holding onto each other's arms. They usually have a singular expression on their faces that seems to suggest absence of emotion. Their focus seems to be more on physics of movement and athleticism rather than on anything that evokes emotionality. . . . Only Argentine tango danced to Argentine music seems to bring forth a wider range of emotions and more intense connection than any other kind. It's the only kind that embraces all generations rather than be appropriate for a certain age group. The only time I've seen people moved to tears is when they dance authentic Argentine tango.
>
> Tango-L post, 2007

Korey Ireland's description of the floor at the El Motivo *práctica* suggests the difficulty of denying that much of the focus in *nuevo,* or the tango being danced in the city's growing *práctica* scene, lies in the expansive physical possibilities that result from the influx of agile young bodies, many of whom bring significant training and ideas from other movement disciplines. Certain nights, a glance at the floor might reveal the mix of chaos, noise, and messiness that results from serious intentional play. There is no denying its stark contrast to the steady circling flow of a *milonga* peopled by skilled veterans, undeniably meditative on the surface. Of course, this is by no means the defining image in all of the city's *milongas* every day and night of the week.

More importantly, is such flowing, trance-like circulation the only authentic manifestation of Argentine tango? Is the emphasis on feeling and trance not the least bit essentializing, promoting an impoverished, one-dimensional view of Argentine identity? Does it not reinforce an unrealistic goal—limiting dancers to an experience that is often unattainable, statistically speaking and otherwise? For maturity, skill level, desire, and one's partner all play a part in the dancer's ability to achieve the "tango trance." Such a demand raises other questions as well: Just what sorts of emotions and experiences are to be deemed "authentic," which are not, and who makes these decisions? How do the emotions and sensations experienced in the embrace reinforce and speak to larger notions of culture?

Reauthenticating *Nuevo*, or Out with the New

> I believe that these two aspects, these two sides . . . of the same coin have always been present, throughout the dance's history. On the one side there's intimacy, the closed embrace, the interaction between the man and the woman, and on the other there's the question of wanting to do things differently, each step differently, of constantly searching for new ways to play with the woman. (τ)
>
> Raul Masciocchi, Argentine, tango professional

When I posed the embrace = feeling = authenticity question to a young American professional, she offered the following frustrated take: "I think it's crazy . . . this idea that unless you're chest to chest you don't feel anything and there's no connection. . . . I feel emotion for all sorts of people that I'm not pressed up against all the time! Whatever emotion there is in the dance is about the joy I feel in moving, the relationship I have with my partner . . . and the music. Those three things" (Deborah, American expat, tango professional).

Nonetheless, the tendency to pit feeling, intimacy, and emotion against play, exhibitionism, and investigation is deeply ingrained in the language of social and professional dancers today. Masciocchi, another of Buenos Aires' rising stars, seems to suggest a historic integration of these values in the opening quote. Still, by using the image of a coin to convey his point, he also reinforces their opposition. A means of resisting clichéd, essentialist ideas about what it means to be Argentine or a *tanguero*, young Argentines insisted that the values of innovation, evolution, and investigation are firmly entrenched within the dance's history. According to this logic, experimentation has its place on the social dance floor—alongside or even integrated into expressions of intimate communion.

During my two-year stay in Buenos Aires, I spent a lot of time at Villa Malcolm, the aesthetically uninspiring social club (that is, until the completion of the Tango Composers mural just before my departure in late 2007) that has become the city's *práctica* central. Though I frequented many other venues, Malcolm is where I felt most at home, the place I could enter alone, knowing I would find familiar faces any night of the week. But despite my comfort there, and despite my pleasure at the growth of sites where *pibes* (kids) are expected to dress, dance, and act their age, there were nights when the floor seemed hijacked by an unspoken celebration of the very attacks I often find faulty, biased, and exaggerated.

January 2006, Villa Malcolm

Pina, a friend of a friend, is visiting Buenos Aires on a brief stopover en route to Brazil. A salsa enthusiast, she's had a brief introduction to tango in the United States before her trip, but when she calls to make plans, she tells me that she's "excited to see the real thing, and what the young kids are doing—the new tango."

It is an oppressively humid January night. We barely finish dinner on Plaza Armenia when the storm hits. Like my Klimt-esque frizz, the scene at Malcolm mushrooms to life with the rain's relief. The "American invasion," that winter-holiday period that for the past few years has drawn a healthy batch of young U.S. tango luminaries, is at its height. The floor is packed, as are the tables surrounding its perimeter, so that extra seating is called for, and packs of waiting, socializing, or resting dancers spill out into the hallway.

I retire to my chair after a couple of tandas, *unable to compete with the crowds and recklessness on the floor. Stilettos slice the air, rebounding from leg wraps in stealth* rond-de-jambes (round of the leg), *drawing circular* boleos *out into full attitudes, and reveling in* patadas (kicks) *every which way. My partner drew me in closer, but it was not much use—it feels more like bumper cars than tango tonight. Everybody is desperate to show off their moves, whether space permits or not. To be honest, part of my frustration lies in my getting cut off each time my partner tries to do anything more than walk. It's important to show what you can do here, and neither one of us was getting anywhere.*

I join Pina for a beer and she congratulates me, saying it "looks like fun," but seconds later turns and asks whether "not dancing to the music is part of nuevo." *Glancing at the floor, it's hard to tell whether musicality is the problem. It's too noisy—the room is full of chatter and the music is loud tonight. But the noise seems more the product of a bunch of excited kids* "tirando pasos," *or throwing steps about. What is missing is communion. Everyone seems to be dancing on their own.*

* * *

A good friend once described *nuevo* as a tennis match: the man and the woman just trying to "one up" the other with every new step. In my interview with Naomi, an American dancer from California, she described *nuevo* dancers in the United States as "just running, on our own, around each other." Admitting that *nuevo* has a somewhat deserved reputation for "not being tango," she noted that many young dancers become addicted to the physical sensation of exploration, and with this focus on movement for movement's sake, lose touch with the essence of the dance:

> People are attracted to *nuevo* because it's fun, it's physically exhilarating, it's physical sensation. And people get really addicted to that. And they want to work on and play with momentum and movement, and tension, and all these different things you can do with each other. And they want to do it all the time and they want to do it in *milongas*. And to me, that's not tango. Tango is about the connection with your partner, and I think that people get really caught up in the physical aspect, the physics of the movement instead of the context for it, which is what tango is, you know, just this hole opening between people.

Patricia Lamberti, an Argentine professional since 1994, lamented that the tango often appears more individualistic—both in the embrace and on the floor; that the man and woman seem to be dancing separately, each performing their own exhibition. With a lax embrace and the loosening of the torso, it has become more common for leader and follower to project outside the embrace and into the surrounding space, and it seems they are losing the sense of connection to one another, which is really the essence of tango. Each time she sees young people dancing together but looking away from one another, Patricia told me, she senses this disconnect and feels that it is "almost violent." (τ)

Adding the gaze to my dance was a revelation when I stumbled upon the classes of an Argentine couple associated with *nuevo* back in January 2005. Beyond the more open, relaxed embrace so common to *nuevo*, here the cues were visual as well, creating a tango that approximates contemporary dance in its use of the entire body to invite and accept. This emphasis on relaxation, freeing of the head, and integration of the gaze is part of the contemporary move away from the clichéd image of sex and passion embodied in the "tango face" mentioned by Pablo Inza in Chapter 3.

Unfortunately, when taken to its extreme, this relaxation can yield a sense of separation and distance, rather than communication and connection, as Pia noted:

> You shouldn't stare into people's eyes or anything, but it's okay to acknowledge that you're with somebody else. It's not just a material substance, it's a person and you're dancing with that person. . . . This coolness . . . it's so easy, it should look so easy and relaxed. You look everywhere and you don't care. Then I think it's not tango anymore. Tango should be about . . . that you really acknowledge the other person, and that you care. It's important, that connection. (ε)

The *prácticas* of Buenos Aires are by no means uniform; not all are places where one finds kids throwing steps about. At any event, one will find couples pasted together at the chest, dancing slowly and simply, oftentimes with eyes closed, encircled by others who will shift, open, and change the embrace within a single song, who may turn their eyes and their bodies away from their partners, whose limbs explore the space around them (occasionally to dangerous effect to others in their path).[11] Likewise, the *milongas*, though often depicted as sites of tradition, are also open to variety and change, and importantly, to a certain degree of playfulness. Evidence that the tango is far more than the steps themselves, and it is never entirely dictated by the place within which it is enacted. Rather, it is a personal expression that is each time "new" because it is improvised and because it "takes two." The dialogue of tango never repeats itself, arising not only from a shared vocabulary but also from the unique chemistry that arises from each partnership in that particular moment. And this all takes place in response to the music, the floor, the codes, the attendees, and the overall feeling of the larger room. Thus, even in the most traditional *milongas*, the improvisational and intersubjective nature of tango suggests that concerns of style provide a rather impoverished framework for thinking about authenticity.

May 2006, Viejo Correo

It is Metropolitano in Buenos Aires—the monthlong, citywide tango competition—and I decide to hit the site of tonight's contest, Viejo Correo, home to a nightly milonga *for a mostly mature close-embrace crowd. The classic black-and-white tile floor is offset by an imposing diorama of Caminito—La Boca's tourist-trap tango walkway—that projects out of one wall, hovering like a crucifix above an altar to bless the dance space. The majority of the attendees are in their fifties or above, save for a table of young dancers who leave soon after I arrive. I sit for what feels an eternity, until finally, after turning my glance one too many times toward my neighbor with the ever-so-slight handlebar mustache, we achieve* cabeceo *and nod.*

Despite some initial confusion, we settle into a pleasant tanda. *I begin with my left arm midway down the right side of his back, my elbow projected slightly out—the position favored by many of the younger professionals these days—but he readjusts so that my left arm drapes fully around his neck, my hand resting over his left shoulder. We do little more than walk around the room. An* ocho cortado *here and there, a few simple turns to keep within the line of dance, but mostly walking. The simplicity and musicality are lovely. As any true tango lover will profess, walking to the music with the right partner can be blissful. But he is testing me out. Unsure whether I am a liability, he is reluctant to allow me a voice in this exchange. As he escorts me to my chair, he asks how long I've been dancing and what style I have studied, then informs me that I will need to take classes at Viejo Correo if I want to dance the particular brand of close embrace favored by the club's regulars.*

Later that night, I dance with a rather short, slight, very serious campeonato *(championship) competitor. Walking into his arms, I realize I am a full head taller than he. As I look down and smile, I notice that he sports on his lapel a tiny golden pin of a couple in an exaggerated lunge. He pulls me so tight I nearly gasp, and a wave of second thoughts washes over me. But as the music begins, his embrace breathes a little, and then, something happens. More than a suggestion, each step seems an undeniable occurrence. Musically thoughtful, playful, he keeps me on my toes as patterns emerge and dissolve. As the* tanda *progresses, I contribute more by slowing him down and adding the occasional adornment, while his moves grow more daring, from* calesitas *to* ganchos, *even a rather elongated* volcada, *a step that nearly trips me up given our surroundings. While I enjoy our* tanda, *my pleasure is offset by a degree of self-consciousness. My eyes are closed, but I feel the attention we are drawing, not all of it good. He is showing off, taking up too much space,* aprovechando *(taking advantage) of the young body in his arms, dancing for himself rather than as a part of the larger room.*

He doesn't place that night, and I can see why. He is too flamboyant for the Viejo Correo crowd. Later that night, he stops by my table and whispers in my ear, "El proximo año bailamos juntos en el campeonato, eh nena?" (Next year we'll dance together in the campeonato, *what do you say, baby?)*

* * *

In Viejo Correo, just as in Villa Malcolm, or any other community for that matter, there is room for tension, variety, even conflict. The steps and codes that together make up the larger genre of tango and that are manipulated to create stylistic divisions like *nuevo*, *milonguero*, and *escenario* are open to change, as evidenced in the surprisingly expansive moves introduced by my second partner. It is the members of any community themselves who break the rules and bring about the evolution that is necessary to survival. Competence and status are also key here, however. Anyone can introduce change, but innovation is embraced widely only if the rule breaker is admired for her or his skill.

In other words, examining the purported connection between style and authenticity in tango venues, old and new, reveals the fluid character of both dance vocabularies and communities. The range of physical experiences and emotions evoked in different manifestations of tango in Malcolm and Viejo Correo point to such fluidity. The interactive nature of the dance and the ease with which practitioners pass through these sites complicate efforts to limit dance venues and the bodies within them according to static notions of culture or tradition. Indeed, both Club Villa Malcolm and Viejo Correo have played host to more than one event since at least 2005, while the events, the organizers, and, in turn, the attendees, continue to evolve. In 2010, Práctica X relocated to the Viejo Correo space, complicating the club's image, and as recently as 2012, friends reported that Malcolm was home to a new event that attracted a decidedly traditional crowd of dancers. While critics of *nuevo* often assault it as the tossing aside of heritage, or worse, the transformation of a sacred tradition into a more easily digestible, soulless "world" product, it is worth remembering that young Argentines move in the modern world, that artistic development does not negate authenticity, and that innovation is one path to ensuring that preservation does not mean Disneyfication.

Embracing Theory

Given Argentina's and the tango's long struggles with self-definition, the confusion and contention surrounding *nuevo* are perhaps less surprising. Always relational and performative, culture and identity have become that much more complicated in our postcolonial, postmodern, globalized era, even more so in formerly colonized locales that are increasingly shaped by or dependent on tourism. As Adams (1996) demonstrates, tourism economies can yield identity crises among local populations; among Himalayan Sherpas, for instance, identity is carefully shaped in response to foreign desires. Neither totally real nor entirely fake, modern-day Sherpa identity is a partial performance of a mythic past, a legitimate aspect of the Sherpas' heritage that is exaggerated and romanticized because it yields financial rewards in an otherwise depressed local economy.

While I agree with Juan Carlos Copes's claim that the tango was destined to rebound like a cork in the water, young Argentines also have an incentive to embrace the tango today. But this is not a clear-cut causal relation. Tango's exchange value is undeniable, but economics alone cannot fully explain artistic and cultural phenomena. Moreover, not all aspiring tango entrepreneurs are necessarily financially successful, nor by any means does success in the global tango industry require performing an anachronistic or clichéd version of Argentine or tango identity.

The tango's transformation into global phenomenon and the tensions surrounding *nuevo* speak to the weakening link between culture and place in an era of heightened globalization. Tracing *nuevo* through multiple sites, virtual spaces, and transnational flows—of bodies, media, ideas, and more across borders—I follow the lead of the dancers who constitute this world, as well as that of scholars who have developed creative strategies to the problems of "de-territorialization," or the uprooting of culture from place. At the same time, contemporary tango and its practitioners do not float around in a netherworld disconnected from culture, politics, and structures of power. Opposing processes work to re-situate tango back into specific locales, and they do so in ways that underscore the uneven nature of globalization. So it is that tango thrives at home thanks, in part, to the support it receives from abroad, and that Argentines pursuing a career in tango are driven to construct that career with an outward glance, through foreign students at home and travel and teaching gigs abroad. Still, the soul of the global tango community remains somehow fixed in Argentina; through portraits of the continued potency of place and tradition, I challenge simplistic notions of globalization as homogenization or Westernization.[12]

Though anthropology was founded on the desire to understand the human experience through the study of "the other," the discipline and the world we inhabit have evolved enormously since those early days. Moreover, the difference that separates—you from me, native from foreigner, "first world" from "third"—is never entire, else there would be no point of contact (Kaminsky 2008). Building on this premise, I explore the pursuit of tango through the prism of postcolonial and tourism studies, noting the global context within which culture is exoticized as "difference," "authenticity" is constructed in relation to place, and cultural consumption becomes a solution (for those with means) to postmodern yearnings for the comfort of "authentic experience," best accessed in distant locales, the lesser "developed" the better. Yet even as these power dynamics are perpetuated, tango is a site of democratic potential, where strangers can communicate and connect across the arbitrary (though nonetheless real) divisions of culture, language, and nation, and political and economic inequities are open to disruption.

In similar fashion, the practice of tango can be a profound means of resistance to the local circumstances of everyday life. Historically shocking as a site where class boundaries were crossed, tango was a salve against the bitter reality of economic and political disenfranchisement, a site where poor and working-class *porteños* sought freedom and protagonism. In contrast, today's global tango community is a largely educated, upper-middle-class cadre of practitioners. The current emphasis on tango as therapy—as opposed to social capital or status—speaks to the transformation of its audience. As therapy, tango has much to say about the disconnect that plagues people in many parts of the world, despite the technological connection that abounds. At the same time, the luxury of this preoccupation, with constructing and healing the self, is worth considering if we examine tango through the lens of history and cross-cultural comparison.

An example par excellence of the ways in which individuals go about constructing the self and community with the aid of virtual media, communication technologies, and accessible travel, contemporary tango is also the site of much rupture and conflict. Anything but the picture of stasis or cohesion, the global tango scene reveals the difference necessary to any vibrant community, as well as the inevitable fact that choice—the conscious decision to leave certain things behind and to preserve others—is inherent to cultural survival. This is as true of tango as it is of fashion or car design, though *tanguera/os* might argue that the choices are far more charged when it comes to tango. For more than hobby, passion, even obsession, tango represents a way of life.

Which brings us back to the question of *nuevo*, and whether it is an appropriate term for describing contemporary trends in the dance. While I agree with many who said that "*no existe*," I use the term *nuevo* because there is no denying the existence of a growing and rapidly evolving global community of young *tangueros*, many of whom continue to push the bounds of the dance's vocabularies. The tango as it is danced by these practitioners is arguably evolved rather than new. However, the recent explosion of Buenos Aires' *prácticas* is new, as is the heightened circulation of dancers, media, and ideas across borders. More than the dance itself, the impact of global economics and the larger sociopolitical context within which these dancers, ideas, and media circulate demands a reexamination of the very meaning of tango in the twenty-first century. While this "new" tango represents continuity through transformation, the results on the dance floor are no less contested. The circulation of global norms, desires, attitudes, and currency in contemporary tango challenge simplistic notions of the location of culture and cultural survival. And in a practice guarded with quasi-religious fervor, survival and renewal can be an uneasy business.

La vida es un tango (Life Is a Tango)

> I had become again a person who rode escalators and watched the ads skim by.
>
> Helen Stevenson, *Instructions for Visitors* (2000)

There are escalators and ads in Buenos Aires. All the same, Stevenson's words bring tears to my eyes, even months before I am to leave Buenos Aires. For I, too, will soon relinquish a way of life that has become precious to me and return to something more familiar, arguably more stable, decidedly less romantic, financially more rewarding: but at what cost? As I dig through two years of journal notes, I come across an entry whose prematurity does not obscure its contradictory truths—the endurance of romance in the face of globalization, its lure and accessibility to those who are open to it. And I remember what a tango historian told me one day in Caminito: "*La vida es un tango.*"

February 2006, Avenida Jorge Luis Borges, Palermo Viejo

The lack of change in Buenos Aires is one of those idiosyncratic quirks that wakes me from the drowsy comfort of familiarity. Spending so much time in the tango scene, where nearly everyone speaks English and it seems at least half the population is foreign, it's easy to forget where I am at times. I exist in this very strange bubble of transient foreigners and natives who both depend on and profit from these visitors.

Despite the fact that "place" is arguably what brings most dancers here, the production and sustenance of the tango scene demand a constant flux of people who arrive from (and return to) elsewhere, creating a space within the city that encapsulates the modern anthropologist's conundrum: how to investigate and talk about culture in a time when people and phenomena aren't neatly encompassed by the confines of place.

Strolling the streets in Palermo Viejo, I note the palpable presence of foreigners. A division of the larger barrio *of Palermo that caps the northern edge of the city, Palermo Viejo's tree-lined, cobblestoned streets are increasingly populated by trendy eateries and designer boutiques, patronized by beautiful locals and hip foreigners with money to burn. While real estate is advertised in U.S. dollars everywhere in the city, prices are significantly steeper here, and the cost of ownership prohibitive for the average Argentine. In the rental industry, two markets operate in parallel: one for locals and another for foreigners, the rates for the latter jacked up to meet the earning potential represented by the growing tourist and expat presence. Many of my* porteño *friends regularly vacate and rent out their apartments as a sort of second job. Confounding the distinction between host and guest, they have become visitors in their own homes.*

In the midst of all this, there are moments that bring to mind a mentor's sage reminder: if the world were as homogeneous as the nearly ubiquitous presence of McDonald's might lead us to believe, any international airport would be the perfect site for studying culture. Walking home tonight from dance class, I do a double take as a fashionable young porteña *makes the sign of the cross as she passes me, her small gesture speaking volumes in a matter of seconds. Somehow I'd missed the presence of the church in the twenty or so times I'd passed that block before. Along with plazas, churches are the buildings around which the city's neighborhoods were constructed. More than* porteño *history, there is something of family, innocence, and the safety of* barrio *encapsulated in the discreet reverence of her hands. In contrast, her gesture brings home the distance I feel, not only from my own upbringing in the Catholic faith, but from an earlier time in my life, when the bonds and protectiveness of home were ever present. Frozen in photographs and tucked away in the mental spaces of remembrance, these memories grow more ambiguous and more poignant with time.*

And yet, here, at the other end of the world, I am closer to them than ever before. In the Paris of the South that couldn't quite keep pace with the cultures it looked to, I see my past everywhere. The milongueros *are my great uncles' former selves—their wide ties, their wing tips, and the keychains that dangle from their belt loops trick me, filling me with a false sense of comfort and familiarity. In the* milongas, *pale blue industrial fans, Styrofoam ceiling panels, deadening fluorescent lights, and fake wood paneling combine to transport me to that ten-year span during my childhood when every few months meant a banquet of some sort—basketball, bowling, softball—in strikingly similar environs. As I dig through the dance photos in the National Archives—those neglected black-and-whites tossed into an old shoebox, their corners torn and folding—I am leafing through my family history in the wake of a grandmother's, an uncle's, and a great aunt's passing.*

Separation

Your absence has gone through me
Like thread through a needle.
Everything I do is stitched with its color.

W. S. Merwin, "Separation" (1993)

By the time I leave Buenos Aires, the impact of everything I've experienced in two years is most evident when I look at my videos from El Galpon. The excitement and openness I felt at the time—to all things new, experimental, alternative, innovative—are tempered by a profound reverence for the enduring beauty of what may best be described as "the traditional" in tango. The techno music, the contact improv, the messiness—these fill me with laughter. Many of the electronic tangos I couldn't get enough of then sound dated now, but "Bahia blanca," "Melodía del amor," and "Nada" (to name just a few) still send me into a rapturous state of melancholy. Watching these videos, I know that I have matured, that I shared a fleeting moment in the history of the dance with a group of like-minded, irreverent young dancers. Displaced to my other home in the States, I realize that my dance has, in a sense, come full circle. Once defensive about the right of young dancers to "do their own thing," I am a little less forgiving now, a little less tolerant of the tango dancer who does not understand, or at least aspire to understand, the roots and the development of the dance, its music and poetry. While I remain a great admirer of Naveira and Salas's tango revolution, spellbound by Naveira and Giselle Anne's pedagogic skills, and happy at the growth of new spaces catering to young dancers, I find a romance in the *milongas* that speaks back to experimentation. This is what draws packs of kids across town at the close of the *prácticas* each night: an experience that draws tango lovers young and old, that calls with the enduring significance of place and tradition.

Countless dancers from abroad commented on the mixing of generations on *porteño* dance floors, connecting it to scenes observed in daily life in the Argentine capital. It is this contact between generations that will ensure the dance's future. In the midst of stylistic wars and generational conflict, there is also gratitude among older *tangueros* that their dance will survive, met with an attitude of reverence and respect among many young *tangueros*, encouraged by the knowledge that the practice of tango can be a lifelong one, though its execution may demand alteration with the passage of time.

Back in the States, I find myself singing along to tangos I never realized I knew the words to. I will my *yanqui* partners to hold just a few bars at the start of each song, even if they are pretending, to extend the illusion that they are locating the orchestra, the singer, maybe even the year of each particular recording. As I settle into the comforts of my old home, I also fantasize about returning south, to a house in Boedo, to a lifetime in the birthplace of tango. As my body moves through time and space to a music that celebrates the loss of a place that was never mine to begin with, I am reminded where it is that I come from. At the same time, I stake my claim to the place where I now belong, which resides within me wherever I might go.

Epilogue

Las vueltas de la vida (Life's Twists and Turns)

By what strange ways have we been led back here? . . . I seem to appraise the scene from a perspective where, against its custom, the past rises to bless, not haunt, and where every impossibility seems possible again.

Vikram Seth, *An Equal Music* (2000)

Living abroad facilitates treating life as a spectacle—it is one of the reasons that people of means move abroad. . . . The expatriate's dancing city is often the local reformer's or revolutionary's immobilized one, ill-governed, committed to injustice. Different distance, different cities. The Cavaliere had never been as active, as stimulated, as alive mentally. As pleasurably detached.

Susan Sontag, *The Volcano Lover* (1997)

June 2010, the Dancing City

*Back for a month in Buenos Aires, I find myself falling in love all over again with this city, and with my life and my self as I am allowed to be here. Beyond the romance of life abroad, where even the most mundane things become, as a good friend so aptly put it, "more vibrant," there is a film-like quality to living life in another language. Carrying out my life in Spanish finds me awash in vibrant impressions, at moments all too conscious of myself and of that immersion. At once protagonist and audience, I give myself over to the life of this city, only to float and to watch, as if from above, this character create the script that is her life in a foreign tongue. Trying on those superfluous turns of phrase—*como, así que, digamos, este (like, so, let's say, uh)*—culturally priceless if literally meaningless, has something in common with learning to dance. From mimicking to incorporating the movements or words of another, there is a mysterious element to fluency: beyond sheer will and the desire to appropriate, to make uniquely personal something that was not one's own to begin with, a distance must be closed.*

There is a degree of performance, appropriation even, to this whole business of dancing tango that mirrors the spectacle of Buenos Aires as expat haven and tango mecca. And if we take to heart tales of the dance's dying essence, of the disappearance of the tradition of tango through acquisition, this appropriation pervades the city nearly to its core. If the purists have it right, even the Argentines are as detached as Sontag's Cavaliere, reveling in the chaos wrought by nuevo, *displaced from their own tradition.*

But what of recent efforts to bridge that distance, to return to "the essence" of tango, as many young dancers claim to be their goal these days? Can the dancing city become the site of another (r)evolution? Where this latest turn is a folding in upon so much investigation, and preservation becomes the heart—no longer just the by-product—of evolution? Where tangueros *local and global mobilize to redraw the boundaries, dirtying their hands, to use Sartre's words, "right up to the elbows" (1955: 224) in the messy work of rejecting spectacle, demanding a truth that balances reverence for the past with the life of the present and the possibility of the future?*

* * *

Contemporary tango continues to evolve. In the brief span of time between my return to the United States in late 2007 and a monthlong stay in Buenos Aires in mid-2010, evidence of a backlash, a turning inward from experimentation and expansion, has slowly accumulated. From the disappearance of a once-popular festival dedicated to *nuevo*, to the growing cadre of foreign disc jockeys dedicated to studying and amassing traditional music, promotional images and video footage of young couples dancing in a closer embrace, and reports from rebel leaders denouncing the obsession with novelty and advocating a return to the essence of the dance, this shift has manifested in Argentina and abroad.

By 2010, a handful of new *prácticas* and *milongas* had emerged in Buenos Aires, more than one situated somewhere between traditional and *nuevo*. These new *prácticas* are still organized by and cater to younger dancers. However, there is a palpable feeling that something new is occurring yet again. In these spaces, one can see a return to tango's essence in the closeness of the couple (as opposed to the more open embrace that had become common in the *prácticas*); a return to the tradition of dancing in *tandas*; the relatively ordered look of the floor; and the decidedly classic costumes donned by the city's hottest young tango stars during their exhibitions.

PRAKTIKA8 and MILONGA10 are two new events held in the same neighborhood social club, El Club Fulgor de Villa Crespo, where attendees are primarily in their twenties and thirties, but the look of the floor is decidedly more traditional than that at the *prácticas* that arose just years ago. The classes offered here are grounded in the approach of renowned teachers Carlos and Rosa Perez, longtime instructors at the famed Club Sunderland and the coaches of the last six *tango de salon* champions in the Mundial competition. Yet again, young dancers, it seems, have new needs. In language oddly reminiscent of Luciana Valle's description, less than ten years before, of the need for an alternative to the *milongas,* the text of the Web site for PRAKTIKA8 and MILONGA10 deliberately separates these events from the *prácticas* of the past decade: Young dancers need "an alternative to the new *práctica* scene," where the floors are monopolized by dancers of such a "*high level*" that nobody feels free to dance. Further distancing themselves from contemporary tango, the organizers profess their rejection of "accelerated learning," an approach to instruction they link to foreigners. Citing the reinvigoration of tango's Argentine identity as their goal, they assert that they are dedicated to cultivating a young, local community of *tangueros.*

El Gardel de Medellín, a cultural center and *milonga* opened in 2008, is described to me by co-organizer Julio Bassan as "a place for everyone." Breaking down the divide between art and life, the organizers envision a tango that acknowledges its popular roots without denying the importance of artistic excellence. A place where "you don't need to study ballet for twenty years to dance tango," as Bassan said, El Gardel de Medellín provides the Argentine interested in tango access to top-notch performers, instructors, live music, and art exhibits, all in a comfortable, neighborhood setting.

Similarly, the Estilo Parque Patricios (Parque Patricios Style) tango festival was inaugurated in 2010 with the express goal of reclaiming the roots of tango as a popular, Argentine social dance. Indeed, it is named for the *barrio* in which the festival takes place (it was held in El Gardel de Medellín in 2010). The organizers describe *estilo* Parque Patricios not so much as a style of dance, but as an Argentine worldview that is encapsulated in the tradition of tango. Evoking the heart of the dance in this approach, they describe *estilo* Parque Patricios as a way of life that calls to mind a simpler time and place: "a return to neighborhood streets, a code amongst friends, a mischievous gesture that makes you smile, a toast that is always shared with others, a *maestro* who remembers his students and a student who never forgets his teachers" (τ; Daniel Fratantoni quoted in Valbuena 2010). Like MILONGA10 and PRAKTIKA8, the efforts are addressed to natives. Though foreigners are welcome, their Web site notes that the festival is directed toward a local public and available at "neighborhood prices."

The language employed by some of the new arrivals to the *porteño* tango scene is noteworthy. It suggests that a return to the essence of the dance is not only about movement vocabulary, codes, music, or dress but also a decidedly populist move, the goal being to cultivate tango's future guardians and return the dance to its rightful owners: not the foreigners, or the world-traveling tango luminaries, but the people, *los argentinos*. It is a political statement that calls to mind the *nuevo* rebels' rejection of the label that others had been so eager to place upon them. While these young rebels sought to locate experimentation and innovation firmly within the historical trajectory of an Argentine cultural tradition, the most common path to success combined selling this idea abroad and building a globalized clientele at home. Now, in contrast, some of today's emerging dancers and organizers are projecting an almost protectionist attitude, where the future of tango rests first and foremost on local consumption.

This is interesting for the simple fact that some of the *tangueros* associated with these new locales are already traveling and teaching abroad. In my interview with Marco Bellini, singer with the acclaimed Orquesta Típica El Afronte, he described a similar desire to cultivate a local audience and the particular challenges this presents. Since February 2005, El Afronte has gained fame by playing just off of Plaza Dorrego on Sunday afternoons during the San Telmo antiques and artisans' fair (itself a well-attended event that has exploded with growing tourism). In six years, the orchestra has self-produced four CDs and sold 60,000 discs with no record label or outside assistance; all sales are entirely hand to hand. More recently, the band has joined a fledgling movement to resuscitate the tradition of the live-music *milonga*. Every Monday and Wednesday evening, El Afronte presents Milonga Bendita and Milonga Maldita, playing an hour-long set that provides a respite for the disc jockey and notably keeps attendees dancing.[1] El Afronte has toured Europe and has undoubtedly profited from tourism and tango pilgrims in Buenos Aires. Nonetheless, Bellini cited Argentine youth as the orchestra's target. Reaching this audience is also its biggest challenge, he told me, for not only do rap, *cumbia*, and rock dominate the airwaves, but the hypersexualized image of much of that music is more attractive to young listeners. Teenage boys want to meet girls, he said, but when they turn on the television and see tango, they usually see people who look like their grandparents. What's more, government funding of tango often supports already-established luminaries, so bridging the generational gap and exposing young Argentines to the contemporary tango scene is a labor of love, at odds with not only commercial but also government interests.

Buenos Aires' shifting political climate is undoubtedly affecting efforts to cultivate a local audience and reinvigorate tango's Argentine identity. When conservative candidate Mauricio Macri was elected mayor of the city in late 2007, rumor had it he intended to do away with funding for tango programming, including the city's beloved tango festival. Since 1998, the February–March (late summer in South America) festival has fostered large-scale *porteño* engagement with tango through a week-long, citywide program of free classes, concerts, and an open-air *milonga* where tango lovers, professionals, and novice residents came together to dance under the stars, set against the dramatic backdrop of the obelisk. In the end, Macri replaced the festival staff and moved the event to the week preceding the world tango championship in August, making it a decidedly global event occurring at a time of year that profits from Northern Hemisphere summer holidays. The new administration also updated the city's tango Web site: now dedicated to the festival and the Mundial, an important two weeks for tango in Buenos Aires, it supplanted the tango data.com portal, which had provided a wealth of information on social tango events year-round; now that resource has, sadly, disappeared.

It is rumored that tango was not even incorporated into the capital city's bicentennial celebration until Juan Carlos Copes questioned this in a televised interview just days before the festivities were set to begin. In less than one week, a tango program was prepared, bringing together such luminaries as Horacio Salgán, Ubaldo De Lío, Tata Cedrón, Rodolfo Mederos, Leopoldo Federico, and Susana Rinaldi, and for the first time in ten years, Copes and María Nieves danced together. In an interview with La Milonga Argentina, Copes notes that he spoke out not for himself, but for the many talented young tango artists "waiting in the wings" (quoted in Rojas 2010).

Indeed, even El Indio's *milonga*, an institution in San Telmo's Plaza Dorrego, recently appeared in danger of disappearing over a dispute with the plaza restaurants. For nearly twenty years, donations collected at this free Sunday event following the weekly antiques and artisans' fair that draws hordes of tourists have gone to charitable causes. The plaza businesses would like to convert this *milonga*, which they see as prime real estate, into more tables and chairs. (The strange thing is that El Indio's *milonga* arguably keeps tourists in the plaza long after the fair closes down, and the surrounding restaurants likely benefit from the many *tangueros* who descend upon the square every Sunday.) Not only did an international online petition quickly circulate via social media and e-mail networks, but El Indio also turned to local sources for support, and in June 2010, La Milonga del Indio was symbolically transferred to the Mothers of the Plaza de Mayo and renamed La Milonga Placita del Pañuelo Blanco (the White Kerchief *Milonga* of the Little Plaza) for the headscarves women wore, adorned with their missing children's names and images, during the Dirty War; and to this day, many still march in their headscarves in a weekly protest in front of the Casa Rosada. In teaming up with the Madres, El Indio is smartly aligning himself with powerful political allies, who may help in negotiations with the city and plaza businesses.

Despite its cachet, then, tango's star appears to have descended a bit with recent power shifts, thus the potentially political bent of young *tangueros*' efforts to re-create its popular spirit.

Still New?

The term *nuevo* is still tossed about and debated, and the reinvigoration of tradition has not yielded a rejection of innovation by any means. The "return to the embrace" so evident on my most recent trip to Buenos Aires is not a mere reversion to a former image. Rather, young *tangueros* appear to be integrating the creativity and experimentation of so many years of "investigation" within the frame of a more closed embrace. Situating themselves in a hundred-year-old lineage, they are the most recent protagonists of the tango's continued evolutions, recognizing El Cachafaz, Petróleo, and Naveira as their forebears. In these newer *prácticas*, as well as in their predecessors, there are a maturity and an assuredness on the floor that contrast with the rebelliousness (and occasional chaos) of only a few years earlier.

Flesh-and-blood evidence of yet another "new" era, Ariadna and Federico Naveira, the children of Gustavo Naveira and Olga Besio, are today's rising tango stars. An exquisite dancer who blends femininity and power to stunning effect, and who dances both roles flawlessly, Ariadna is known to exchange lead and follow on the social dance floor and in exhibitions with partner Fernando Sanchez.

At the same time, young dancers continue to wrestle with the tango's fundamental contradictions. For instance, while the organizers of the Estilo Parque Patricios festival evoke in their promotional materials a simpler time, when groups of men met on street corners to practice steps, a promotional flyer for a new *práctica* features an anonymous woman's torso, her crotch barely concealed by a dangerously low-cut *bombacha* (panty) from which a tattoo of revered composer and orchestra leader Osvaldo Pugliese emerges. In this image, a return to the essence of tango does not preclude a more modern aesthetic when it comes to marketing, and the *tanguera* appears not necessarily as a dancer, but as an object to be gazed upon or a body part to be fetishized.

Testing the boundaries of definition, some young dancers continue to push the envelope through expansive vocabulary, nontraditional clothing, or promotional materials absent, even, of tango imagery. And *filete*[2] artist Jorge Muscia's recent collaboration with some of the city's most talented young female dancers is an ingenious alchemy of old and new, where this traditional *porteño* art form is inscribed onto the contemporary *tanguera*'s body, as in his painting of Guillermina Quiroga for the April 2009 cover of the *El Tangauta* tango magazine. And by 2010, in the spirit of the young dancers who serve as canvas, Muscia had begun to push the boundaries of *filete* in his body-painting project, infusing the designs with mythological references, rendering the bodies themselves modern-day tango mashups.

Mecca or Disneyland?

> A Házam danced on the precipice of overpopularity; everyone felt that their secret had slipped out of their control. The very hippest Hungarians felt there were too many foreigners. The very hippest foreigners had the impression there were too many uncool foreigners. The rest of the foreigners, unaware they were uncool, were noticing too many obvious tourists. By September, it would become a favorite bar from the past that you couldn't really go to anymore without aching for the good old days when it was yours alone. But for a few weeks in July of that year, before it won praise in a college-published budget travel guide for its authenticity as a locals' hangout, A Házam was everyone's first choice.
>
> Arthur Phillips, *Prague* (2002)

Reflecting on the meaning of homeland, author Milan Kundera (2002) contends that our short time on this earth necessarily limits such feelings to a single place (121). Kundera may not have danced tango, but he did drop his native Czech for French after having lived for many years in exile and eventually becoming a citizen of France. *Tangueros* similarly appropriate other ways of moving, hearing, speaking, and being in their pursuit of the dance. While we do not necessarily relinquish our homelands, dedication to the dance drives many to forsake the comforts of home, often for months or years at a time. Perpetual border crossers, we regularly traverse city, state, and country lines for a good dance. And in this world, the pilgrimage to Buenos Aires still stands as the ultimate sign of membership—a form of naturalized citizenship in a decidedly global community that trades in experience. As tango continues to expand around the world, a return to tradition is also a means of safeguarding the significance of that place, of ensuring that *tangueros* will still have a homeland in the years to come.

In September 2009, tango was declared part of the world's Intangible Cultural Heritage of Humanity by the United Nations Educational, Scientific, and Cultural Organization (UNESCO), an initiative conceived to safeguard cultural traditions passed from one generation to the next, which give "communities and groups a feeling of identity" (BBC 2009). But protecting that sense of identity is tricky when a tradition goes global, for not only are the tradition's global pilgrims driven to a brand of devotion that threatens the very altar at which they bow down, but in an age of experiential travel, tourists are increasingly demanding "authentic" experiences. Once content with neatly packaged *cena* shows, nowadays tourists often demand "real tango," and are thus a growing presence (or nuisance, depending on your perspective) at some of the city's better-known *milongas*.

On my most recent trip, I squeezed my way into the last available seat at MILONGA10 and quickly befriended a table of American and Japanese expats and Argentines. During our conversation, Henry, an American who relocated to Buenos Aires in 2008, told me that he feels more *porteño* dancing salsa than dancing tango: "The funny thing about tango in Buenos Aires is that you feel like an expat. I feel more like a *porteño* when I dance salsa, where everyone in the class is Argentine. When you go tango dancing, the *milongas* are full of foreigners" (Henry Nguyen, American expatriate, lawyer). Even the proper place of these foreigners in the *porteño* tango scene continues to provide fodder for seemingly endless debate. Following uproar over the restriction and the participation of foreigners in the 2011 citywide Metropolitano tango competitions, the prequalifying rounds for the Mundial, a foreign team won the salon competition at the

Mundial, and the highest-ranking Argentine couple came in at eighth place.[3]

In a December 2009 interview, Chicho Frúmboli—star pupil of Naveira and Salas, who, despite his objections, is often cited as a global ambassador of *nuevo*—confessed to dismay over the current state of tango. Among the last to learn from that great generation who inherited the tango through acquisition, he regrets, he said, that an obsession with experimentation has led many young dancers astray. Without that link between past and future, he argued, young rebels are pushing the boundaries of tango with no context, and the result is a dance with no depth—a tango that has lost its soul (Plebs 2009). Like that of the new generation of dancers and organizers, Frúmboli's return to tradition is about identity: it is a return to the cultural grounding of the form that acknowledges its popular roots.

Tango's increasing presence in the global imaginary may also play a part in its latest turn. From television programs like *Dancing with the Stars* and its international versions in over thirty countries, to Sandra Bullock's forthcoming film version of *Kiss and Tango*, to mattress and pharmaceutical ads, tango has become a household name in the United States.[4] Popular dance competition shows like *So You Think You Can Dance?* and *Dancing with the Stars* have eroded tango's status as exotic by bringing it to millions of households each week. At the same time, they have tended to play up its exoticism by substituting a combination of ballroom and stage for Argentine tango, while guest appearances by stage-show companies like the cast of Luis Bravo's *Forever Tango* in 2010 have reinforced that image. Popularizing a version of the dance that has little relation to social tango as it lives and breathes, these shows package and sell a spectacle of sex, drama, and passion to the sounds of the *bandoneon* that is subsumed under the exotic umbrella category of "Latin dance." In this sense, the reinvigoration and safeguarding of tradition create a distinction from the commercialized tango that a largely uninformed public happily consumes.

Tango communities outside Argentina have evolved as well. When I returned to Philadelphia in fall 2008, the community there was starting an exciting growth phase. Meredith Klein and Andrés Amarilla had opened the Philadelphia Argentine Tango School that February, bringing the city its first full-time, resident Argentine instructor. By October 2009, they had purchased a building and greatly expanded opportunities for tango education in the city, most importantly by inviting revered dancers from Argentina and other U.S. cities to teach workshops on a regular basis, and bringing the city its first international tango festival in May 2010. In July 2010, a second Argentine professional, Damian Lobato, joined the school full-time.

In many ways, the evolution of their dance and the school have mirrored larger shifts in tango at home. Though dedicated to providing students a solid foundation in tango and the ability to dance in any style, Amarilla and Klein quickly became known for their stunning and occasionally ballet-inspired performances and for their advanced seminars in *tango nuevo*. In two years, more than a dozen accomplished and creative young couples have visited as guest artists, and Amarilla and Klein brought two of Argentina's premiere electronic tango bands, Otros Aires and Tanghetto, to Philadelphia. In 2011, they introduced an iPhone app that trains dancers to read and write tango steps using a code developed by Amarilla. At the same time, however, they emphasize tradition through an approach to instruction that integrates Naveira's deconstruction with the basic elements of traditional tango, most importantly, beginning all students with and explaining all steps from the eight-count basic step. More recently, they have offered an advanced close embrace class, shifted toward a more classic look in their promotional imagery, and announced plans to bring some of the most revered elder teachers of traditional tango to the school.

My relationship to the dance has also changed. Breaking my own rule, I have become seriously involved with a fellow dancer. He was a beginner when we met, and seeing tango through his eyes has brought me back in touch with the romance of my early days, when nearly every dance was wonderful, as well as all the trials and travails that await one in learning to dance. I have watched in amusement as he has redrawn renovation plans, recalculating square footage, moving furniture, somewhat painfully negotiating the release of unnecessary items to accommodate for tango practice and parties in the home we now share. An experience that offers a new set of rewards and challenges, this relationship also brings to mind an informant's sage warning regarding tango, love, and the all-too-simplistic association between tango and therapy.

October 2009, Tango in the Square

I have reluctantly entered into my first serious tango relationship. A beginner, he insists he isn't ready for the milongas *yet. He is reluctant to go with me—to watch me in the arms of other men all night. But he doesn't much like the idea of my going without him, either. He teases me that I will fall in love on the dance floor—with someone younger, more Argentine, more advanced. He grills me about what I feel in the embrace. When I ask him, he tells me he has felt love. I am left to wonder what will happen as he progresses.*

I bump into Alicia, a tango friend and Argentine expat who discovered the tango only after she was displaced from her homeland, who learned to dance in Philadelphia with gringos. She asks where I've been and I have to confess I've been happier to skip out on tango than on this new man in my life. "I'm so happy for you," she exclaims, but her smile quickly fades. "Better to keep him to yourself for a while," she suggests. Men are a scarce commodity in the tango world outside Argentina—a factor, I believe, in the near-deification of male professionals, and the reason for which machismo *and violence toward women still manifest in subtle and not-so-subtle ways. Once he gets better, she warns, he'll be the apple of every woman's eye. Enjoy it while it lasts, the unspoken implication.*

We laugh when I recount this exchange later. Because it is far-fetched? Or to defuse the tension in the room? It would be convenient to blame the possibility of jealousy on tango, but I see the faulty logic there. The dance does not precipitate rupture, it simply brings such things to the surface more quickly. As one of my informants put it, tango can be therapeutic, but therapy is no walk in the park.

¡Que siga la milonga! (On with the *Milonga*!)

The reining in of tango innovation is hardly surprising, for the boundaries of any genre can be pushed only so far if it is not to become something other entirely. As in other artistic movements oriented around a rejection of the past in favor of novelty, this break is never complete, for the very notion of tradition is implicated at an ideological level. Ever-present referents, modernity and progress can be constructed only in light of that which came before, even if only to move away from or against it. As Jauss (1988) points out, failure to recognize the "symbiotic unity," or the necessary interplay, between traditionalism and modernism results in either lifeless imitation or uninformed dilettantism.

Such artistic revolutions (or evolutions) also point to the insufficiency of labels. Despite the entirely human drive to organize our experiences to better explain and comprehend them, categories necessarily confine. And in a practice like tango, where landscapes of sentiment and feeling feature so prominently, the circularity of evolution is all the more inevitable. For despite the investigations and innovations of the past thirty years, tango has remained a feeling. Though that feeling may vary in its contours, Discépolo's "sad thought danced" encapsulates the heart of tango, which lies in sentiment. That today's dancers have a language for conceptualizing and dissecting the physical mechanics that make that feeling achievable through dance does not negate its essence. The challenge of moving forward is not only in digesting novelty and perceiving its connection to the past but also in allowing familiar things themselves to become new, to endow them with the possibility of life.

June 2010, Coffee with a *Milonguero*

The lines that run the length of Daniel's face hint at the cost of a life spent chasing the tango. Not, like so many of his foreign counterparts, across county, state, or country lines, but across the span of years in which time was marked by the hours that separated one milonga *from the next: home from work at 2:00 p.m., to eat and nap until 10:00 p.m., to dance until 4:00 a.m., to arrive back at work and begin again at 6:00 a.m. With a wistful smile, he recounts dancing foxtrot and rock 'n' roll as a young boy with his mother, sneaking out of the bedroom he shared with a younger brother and accompanying his parents to the* milongas, *sitting enraptured by the scene before him, falling in love with a world that would become his livelihood, his passport to protagonism. His eyes well up as he observes the five-year anniversary of his great* tanguero *friend's passing, then brighten as he recalls afternoons spent practicing on street corners, years of* milonga-*hopping until the sun came up, the code of respect among serious dancers, the last of a class of self-taught* tangueros. *Tango was everything, he tells me, but for all her gifts she exacted a price. A relationship, a wife, children—how can these be sustained from halfway around the world? So tango took their place.*

Another year or two of traveling, and he'll retire the floor to the next generation. He is no longer able to maintain the lifestyle of a milonguero, *and the spaces that for so long contained him in a loving embrace are increasingly inhabited by ghosts. He tells me to enjoy it, to share that message with others. "Long live the tango" are his last words before I turn off my recorder.*

As we prepare to part ways, he asks if I'll be dancing that night. "Ah, Niño Bien [milonga]*," he exclaims when I tell him, "it is one of the best," the sparkle in his eyes revealing the tiniest hint of everything those four walls enclosed for him. He squeezes my hand, kisses my cheek, and tells me we'll see just what kind of dancer I am that night.*

Appendix 1

Law 130

Tango as Cultural Patrimony (author's translation)
Law N° 130 Buenos Aires, December 14, 1998

The Legislature of the City of Buenos Aires

sanctions with the force of Law

Title I

Article 1—The City recognizes Tango as an integral part of its cultural patrimony, and as such guarantees its preservation, recuperation and diffusion; it promotes, foments and facilitates the development of all artistic, cultural, academic, educational, urbanistic and any other nature of activity related to tango.

Article 2—In order to meet its objectives, the Government of the City, on its own or through the establishment of cooperative agreements, may carry out academic, research, study and creative activities, as well as programs with content that support its goals. Additionally, it will organize and provide for the preservation of a general archive on tango, which will gather together all artistic and cultural expressions related to tango.

Article 3—It grants the widest possible diffusion of tango through all available media, privileging direct contact with the city's residents through activities of local or community insertion. Also, the circulation of tango at the national and international level will be amplified. The government will organize, sponsor and promote exhibitions, shows, and events geared toward a mass audience, within the city as well as at the national and international level.

Article 4—The Executive Branch may propose the creation of decentralized entities to the Legislature of the City of Buenos Aires, in order to implement the objectives of this Law.

Article 5—The City Government may subsidize neighborhood associations and nonprofit organizations related to tango. Additionally, it may arrange the joint venture of commercial entities whose business proposal is focused on tango.

Article 6—In its educational programs and material, the Executive Branch must include references to the City of Buenos Aires, tango and its artistic manifestations as one of the identifying cultural expressions of the city and the country.

Article 7—The City Government will promote the touristic value of tango, designing activities for this market in collaboration with the Secretariat of Tourism of the City and of the National Government.

Article 8—The City Government must guarantee the protection of the cultural patrimony of tango, with regard to emblematic architectural and urban sites. Additionally, it will contribute through the appropriate means to works and planned activities to enliven public space in the City, with the goal of creating a particular urban aesthetic through the imaginary of Tango.

Article 9—The City Government will make a special effort to protect the patrimony represented by the musical instruments that belonged to the great interpreters of tango. It will promote the preservation of *bandoneons* in the City, and it will encourage their local production.

Article 10—The City Government will encourage, promote and circulate the avant-garde trends in tango—music, lyrics, interpretation and dance—as a means of ensuring its historical development.

Title II

Article 11—It creates the Popular Tango Festival, to be carried out annually, its culmination coinciding with the day of tango, which is celebrated on December 11.

Article 12—The objective of the Popular Tango Festival will be the exhibition, promotion and diffusion of all artistic, cultural and scientific products related to the genre of "tango" in the broadest sense of the term.

Article 13—The Popular Tango Festival will take place over the course of several days on both closed and open air stages, in venues in the city center and in the *barrios*, free of charge, and all the residents of Buenos Aires, as well as the national and international community, will be invited to participate.

Article 14—The Popular Tango Festival will include a wide range of offerings and recreation including performances, exhibits, dances, interactive entertainment, roundtables, book and research presentations, recorded material, film and video showings and art exhibitions, offering participation in the styles and expressive languages of different generations.

Article 15—During the course of the Festival, there will be a competition for new figures in the following categories: (a) singer, (b) composer, (c) lyricist, (d) orchestra, (e) dance couple or group, (f) soloist, according to the rules of the present Law. There will be a public announcement / call for entries broadcast via the mass media.

Additionally, the winners of the "Hugo del Carril" tango certification, in the areas of lyrics, music, song and dance, will participate in the competition, in accordance with Ordinance N° 43.156, B.M N° 18.443.

Article 16—[The Festival] is empowered with the authority to apply and sign agreements with radios, television and/or cable networks for the mass circulation of the Festival within and outside the country; and with record companies, for the effects of the issue and sale of acoustic material.

Article 17—[The Festival] is empowered with the authority to apply and sign agreements with Foundations and/or public and/or private companies for the effects of cooperating in the economic investment required by the Festival. In the case that the funds invested surpass the total costs incurred in the organization and production of the event, the corresponding surplus will be designated exclusively toward activities that coincide with the objectives set out in article 14 of the present Law.

Article 18—The costs required for the completion of the Festival will be charged to the corresponding budgetary party.

Article 19—Communications, etc. ANIBAL IBARRA—MIGUEL ORLANDO GRILLO

LAW N° 130 *Sanction: 14/12/98 / Promulgation: Decree N° 37/99 of 14/01/99*

Publication: BOCBA N° 616 of 22/01/99

Appendix 2

Evaluation Criteria, Tango World Championship, Salon Tango Competition

It aims at a worldwide promotion of this social dance as an authentically Río de la Plata popular practice. Evaluation criteria will comprise good taste and popular dance guidelines, i.e., an unbroken embrace, style, movement around the floor, closeness to the floor, cadence and rhythm.

Once a dancing couple is formed, the partners will not separate as long as the music is playing. This means that they cannot break the embrace, which is considered to be the tango dance position.

For the position to be considered correct, the partners must constantly hold each other by means of the embrace. Even though—during certain figures—the embrace may be flexible, this shall not prolong throughout the entire piece.

All the movements should be performed within the space allowed by the couple's embrace.

The Jury will give special relevance to the couple's musicality, elegance, walking style and movement around the floor.

Within these guidelines, the participants may perform any figure commonly used, including *barridas, sacadas* close to the floor, *enrosques*, etc.

Ganchos (hooks), *trepadas* (climbs), leaps, and any other typically stage tango possibility shall be completely excluded.

Couples, as in an actual dancehall, shall constantly move counterclockwise and avoid remaining in the same place for over two musical measures.

No contestant may raise his/her legs above the knee line.

(www.mundialdetango.gov.ar/reglamento_e.php)

Glossary

abuelos: literally "grandparents," but more generally, the elderly
academias: academy; *tango academias* are tango schools
adornos: adornments, embellishments
alteraciones: changes of direction
apilado: another term for the "close embrace" style of tango
arrabales: slums located on the outskirts of the city
attitude: from classical ballet; the dancer lifts the working leg with a bent knee, generally in a ninety-degree angle to the floor
bailarín: dancer; also, ballet dancer
bandoneon: signature tango instrument whose sound can at best be compared to that of the accordion
barrio: neighborhood; *clubes de barrio* are neighborhood social clubs
boleo: from the verb *bolear*, "to throw," a circular boleo results from a quick, light torsion of the spine that causes the leg to release and trace a circular shape in the air, either in front or in back of the dancer. A linear *boleo* is a throw of the leg straight forward or back.
bolero: A musical tradition rooted in nineteenth-century Cuba, with roots in Spanish *bolero* and French *contredanse*, the bolero arose from the blending of the Cuban *danza*, habanera, *trova*, and *son* with other Cuban, African, and European rhythms. A slow and romantic music, *bolero* spread throughout Latin America and beyond in the early to mid-twentieth century.
cabeceo: the invitation to dance initiated by shared eye contact often across a crowded room; it might include the slightest of nods, the tiniest of twirling gestures with the hand, or mouthing "*Bailamos?*" (Shall we dance?)
calesita: carousel; the follower stands with weight centered and pivots on one foot as the leader walks around the follower's supporting leg
campeonatos: competitions or contests; also *concursos*

candombe: an African-derived rhythm imported to Uruguay and Argentina by black slaves; candombe in nineteenth-century Buenos Aires referred to the dance, music, and gatherings of blacks

canyengue: a "funky," older style of tango as it was danced in its earliest days, around 1900

cena: dinner; *cena* shows, or dinner shows, featuring Argentine beef, wine, and ninety-minute spectacles of tango history

colgada: from the verb *colgar* ("to hang"); in a *colgada*, the follower moves off-axis in a direction away from the leader, who supports her

compadrito: hoodlum in early-twentieth-century Buenos Aires; also a common character in tango stage shows and mythology

confitería: tearoom; a place where coffee and sweets are served; *confiterías bailables* served cocktails and played recorded music for dancing tango

contact improvisation: an improvisational dance form based on the give and take of weight with one or more partners that emerged in the United States in the early 1970s

conventillos: tenement houses

cortina: a splice of non-tango music (from as short as thirty seconds to as long as an entire song) that signals the end of the *tanda* (set) when dancing tango socially

cumbia: musical genre that originated in Colombia in the early nineteenth century, through the merging of African, Hispanic, and Native American traditions

disociación: separation at the torso, of the ribs and chest from the hips and legs to allow torsion

escenario: stage; *tango escenario* is tango choreographed for the stage, as opposed to social tango

fantasía: fantasy; though sometimes used interchangeably with *tango escenario*, *tango fantasía* has been distinguished by professional dancers as less spectacular and originating in the 1940s Club Nelson tango practice sessions

ganchos: hook; generally a sharp move, when one dancer "hooks" a leg around their partner's leg at the thigh, by bending and then releasing the knee

gaucho: cowboy

habanera: a creole music and dance that arose in nineteenth-century Cuba with roots in the Spanish contredanza and candombe

investigación: a closed practice session where a small group of dancers gathers to work on steps; also refers to research more generally

lunfardo: a slang of Argentine Spanish that has its origins in lower-class, immigrant *barrios* of late-nineteenth-century Buenos Aires, where it arose among the children, or second generation, of primarily European immigrants

mazurka: a Polish folk dance and music, written in 3/4 or 3/8 time

milonga: social gathering where people dance tango; also a precursor to the tango, *milonga* referred to an improvisational dance executed in an embrace by early-twentieth-century blacks, lifted and mocked by the city's *compadritos*; *milonga* today refers to one of the three varieties of tango music played at social tango events (*milongas*), and the dance as it is executed to that music. Generally *milonga* is the fastest of the three musics. A main characteristic of *milonga* is the use of *traspiés*, steps in which the leg is sent in a direction (front, back, or side) without a complete transfer of weight, such that the same leg is used again in the following step. While a primary interest in tango may be to create complicated sequences of steps, a primary interest of *milonga* is to use simple steps to articulate complex rhythmic ideas.

milonga clandestina: "underground," secret *milonga*

milonguero/a: someone who attends the *milongas* frequently, sometimes every night. Historically, the term *milonguero* sometimes carried negative connotations, to refer to a man who lived in the *milongas*, barely held down or had no job, and in many cases was supported by a woman or family. The term was appropriated by a sector of *porteño* dancers and organizers in the 1990s to brand a style of tango danced in a close or chest-to-chest embrace, featuring a simple vocabulary that stresses rhythmic complexity, and that was quite successfully marketed locally and abroad as the "real" tango danced in Buenos Aires' *milongas*, where the crowded dance floors might not permit a more open frame.

ocho: "eight"; a forward step preceded by a forward step (forward *ocho*), or a back step preceded by a back step (back *ocho*), in which the trailing leg follows a figure-eight pattern, giving the step its name

ocho cortado: "cut eight"; in an *ocho cortado*, the two forward steps that make up a forward *ocho* are "cut" and two side steps are placed in the middle, creating the pattern: forward step–side step–side step–forward step

orquestas típicas: bands of ten to fourteen musicians, typically composed of piano, strings (violin, and sometimes cello or violoncello), *bandoneon*, double bass, and vocalist

pampas: plains

patadas: kicks
peñas: folk music and dance parties
pensión: guesthouse
pibes: kids
polka: a folk music and dance that originated in nineteenth-century Bohemia
porteño/a: a native of the port city of Buenos Aires
práctica: practice event; somewhere between a class and a *milonga*, a *práctica* is a space in which to practice without the strict codes of the *milonga* (which regulate the line of dance, musical programming and dancing in sets, the invitation to dance, clothing, and more). Buenos Aires' growing *práctica* scene functions as both a supplement and an alternative to the *milongas*, but with codes deemed more appropriate for younger practitioners.
rond-de-jambe: "round of the leg"; from classical ballet, the dancer stands straight on one leg while extending the free leg along the floor in a semicircle, from front to back or the reverse; rond-de-jambes can also be executed "en l'air," with the working leg executing a circle in the air
sacada: displacement of a partner's leg or foot by stepping into that space
tanda: a musical set of three to four songs of tango, *tango vals* (waltz), or *milonga*, separated by a *cortina*
tango canción: tango song
tango para bailar: tango song for dancing
tango para escuchar: tango song meant for listening rather than dancing
tanguería: tango café or concert hall
tanguero/a: male/female tango dancer
vals: waltz; one of the three varieties of tango music
volcada: from the verb *volcar* (to tip over, upset, spill); in a *volcada* the follower moves off-axis in a direction toward the leader, who supports her
yanqui: a North American
zapateo: Andalusian tap; the 1940s Club Nelson practitioners are said to have integrated *zapateo* (among other movement disciplines) into tango
zouk: also Zouk Lambada, Lambazouk, and Lambada Zouk; a partner dance that originated in Bahia, Brazil, with influences from the French Caribbean and Portuguese-speaking countries

Notes

Prologue: Travels in Tango

1. In 2005, *La Nación* reported that four out of every ten visitors mention tango as a reason to visit Buenos Aires, a $400 million per year global industry (Barco 2005). A more recent report by the *International Herald Tribune* (Ortiz 2008) sets the number of tango tourists at 25,000 per year. In 2009, the *Observer* reported that the tango industry brings $100 million annually to Buenos Aires (Carroll and Balch).

2. The lyrics of tango abound with *lunfardo,* a slang of Argentine Spanish that has its origins in lower-class, immigrant *barrios* of late-nineteenth-century Buenos Aires, where it arose among the children, or second generation, of primarily European immigrants (Gobello and Olivieri 2004).

3. A dancer's experience will vary greatly depending on which events and even which day or time he or she goes dancing, for many sites host different events and thus have a very different feel and crowd from day to day, or afternoon to evening. Add to this the fact that events come and go, switch locations, and go in and out of fashion, and the impossibility of giving a complete picture of Buenos Aires' tango scene becomes clearer. Overall, my research was situated in a local and global circuit of *prácticas* and *milongas.* The sites I attended most regularly were populated by a mix of locals, foreigners, and expats, as opposed to the neighborhood clubs that might be populated largely or entirely by locals.

4. Bill T. Jones, Liz Lerman, and Anna Halprin are three established American choreographers who have long broken with this tradition.

5. My obvious forebear here is Julie Taylor, a ballerina-turned-anthropologist and tango dancer, whose *Paper Tangos* is an artful blend of memoir, allegory, and ethnography.

6. See also Csordas 1990, Desjarlais 1992, and Jackson 1996 on embodied scholarship; Browning 1995, Connerton 1989, and Novack 1990 offer fascinating accounts of bodily constructions of culture.

7. There were important feminist precursors to this text. See di Leonardo 1993 and Mascia-Lees et al. 1993.

8. For instance, see Fabian and de Rooji 2008; Scheper-Hughes 2000.

Chapter 1. There Is No New Tango

1. An *investigación* is a closed practice session where a small group of dancers gather to work on steps. See Chapter 2 for a discussion of the famed 1990s "investigation sessions" that many cite as the breeding ground for *tango nuevo.*

2. The famed bandoneonist (1921–1992) is largely credited with bringing tango music into modernity, and for keeping tango music alive among international audiences when it had gone largely out of fashion in Argentina from the mid-1950s through the mid-1980s.

3. Angela Rippon famously labeled the tango "the vertical expression of a horizontal desire" (1993).

4. Osvaldo Pugliese (1905–1995) was a pianist, a composer, and an orchestra leader who left behind a body of compositions created from the 1920s through the 1970s. Especially known for powerfully dramatic orchestral arrangements, Pugliese is considered a link between traditional and avant-garde in tango music, and an important precursor to Piazzolla's innovations.

5. The small size of many communities outside Buenos Aires has facilitated the growth of tango festivals, multiday, intensive programs of classes, workshops, *prácticas*, *milongas*, concerts, lectures, and shoe and clothing sales, many of which draw crowds into the hundreds.

6. An all-female-run *práctica*, tango academy, and teacher-training program opened in 2004 by Luciana Valle, Valeria Batiuk, and Dina Martínez, El Motivo is a powerful symbol of the expanding role of female professionals in the tango world. Valle was crucial in the early dissemination of *nuevo* principles in the United States, following her participation in the investigation sessions that many cite as the breeding ground for *nuevo*.

7. Law No. 130 of the Legislature of the City of Buenos Aires, passed on December 14, 1998 (see Appendix I; Buenos Aires 1998).

8. Argentina's 2001 economic crisis and its impact on tango tourism in Buenos Aires are discussed in detail in Chapter 3.

Chapter 2. Finding Tango: From the Golden Age to the Twenty-First Century

1. See Baim 2007; Benarós 1999; Castro 1999; Collier et al. 1995; Del Mazo and D'Amore 2001; Ferrer 1980, 1998; Gazenbeek 2008; Nau-Klapwijk 2006; Savigliano 1995; Selles 1999; Thompson 2005; Varela 2005; Vila 1991, 2000; and Zalko 2001.

2. This brief account of Argentine and *porteño* history is informed by Bergero 2008; Blustein 2005; Collier et al. 1995; Del Mazo and D'Amore 2001; Harnan 2002; Kaminsky 2008; Nouzeilles and Montaldo 2002; Rock 1987; Savigliano 1995; Vila 2000; and Zalko 2001.

3. Baim (2007) suggests that the earliest written account of tango as dance comes from a municipal court of Montevideo, which prohibited public performance of *tangos de negros* (tango danced by blacks) in 1856, while Savigliano (1995) cites Vicente Rossi, who describes the *tango de negros* of Montevideo as an "Ur-Tango" that was "ruined and disfigured" when it made its way to the "underworld" of Buenos Aires (1926/1958).

4. Even if public performance was not sanctioned for ladies, women did have access to the tango at home, where they might practice with male relatives. Also, early accounts of tango and its practitioners came from those who were literate—the upwardly aspiring and arriviste and established upper classes—so its salacious profile likely derived from a desire to reinforce class divisions through ethnic and cultural discrimination.

5. The 1902 Residency Law and the 1910 Social Defense Act curbed radicalism by threatening immigrants with expulsion, and on May 1, 1909, police opened fire on citizens as they dispersed from an International Workers' Day rally, leaving fourteen dead and eighty injured. Understood as part of the oligarchy's efforts to "beautify" the city center for the 1910 centennial celebrations, the massacre set off the "Semana Roja" (Red Week), a weeklong general strike.

6. Guy (1991) suggests that European fears of Latin America were exacerbated by hyperbolic tales of middle-class European women who were either drugged or tricked, abducted, and sold into bordellos in Buenos Aires and Rio de Janeiro. She argues that most of the European women who landed in South American brothels had engaged in prostitution beforehand and had come to the New World seeking refuge from devastating poverty, from family, or from religious or political persecution.

7. Many cite Contursi's "Mi Noche Triste," famously recorded by Carlos Gardel in 1917, as the first true tango song, for its unparalleled pairing of music and verse and an emotional depth that would mark so many tangos from that point forward.

8. María Eva ("Evita") Duarte de Perón is the rare female who triumphed on this path, overcoming poverty and illegitimacy to achieve fame in her own right in Buenos Aires' radio and theater world before marrying General Juan Domingo Perón and becoming Argentina's most famous first lady. One of the most divisive figures in the nation's history, she was revered as a saint and a tireless advocate of social reform by her supporters, and demonized as a whore and a tyrant by her detractors. Claims of Evita's sexual cunning illuminate fears of female sexuality (especially lower class) in modernizing Argentina, a familiar trope in tango.

9. El Proceso de Reorganización Nacional (The National Reorganization Process) was the euphemistic term employed by the military government that seized power in 1976 for the "process" that included the systematic "disappearance" or internment, torture, and murder of some 10,000–30,000 Argentine citizens.

10. Juan Domingo Perón was president of Argentina from 1946 to 1955 and 1973 to 1974.

11. The singer was generally understood as simply one of the instruments in the *tangos para bailar* (tangos for dancing) of the Golden Era, though this changed with artists of the late 1930s and 1940s, including Francisco Fiorentino, Angel Vargas, Alberto Castillo, and Roberto Ruffino. The downsizing of ensembles and the dissolution of dance spaces in the 1950s facilitated the resurgence, in the tradition of Gardel, of *tangos para escuchar*, led by artists like Julio Sosa, Edmundo Rivero, Roberto Goyeneche, and, later, Susana Rinaldi and Tata Cedrón. Lydia Borda and Ariel Ardit are among Gardel's descendants today, while the recent revival of young *orquestas típicas*—Fernandez Fierro and El Afronte being two of the more renowned—represents an interesting new trend in music that might be categorized as "for listening" but that is often danced.

12. Varela (2005) suggests that resistance lay in Piazzolla's ultimately musical identification with the tango, often at the expense of the poetry or lyrics.

13. A *milonguero/a* is someone who attends the *milongas* frequently, sometimes every night. Some use the term to refer specifically to those elder dancers who danced during the Golden Age of tango. I use the term generally to refer to elder social tango dancers, though, according to the first sentence, a *milonguero/a* can be of any age. I also

use the term *tanguero/a* (male or female tango dancer) to refer to social tango dancers, and the term *bailarín/rina* to refer to revered social dancers (also connotes "professional" or "ballerina"). Historically, the term *milonguero* sometimes carried negative connotations, to refer to a man who lived in the *milongas*, barely held down or had no job, and in many cases, was supported by a woman or family. The term was appropriated by a sector of *porteño* dancers and organizers in the 1990s to brand a style of tango danced in a close or chest-to-chest embrace, featuring a simple vocabulary that stresses rhythmic complexity, and that was quite successfully marketed locally and abroad as the "real" tango danced in Buenos Aires' *milongas*, where the crowded dance floors may not permit a more open frame. Of course, the *milongas* of Buenos Aires come in all shapes and sizes, while attendance varies throughout the night and more generally throughout the year, so there are certainly many venues (or times in certain venues) where the floor may not be crowded.

14. See Paz 2008.

15. Zalko (2001) reminds the reader that the friendship between the two countries was a complicated one. While France received Argentine exiles fleeing state-sanctioned terrorism, the Argentine junta was an important client of the French defense industry, which supplied the military government with the weapons, tanks, fighter planes, helicopters, and boats it employed to wage war on "subversives" and guerilla forces. At the same time, France provided significant technical support and military intelligence to the British during the Malvinas War, arguably contributing to Argentina's defeat and ultimately bringing an end to the junta's rule (311–12).

16. See Taylor 1998 on Pino Solanas's 1986 film *Tangos: El exilio de Gardel.*

17. Gabriel Angió is an Argentine dancer whose Web site includes an archive of writings by Petróleo, an interview with his contemporary Lampazo (José Vazquez), and a note from Mingo Pugliese, the youngest of the dancers to participate in the Club Nelson practice sessions.

18. Eduardo Arquimbau (quoted in Valentino n.d.) distinguishes between *fantasía* ("fantasy," an expansion of the 1940s style of tango that allowed for a complete rupture of the embrace and prolonged pauses for embellishments) and *tango escenario* (stage tango), also known as "show," which includes larger jumps and lifts and incorporates elements from other disciplines including ballet and contemporary dance. Arquimbau's description of *fantasía* is complicated by accounts that the Nelson men were already freely importing elements from other dances.

19. Todaro (1929–1994) is hailed as one of the great tango teacher-choreographers, responsible for training many star stage performers in the 1980s and early 1990s.

Chapter 3. What's So New about *Tango Nuevo*?

1. From the verb *bolear,* "to throw," a circular *boleo* results from a quick, light torsion of the spine that causes the leg to release and trace a circular shape in the air, either in front or in back of the dancer. A linear *boleo* is a throw of the leg straight forward or back. A *gancho* is generally a sharp move, when one dancer "hooks" a leg around the other's at the thigh, by bending and then releasing the knee.

2. *Esa ansiosa búsqueda de la libertad* is the subtitle of Rodolfo Dinzel's *El Tango: Una danza* (1997).

3. See Blustein 2005 and Hornbeck 2002 on Argentina's 2001 economic crisis, and Barrionuevo 2008 and Gabino 2007 on doubts surrounding the nation's inflation rate in the mid- to late 2000s.

4. See Patterson 2006 and Shipley 2007 on sincerity versus authenticity.

5. Co-owner Luis Solanas admits that "there are crashes on the dance floor from time to time" but argues that "nobody does this with bad intention" (quoted in Bevilacqua 2003). See also Gambarotta 2006.

6. A *milonguero* admits to and laments this tendency toward surveillance and critique in *Tango: Baile nuestro* (Zanada 1988).

7. While the city is famed for its nocturnal tango scene, there are several "matinee *milongas*" attended by traditional dancers during the same time frame in Buenos Aires.

8. Rumors of drug use among the *milongueros* and drug sales in *milonga* bathrooms (especially cocaine, which helps dancers keep going until 6 a.m. after working all day) are common.

9. Famed composers associated with different periods of the Golden Age. Interestingly, the majority of the music played in Buenos Aires' *prácticas* is traditional tango.

10. As Juan Carlos Copes famously put it, "one heart and four legs" (quoted in Chiori and Groisman 1993: 154).

Chapter 4. *Manejame como un auto* (Drive Me Like a Car)

1. The *piropo* is widely documented in many Spanish-speaking cultures. Here, I draw attention to its use in defining dance style and community in Buenos Aires' tango scene.

2. See Quistgaard 1999 for a discussion of the *piropo* as "refined machismo" in contrast to the "white-trash catcall," and France 1999 on collective ownership of the female body on the streets of Buenos Aires.

3. Generally framed as a representation of traditional gender norms, it is also plausible that the *piropo* functions as a reaction to so much noise. While Sebreli (2003) cites Buenos Aires as the world's third-noisiest city (280), a 2006 World Health Organization report ranks it the noisiest city in Latin America. Sergio Avello's exhibit, Volumen, which ranked the city's ever-changing decibel level via a system of noise-sensitive lights installed on the front steps of the Museo de Arte Latinoamericano de Buenos Aires (Museum of Latin American Art of Buenos Aires [MALBA]), speaks to the often oppressive character of the city's noise (see http://volumenurbano.blogspot.com/).

4. See also Nau-Klapwijk 2006 and Ortiz 1986–1987.

5. See, for example, Mariano Chicho Frumboli on the woman as protagonist in the tango couple today (quoted in Karpen 2009). Also, see comments by Olga Besio and Luciana Valle in "A Nuevo Machismo?" (this chapter).

6. See Benarós 1999; Collier et al. 1995; Dinzel 1994; Nau-Klapwijk 2006; Pujol 1999; Saikin 2004; Savigliano 1995; Taylor 1998.

7. See Dempster 2003 on visual kinesthesia.

8. See Duvall 2000; Orezzoli and Segovia 1985–1986, 1999–2000; Romay 2007; Saura 1998; Zotto and Plebs 1988.

9. See also Garramuño's *Modernidades primitivas: Tango, samba y nación* (2007), in which she discusses the cultural processes that have facilitated the integration of "primitive" elements into "modern" tango and samba, as a means of amplifying understandings of the modern and demonstrating how once-primitive cultural products transform themselves to become acceptable national symbols.

10. Of course, tango is not always learned in a classroom setting. See Chapter 3 for a discussion of the tradition of tango through "acquisition." Also, see Del Mazo and D'Amore 2001; Gavito in Quiroga 2001; Savigliano 1995; and Thompson 2005.

11. See Carlos Gavito's explanation of being a *milonguero* and the "men's table" in *El Abrazo del Tango* (Trotta 2006).

12. It is worth noting, too, that the rate of eating disorders in Argentina has been estimated as three times that in the United States (Renfrew Center Foundation 2003).

13. See Savigliano 2003. Also, see Kershaw 2010 on the scandal surrounding the CougarLife dating Web site.

14. Although I have heard and observed over the course of my visits to Buenos Aires that *milonga* attire has become less formal over the past few years, young dancers maintain the distinction between the "traditional" and *nuevo* scene, changing, as noted in Chapter 3, shoes, dress, hair, and posture when in the *milonga*; they thus reinforce the traditional notions of gender identity that they relinquish when in the "laid-back" *práctica* space.

15. More than one dancer argued that these themes could describe expert "traditional" training for women as well. An arguable change in the look of tango when one travels from the *milonga* to the *práctica* is the increased distance that may separate the partners, the more frequent rupture of the embrace, and the increasing integration of non-tango vocabulary onto the social dance floor. That such themes are championed by *tangueras* with "traditional" training underscores the difficulty in defining *nuevo;* furthermore, it demonstrates the tendency to assert independence from predecessors through a linking of style, generation, and culture (see note 5 above).

16. Many dancers insist that leader and follower maintain their own axes in *milonguero* style—at least to the extent of being able to recuperate them instantaneously—but discussions with dancers revealed a greater tendency for the follower to lean on the leader when dancing in close embrace, whether this is technically correct or not. While this image is not representative of traditional tango in a more general sense, younger dancers might see the woman standing on her own axis as something "new" because they had previously been exposed primarily to *milonguero* style.

Chapter 5. *¿Droga o terapia?* (Drug or Therapy?)

1. www.medicine.mcgill.ca/spot/research.htm.

2. Stephen Miller, *Conversation: A History of a Declining Art*, in Ogunnaike 2006.

3. The idea of this image came to me in part from *Precipice*, choreographed by KC Chun (2000), and Pema Chodron's notion of groundlessness (1991).

4. An exception to this rule might be the handful of professional expats whose residency in Argentina or partnership with an Argentine dancer muddies their status and arguably increases their cachet.

5. In late 2007, the city's *Tango Guide* listed approximately 156 *milongas* (including *prácticas* that function like young *milongas*), and 324 classes and *prácticas* per week. By March 2008, a search on the city government Web site yielded a weekly return of 214 *milongas* and 504 classes.

6. In the span of seven years (2003 to 2010), inflation has driven up the price of many commodities and services, while prices in the tango world have risen as well, perhaps in tandem with inflation or perhaps in response to the purchasing power of all these foreign pilgrims.

7. Of course, this depends on the individual and their life experience. One young *porteño* told me he earned much more as a dentist (up to US$10,000 per month before the crash), while another was unable to make ends meet with a degree in engineering, earning a mere AR600 per month after the crash (at the time equal to US$200).

8. Congreso Internacional de Tango Argentino, one of the largest annual tango festivals in Buenos Aires, features classes with some of the most famous contemporary and traditional dancers; pricewise, it is targeted to foreigners.

Chapter 6. Locating the Tango

1. Homero Manzi, "Manoblanca" (1941).

2. See www.lasvioletas.com/site/esp/html/anecdotas/index.html and www.todotango.com/Spanish/biblioteca/CRONICAS/ivette.asp.

3. Myers's analysis of Pintupi acrylics, which were subsumed under the rubric of "Aboriginal" or even "Australian" art once they began to circulate internationally, is a thoughtful portrait of the difficulties of negotiating local identity and global reach.

4. A few examples include *Boedo* by Dante Linyera (1928); *Barrio de tango* (1942), *Yuyo verde* (1944), and *Sur* (1948) by Homero Manzi; *Nada* by Horacio Sanguinetti (1944); *Volver* by Alfredo La Pera (1935); *Almagro* by Iván Diez (1930); *Pedacito de cielo* by Homero Expósito (1942).

5. See Savigliano 1995.

6. Differential pricing for foreigners and Argentines in Buenos Aires' *milongas* caused heated debate on the Tango-L listserv back in 2005. The extent to which this practice continues at all is questionable; however, it is very common for tango professionals, revered *milongueros,* and friends of organizers to enter social dance events free of charge in Buenos Aires. A *porteño* friend argued that La Viruta is the only site whose moderate pricing allows locals to study at the same pace as tourists in the host of schools and academies targeted to foreign income.

7. European dancers cannot legally work in the United States without an artist visa; however, they can enter on a visa waiver and then work illegally, as some Argentines might have before the crisis between 1996–2001.

8. *Si sos brujo* is a documentary and tribute to Emilio Balcarce, director of the Orquesta Escuela de Tango.

9. See Anderson 1983 and Foster 1991.

10. Another term for the chest-to-chest style, which has also been referred to as "club" and "*confitería,*" www.totango.net/eduardo.html.

11. Again, it is important to note that such behaviors—arguably censored everywhere—do manifest in events of all stripes; see Cecilia Gonzalez on the generational tensions in the *milongas* of the 1990s in Chapter 3.

12. Appadurai 1988; Averill 1995; Bhabha 1994; Chambers 1994; Gupta and Ferguson 1992; Hannerz 1990; Kearney 1995; Myers 2002; and Shepherd 2002.

Epilogue: *Las vueltas de la vida* (Life's Twists and Turns)

1. Although a host of orchestras play in the *milongas* of Buenos Aires, the revival of a resident orchestra is a recent phenomenon. While Fernandez Fierro, perhaps the first of the new young orchestras to make a name for itself, opened its own club in 2004, its tango is generally geared toward listeners rather than dancers. At Milonga Bendita and Milonga Maldita, attendees often dance during El Afronte's set.

2. "A fine line that serves as decoration," from the Latin *filum*, *filete* has its origins in late-nineteenth- and early-twentieth-century *porteño* society, when it was a decorative art form that appeared on grocers' and vendors' carts, before expanding to buses and trucks. Tango and *filete* have a long association, as the decorative phrases adorning buses and cars were often taken from tango lyrics (personal communication, Jorge Muscia; Gambarotta 2009).

3. In response to the new restriction that Metropolitano participants be Argentine nationals (with at least one being a resident of Buenos Aires), two antidiscrimination petitions were filed with local judges, and the Metropolitano results were declared null. This decision, in turn, caused more uproar and was heralded as unfair to the winners, as the Metropolitano competition had already concluded. To appease all sides, an additional citywide competition was held, open to any couple so long as one member of the couple was not an Argentine native, and the winners of both competitions went on to compete in the Mundial (Guillouche 2011; Merchant 2011).

4. Sleepy's "Restless Tango" advertisement won the Communicator Awards Award of Excellence in 2008.

Works Cited

Adams, Vincanne. 1996. *Tigers in the Snow and Other Virtual Sherpas: An Ethnography of Himalayan Encounters*. Princeton: Princeton University Press.

Amarilla, Andrés, and Meredith Klein. 2008. *Villa Urquiza-Style Tango with a Nuevo Twist*. AndresAmarilla.com. www.andresamarilla.com/urquiza.htm.

Anderson, Benedict. 1983. *Imagined Communities: Reflections on the Origin and Spread of Nationalism*. London: Verso.

Angió, Gabriel. n.d. http://nataliaygabriel.com/segun-petroleo/item/69-neo-danza-o-tango-nuevo.html.

Appadurai, Arjun. 1996. *Modernity at Large: Cultural Dimensions of Globalization*. Minneapolis: University of Minnesota Press.

Archivo General de la Nación, Dto. Doc. Fotográficos. (Image). 1903. *Tango criollo*. Caras y Caretas. Buenos Aires: Argentine government.

———. (Image). 1912. *Un tango en el agua*. Buenos Aires: Argentine government.

———. (Image). 1936. *Avenida Costanera—Centennial Celebration of the Founding of Buenos Aires*. Buenos Aires: Argentine government.

Asociación Civil Intertango. 2006. "Tango Nuevo." *Tango y Cultura Popular* 72 (Rosario), July. http://tangoyculturapopular.blogspot.com/2006_07_01_archive.html.

Averill, Gage. 1995. "Haitian Music in the Global System." In *The Reordering of Culture: Latin America, the Caribbean and Canada in the Hood*, edited by Alvina Ruprecht and Cecilia Taiana, 339–62. Ottawa: Carleton University Press.

Baim, Jo. 2007. *Tango: Creation of a Cultural Icon*. Bloomington: Indiana University Press.

Bakhtin, Mikhail. 1986. *Speech Genres and Other Late Essays*. Austin: University of Texas Press.

Balch, Oliver. 2006. "Buenos Aires or Bust." *Guardian Unlimited* (London), October 24. www.guardian.co.uk/business/2006/oct/24/argentina.travelnews.

Barco, Gustavo. 2005. "Los turistas llegan atraídos por el tango." *La Nación* (Buenos Aires), May 8. www.lanacion.com.ar/702490-los-turistas-llegan-atraidos-por-el-tango.

Barrionuevo, Alexei. 2008. "Top Official on Economy Steps Down in Argentina." *New York Times*, April 26. www.nytimes.com/2008/04/26/world/americas/26argentina.html.

BBC. 2009. *Tango Gets UN Cultural Approval*. BBC News (London), September 30. http://news.bbc.co.uk/2/hi/8282781.stm.

Benarós, León. 1999. "El tango y los lugares y casas de baile." In *La historia del tango: Primera época*, 205–87. Buenos Aires: Ediciones Corregidor.

Bergero, Adriana J. 2008. *Intersecting Tango: Cultural Geographies of Buenos Aires, 1900–1930.* Translated by Richard Young. Pittsburgh: University of Pittsburgh Press.

Bevilacqua, Carlos. 2003. "Animarse a más." *El Tangauta* (Buenos Aires), August.

Bhabha, Homi K. 1994. *The Location of Culture.* London: Routledge.

Björk. 1995. "Possibly Maybe." Audio CD. London: One Little Indian Records.

Blázquez, Eladia. 1989. "Siempre se vuelve a Buenos Aires" (music by Astor Piazzolla). Audio CD. Buenos Aires: EPSA Music.

Blustein, Paul. 2005. *And the Money Kept Rolling In (and Out): Wall Street, the IMF, and the Bankrupting of Argentina.* New York: PublicAffairs.

Borges, Jorge Luis. 1999. "A History of the Tango." In *Selected Non-Fictions*, edited by Eliot Weinberger, translated by Eliot Weinberger, Esther Allen, and Suzanne Jill, 394–404. New York: Penguin Books.

Bravo, Luis. 1996. *Forever Tango.* Interamerica, Inc.

Brooks, Geraldine. 1995. *Nine Parts of Desire: The Hidden World of Islamic Women.* New York: Anchor Books.

Browning, Barbara. 1995. *Samba: Resistance in Motion.* Bloomington: Indiana University Press.

Brufman, Melina, and Claudio Gonzalez. 2007. *Che tango.* Buenos Aires. www.tangopulenta.com.

Buenos Aires. 1998. Ley 130: Tango: Patrimonio Cultural de la Ciudad de Buenos Aires. www.cedom.gov.ar/es/legislacion/normas/leyes/ley130.html.

Carroll, Rory, and Oliver Balch. 2009. "Latin Rivals Learn It Takes Two to Tango." *Observer* (Manchester), January 25.

Castro, Donald S. 1999. "The Massification of the Tango: The Electronic Media, the Popular Theatre and the Cabaret from Contursi to Peron, 1917–1955." *Studies in Latin American Popular Culture* 18: 93–115.

Chambers, Iain. 1994. *Migrancy, Culture, Identity.* London: Routledge.

Chiori, Santiago, and Adriana Groisman. 1993. "The Tango Is More Than a Dance—It's a Moment of Truth." *Smithsonian* 24 (8): 152–61.

Chodron, Pema. 1991. *The Wisdom of No Escape.* Boston: Shambhala Books.

Chun, KC. 2000. *Precipice (Choreography).* Boston, MA.

Clarín. 2006. "La trascendencia del turismo como industria de exportación." *Clarín.com Viajes.* May 14. Buenos Aires: Grupo Clarín.

Clifford, James, and George E. Marcus, eds. 1986. *Writing Culture: The Poetics and Politics of Ethnography.* Berkeley: University of California Press.

Collier, Simon, Artemis Cooper, María Susana Azzi, and Richard Martin. 1995. *¡Tango!: The Dance, the Song, the Story.* London: Thames and Hudson.

Connerton, Paul. 1989. *How Societies Remember.* Cambridge: Cambridge University Press.

Csordas, Thomas. 1990. "Embodiment as a Paradigm for Anthropology." *Ethos* 18 (1): 5–47.

Dass, Baba Ram. 1971. *Be Here Now.* San Cristobal, N.Mex.: Lama Foundation.

Del Mazo, Mariano, and Adrián D'Amore. 2001. *Quién me quita lo bailado. Juan Carlos Copes: Una vida de tango.* Buenos Aires: Ediciones Corregidor.

Dempster, Elizabeth. 2003. "Touching Light." *Performance Research* 8 (4): 46–52.

Desjarlais, Robert. 1992. *Body and Emotion: The Aesthetics of Illness and Healing in the Nepal Himalayas*. Philadelphia: University of Pennsylvania Press.

di Leonardo, Micaela. 1993. "What a Difference Political Economy Makes: Feminist Anthropology in the Postmodern Era." *Anthropological Quarterly* 66 (2): 76–80.

Dinzel, Rodolfo. 1994. *El tango: Esa ansiosa búsqueda de la libertad*. Buenos Aires: Ediciones Corregidor.

———. 1997. *El tango: Una danza. Sistema Dinzel de notación coreográfica*. Buenos Aires: Ediciones Corregidor.

Discépolo, Enrique Santos. 1930. "Yira, Yira." www.todotango.com/Spanish/las_obras/Tema.aspx?id=hJLVLSi6htM=.

———. 1935. "Cambalache." www.todotango.com/Spanish/las_obras/Tema.aspx?id=T9lldaeHiig=.

Dodes, Rachel. 2004. "Going To: Buenos Aires." *New York Times, Travel Section*, December 12. www.nytimes.com/2004/12/12/travel/12going.html.

Donnay, Lois. 2010. *Dance with Lois Donnay*. www.mndance.com.

Dos Santos, Estela. 2001. *Damas y Milongueras del Tango*. Buenos Aires: Ediciones Corregidor.

Duvall, Robert, writer and director. 2000. *Assassination Tango*. Metro-Goldwyn-Mayer.

Ehrenreich, Barbara. 2005. *Bait and Switch: The (Futile) Pursuit of the American Dream*. New York: Metropolitan Books.

Fabian, Johannes, and Vincent de Rooji. 2008. "Ethnography." In *The Sage Handbook of Cultural Analysis*, edited by Tony Bennett and John Frow, 613–31. London: Sage Publications.

Fabiano, Sharna. 2007. *The Rise of NeoTango Music*. TangoMercurio.com. www.sharnafabiano.com/neotango.html.

Fabio Shoes. 2007. www.fabioshoes.com.ar.

Ferrer, Horacio. 1980. *El libro del tango: Arte popular de Buenos Aires: Tomo 1, crónica del tango*. Barcelona: Antonio Tersol.

———. 1998. *El siglo de oro del tango*. Buenos Aires: Manrique Zago Ediciones.

Fitzpatrick, James A. 1932. *Romantic Argentina*. Travel Talks: The Voice of the Globe. Metro-Goldwyn-Mayer. www.globalimageworks.com.

Foster, Robert J. 1991. "Making National Cultures in the Global Ecumene." *Annual Review of Anthropology* 20: 235–60.

Foster, Susan L. 1988. *Reading Dancing: Bodies and Subjects in Contemporary American Dance*. Berkeley: University of California Press.

France, Miranda. 1999. *Bad Times in Buenos Aires: A Writer's Adventures in Argentina*. New York: Ecco.

Friedson, Steven. 1996. *Dancing Prophets: Musical Experience in Tumbuka Healing*. Chicago: University of Chicago Press.

Fuente, Sandra de la. 2007. "Los estudios culturales son una moda." *Revista Ñ*. (Buenos Aires), August 4, 10–11.

Gabino, Rosario. 2007. "Argentina: Cifras en duda." *BBCMundo.com*. October 3. www.news.bbc.co.uk/hi/spanish/business/newsid_7023000/7023806.stm.

Gambarotta, Lisandro. 2006. "La Viruta: Milonga de Buenos Aires." *El Tangauta* (Buenos Aires), July, 42–44.

———. 2009. "Jorge Muscia: El Fileteador del Tango" (Interview with Jorge Muscia). *El Tangauta* (Buenos Aires), April, 46–47.

Gardel de Medellín, El. 2010. Festival Estilo Parque Patricios. www.elgardeldemedellin.com.ar.

Garramuño, Florencia. 2007. *Modernidades primitivas: Tango, samba y nación*. Buenos Aires: Fondo de Cultura Económica.

Gazenbeek, Anton. 2008. *Inside Tango Argentino: The Story of the Most Important Tango Show of All Time*. Cassville, Mo.: Litho Printers and Bindery.

Gobello, José, and Marcelo H. Olivieri. 2004. *Lunfardo: Curso básico y diccionario*. Buenos Aires: Academia Porteña del Lunfardo.

Gobierno de la Ciudad de Buenos Aires. *Programa cultural en barrios*. www.buenosaires.gov.ar/areas/cultura/cen_culturales/prog_barrios.php.

Graham, Martha. 1991. *Blood Memory*. New York: Doubleday.

Guillouche, Sophie. 2011. "The Metropolitan Tango Championship Is Nullified by Segregation." *2xTango.com*. May 24. www.2xtango.com/anulan-el-campeonato-metropolitano-de-tango-por-segregacion/?lang=en.

Gupta, Akhil, and James Ferguson. 1992. "Beyond 'Culture': Space, Identity and the Politics of Difference." *Cultural Anthropology* 7 (1): 6–23.

Guy, Donna. 1991. *Sex and Danger in Buenos Aires: Prostitution, Family, and Nation in Argentina*. Lincoln: University of Nebraska Press.

Hackney, Madeleine E., Svetlana Kantorovich, and Gammon Earhart. 2007. "A Study on the Effects of Argentine Tango as a Form of Partnered Dance for Those with Parkinson Disease and the Healthy Elderly." *American Journal of Dance Therapy* 29 (2): 109–27.

Hannerz, Ulf. 1990. "Cosmopolitans and Locals in World Culture." In *Global Culture: Nationalism, Globalization and Modernity*, edited by Mike Featherstone, 237–52. London: Sage Publications.

Harnan, Chris. 2002. "Argentina: Rebellion at the Sharp End of the World Crisis." *International Socialism Journal* 94: 3–48.

Hornbeck, J. F. 2002. *The Argentine Financial Crisis: A Chronology of Events*. U.S. Library of Congress: Congressional Research Service. fpc.state.gov/documents/organization/8040.pdf.

Howard, Mel, and José Libertella. 1993. *Tango pasión*. New York: Concert Productions International.

Jackson, Michael. 1996. "Introduction: Phenomenology, Radical Empiricism and Anthropological Critique." In *Things as They Are: New Directions in Phenomenological Anthropology*, edited by Michael Jackson, 1–50. Bloomington: Indiana University Press.

Jauss, Hans Robert. 1988. "Innovation and Aesthetic Experience." *Journal of Aesthetics and Art Criticism* 46: 375–88.

Kaminsky, Amy. 2008. *Argentina: Stories for a Nation*. Minneapolis: University of Minnesota Press.

Karpen, Richard. 2009. Interview with Mariano "Chicho" Frumboli (reposted on *Alex.Tango.Fuego.com*). Translated by Celia Arias. www.alextangofuego.blogspot.com/2009/11/mariano-chicho-frumboli-interview.html.

Kearney, M. 1995. "The Local and the Global: The Anthropology of Globalization and Transnationalism." *Annual Review of Anthropology* 24: 547–65.

Kenyon, Janis. 2000. "Approaching Milonguero Style." *ToTANGO* (reprinted from Tango-L). www.totango.net/janis.html.

Kershaw, Sarah. 2010. "Google Tells Sites for 'Cougars' to Go Prowl Elsewhere." *New York Times*, May 15. www.nytimes.com/2010/05/16/fashion/16cougar.html.

Kundera, Milan. 2002. *Ignorance*. Translated by Linda Asher. New York: HarperCollins.

Ladas, Homer, and Cristina Ladas. 2008. www.TheOrganicTangoSchool.org.

Lepore, Jill. 2008. "Just the Facts, Ma'am: Fake Memoirs, Factual Fictions and the History of History." *The New Yorker*, March 24. www.newyorker.com/arts/critics /atlarge/2008/03/24/080324crat_atlarge_lepore.

Luhrmann, Baz, writer and director. 1992. *Strictly Ballroom*. M&A.

Ma, Yo-Yo. 1997. *Soul of the Tango: The Music of Astor Piazzolla*. New York: Sony BMG Music Entertainment.

Malvinas: Islas de la memoria. 2007. Exhibit shown at the Centro Cultural Recoleta, Buenos Aires.

Manning, Erin. 2007. *Politics of Touch: Sense, Movement, Sovereignty*. Minneapolis: University of Minnesota Press.

Manzi, Homero. 1941. "Manoblanca." www.todotango.com/english/las_obras/letra. aspx?idletra=249.

Mascia-Lees, Frances E., Patricia Sharpe, and Colleen Ballerino Cohen. 1993. "The Postmodernist Turn in Anthropology: Cautions from a Feminist Perspective." *Signs* 15(1): 7–33.

Masiello, Francine. 1992. *Between Civilization and Barbarism: Women, Nation, and Literary Culture in Modern Argentina*. Lincoln: University of Nebraska Press.

Merchant, Shahrukh. 2011. "Debacle of the 2011 Metropolitan Championships in Buenos Aires: SUMMARY." *Tango-L@mit.edu*. August 11. www.limestone.uoregon.edu /~llynch/Tango-L/2006/msg13596.html.

Merwin, William Stanley. 1993. "Separation." *The Second Four Books of Poems*. Port Townsend, Wash.: Copper Canyon Press.

Miller, Marilyn. 2004. "Tango in Black and White." In *Rise and Fall of the Cosmic Race: The Cult of Mestizaje in Latin America*, edited by Marilyn Miller, 79–95. Austin: University of Texas Press.

Miller, Susana. 2010. www.susanamiller.com.ar/editorial.htm.

Moglia Barth, José Luis, director. 1933. *¡Tango!* Buenos Aires: Argentina Sono Film.

Mount, Ian. 2006. "A Moveable Fiesta: Buenos Aires Is the New Expat Haven." *New York Magazine*, February 19. http://nymag.com/guides/changeyourlife/16047/.

———. 2011. "Argentina's Turnaround Tango." *New York Times*, September 1. www.nytimes.com/2011/09/02/opinion/argentinas-turnaround-tango.html.

Myers, Fred R. 2002. *Painting Culture: The Making of an Aboriginal High Art*. Durham, N.C.: Duke University Press.

Nau-Klapwijk, Nicole. 2006. *Tango: Un baile bien porteño*. Buenos Aires: Ediciones Corregidor.

Naveira, Gustavo, and Giselle Anne. 2011. "Who We Are." GustavoyGiselle.com. www.gustavoygiselle.com/english/05_about_us.htm.

Neal, Caroline. 2005. *Si sos brujo: Una historia de tango*. DVD. Buenos Aires: Primer Plano Film Group.

Nouzeilles, Gabriela, and Graciela Montaldo, eds. 2002. *The Argentina Reader: History, Culture, Politics*. Durham, N.C.: Duke University Press.

Novack, Cynthia. 1990. *Sharing the Dance: Contact Improvisation and American Culture*. Madison: University of Wisconsin Press.

Ogunnaike, Lola. 2006. "Pinned between 'Hi' and 'Goodbye.'" *New York Times*, December 17. www.nytimes.com/2006/12/17/fashion/17chatty.html?pagewanted=all.

Orezzoli, Hector, and Claudio Segovia. 1985–1986, 1999–2000. *Tango Argentino*. New York: Mark Hellinger Theatre, Gershwin Theatre.

Ortiz, Alicia Dujovne. 1986–1987. "Etre Porteño (in Buenos Aires)." *Discourse* 8 (Fall–Winter): 73–83.

Ortiz, Fiona. 2008. "Argentina Sees Comeback of Tango." *International Herald Tribune* (New York), January 31. http://ca.reuters.com/article/oddlyEnoughNews/idCAN2232466920080131.

Palmer, Marina. 2005. *Kiss and Tango: Looking for Love in Buenos Aires*. New York: William Morrow.

Palumbo, Tito, ed. 2006. *Buenos Aires Tango: Guía Trimestral*. Buenos Aires: Palumbo.

Park, Chan. 2004. *Tango Zen: Walking Dance Meditation*. United States: Tango Zen House.

Patterson, Orlando. 2006. "Our Overrated Inner Self." *New York Times*, December 26. http://query.nytimes.com/gst/fullpage.html?res=9F05E1DC1E31F935A15751C1A9609C8B63.

Paz, Alberto. 2008. "The 1970s Buenos Aires Milongas, Version 2." *Knol*, November 20. www.knol.google.com/k/alberto-paz/the-1970-s-buenos-aires-milongas/32307hfrzzgo5/5.

Pelinski, Ramón. 2000. "El tango nómade." In *El tango nómade: Ensayos sobre la diáspora del tango*, edited by Roman Pelinski, 27–70. Buenos Aires: Ediciones Corregidor.

Pendziuch, Hugo L. 2012. "Acerca de PRAKTIKA8-MILONGA10; Clases de Tango." *PRAKTIKA8-MILONGA10*. www.praktika8.milonga10.com.

Phillips, Arthur. 2002. *Prague*. New York: Random House.

Plebs, Milena. 2009. "Mano a mano con Milena Plebs" (Interview with Mariano "Chicho" Frúmboli). *El Tangauta* 182 (Buenos Aires), December, 19–22.

Pollan, Michael. 2007. "Our Decrepit Food Factories." *New York Times*, December 16. www.nytimes.com/2007/12/16/magazine/16wwln-lede-t.html?pagewanted=all.

"Por las clausuras hay milongas clandestinas en la ciudad." 2005. *La Nación* (Buenos Aires), January 23. www.lanacion.com.ar/673472-por-las-clausuras-hay-milongas-clandestinas-en-la-ciudad.

Potter, Sally, writer and director. 1997. *The Tango Lesson*. Sony Pictures Classics.

Powers, Richard. 2010. "Ultimate Partnering." *Richard Powers*. http://socialdance.stanford.edu/syllabi/partnering.htm.

Pujol, Sergio. 1999. *Historia del baile: De la milonga al disco*. Buenos Aires: Emecé.

Quiroga, Carlos. 2001. "Tango Is a Shared Moment" (Interview with Carlos Gavito). *Reportango* (New York), January. web.ics.purdue.edu/~tango/Articles/Gavito.pdf.

Quistgaard, Kaitlin. 1999. "The Argentine Art of Flirting." *Salon.com*. San Francisco: Salon Media Group, Inc.

Rabe, Jay. 2009. "Gender Relationships." *TangoMoments.com*. www.tangomoments.com/pages/ATango.htm#gender.

Renfrew Center Foundation for Eating Disorders. 2003. *Eating Disorders 101 Guide: A Summary of Issues, Statistics and Resources.* (September 2002, revised October 2003). www.renfrew.org.

Rilke, Rainer Maria. 1989. The Sonnets to Orpheus II, 4. In *The Selected Poetry of Rainer Maria Rilke*, edited and translated by Stephen Mitchell. New York: Vintage International.

Rippon, Angela. 1993. "Vertical Expression of a Horizontal Desire." *Tango por dos* (concert program). Sadler's Wells, London.

Rock, David. 1987. *Argentina, 1516–1987: From Spanish Colonization to Alfonsín*. Berkeley: University of California Press.

Rojas, Silvia. 2010. "¡Viva la patria, viva el tango!" *La Milonga Argentina*, June, 6–11.

Romay, Diego. 2002, 2005, 2007. *Tanguera*. Buenos Aires: Romay Producciones Teatrales.

Romero, Manuel. 1951. *Derecho Viejo*. Buenos Aires: Emelco-Interamericana.

Rossi, Vicente. 1958. *Cosas de negros: Estudio preliminar y notas de Horacio J. Becco.* Buenos Aires: Hachette. First published in 1926.

Saikin, Magali. 2004. *Tango y género: Identidades y roles sexuales en el tango Argentino.* Stuttgart, Germany: Abrazos Books.

Salessi, Jorge. 1997. "Medics, Crooks, and Tango Queens: The National Appropriation of a Gay Tango." In *Everynight Life: Culture and Dance in Latin/o America*, edited by Celeste Fraser Delgado and José Esteban Muñoz, translated by Celeste Fraser Delgado, 141–74. Durham: Duke University Press.

Sartre, Jean Paul. 1955. *No Exit and Three Other Plays.* Translated by Lionel Abel. New York: Vintage Books.

Saura, Carlos. 1998. *Tango.* DVD. Columbia/Tristar Studios.

Savigliano, Marta E. 1995. *Tango and the Political Economy of Passion.* Boulder, Colo.: Westview Press.

———. 2003. *Angorra Matta: Fatal Acts of North-South Translation.* Middletown, Conn.: Wesleyan University Press.

———. 2005. *Destino Buenos Aires: Tango-turismo sexual cinematografico.* Cadernos pagu 25: 327–56.

Scheper-Hughes, Nancy. 2000. "Ire in Ireland." *Ethnography* 1 (1): 117–40.

Sebreli, Juan José. 2003. *Buenos Aires, vida cotidiana y alienación; Buenos Aires, ciudad en Crisis.* Buenos Aires: Editorial Sudamericana.

Selles, Roberto. 1999. "El tango y sus dos primeras decadas (1880–1900)." In *La historia del tango*, 149–203. Buenos Aires: Ediciones Corregidor.

Seth, Vikram. 2000. *An Equal Music.* New York: Vintage Books.

Shepherd, Robert. 2002. "Culture, Commodification and Tourism." *Tourist Studies* 2 (2): 183–201.

Shipley, Jesse Weaver. 2007. "Real Black: Adventures in Racial Sincerity." *Anthropological Quarterly* 80 (1): 271–75.

Siegmann, Johanna. 2000. *The Tao of Tango.* Victoria, Canada: Trafford Publishing.

Sontag, Susan. 1997. *The Volcano Lover: A Romance.* New York: Anchor.

Stevenson, Helen. 2000. *Instructions for Visitors: Life and Love in a French Town*. New York: Washington Square Press.

Stoller, Paul. 1997. *Sensuous Scholarship*. Philadelphia: University of Pennsylvania Press.

Tango Map Guide. 2006, 2007. Buenos Aires: Caseron Porteño.

Taylor, Julie. 1987. "Tango: Ethos of Melancholy." *Cultural Anthropology* 2 (4): 481–93.

———. 1998. *Paper Tangos*. Durham: Duke University Press.

Thompson, Robert Farris. 2005. *Tango: The Art History of Love*. New York: Pantheon Books.

Tobin, Jeffrey. 1998. "Tango and the Scandal of Homosocial Desire." In *The Passion of Music and Dance: Body, Gender and Sexuality*, edited by William Washabaugh, 79–102. New York: Berg.

Trotta, Mafalda. 2006. *El abrazo del tango*. Italy.

Ueki, Clara. 2009. "Milongueros' Room, Interview Two: Raul Bravo." Translated by Omar Lagos and Mariana Parma. *Inheritingthetango.com*. www.inheritingthetango.blogspot.com/2009/08/interview-two-raul-bravo.html#.

Valbuena, Luz. 2010. "Sensatez y sentimiento: 1 Festival el Gardel de Medellín—Estilo Parque Patricios." *El Tangauta* (Buenos Aires), May, 14.

Valentino, Linda. n.d. "Eduardo and Gloria Arquimbau." *ToTango.net*. www.totango.net/eduardo.html.

van Kokswijk, Jakob. 2006. "'Remaining Authentic'—Between Traditional and Modern Tango" (Interview with Sharna Fabiano). *Eindhoven 4D Tango Festival*. www.4dtango.nl.

Varela, Gustavo. 2005. *Mal de tango: Historia y genealogía moral de la música ciudadana*. Buenos Aires: Editorial Paidós.

Vila, Pablo. 1991. "Tango to Folk: Hegemony Construction and Popular Identities in Argentina." *Studies in Latin American Popular Culture* 10: 107–40.

———. 2000. "El tango y las identidades étnicas en Argentina." In *El tango nómade: Ensayos sobre la diáspora del tango*, edited by Roman Pelinski, 71–97. Buenos Aires: Ediciones Corregidor.

Wikler-Luker, Ruth Juliet. 2007. *Community Arts, Popular Participation and Teatro Comunitario: Buenos Aires' Programa Cultural en Barrios*. Art in the Public Interest / Community Arts Network. www.communityarts.net/readingroom/archivefiles/2007/08/community_arts_1.php.

Wong, Jackie Ling. 2009. "You Know You're a Tango Junkie When . . ." *TangoPulse.net*. www.tangopulse.net/index.html.

Zalko, Nardo. 2001. *Paris–Buenos Aires: Un siglo de tango*. Buenos Aires: Ediciones Corregidor.

Zanada, Jorge, writer and director. 1988. *Tango: Baile nuestro*. Instituto Nacional de Cinematografia.

Zotto, Miguel Angel, and Milena Plebs. 1988. *Tango X 2 / Tango por dos*. Buenos Aires: Tango X 2 Company.

Index

Carolyn Merritt is an anthropologist and dancer. She lives in Philadelphia, where she teaches courses in anthropology and performance studies, and works with the ThINKing Dance project.

* * *

The University Press of Florida is the scholarly publishing agency for the State University System of Florida, comprising Florida A&M University, Florida Atlantic University, Florida Gulf Coast University, Florida International University, Florida State University, New College of Florida, University of Central Florida, University of Florida, University of North Florida, University of South Florida, and University of West Florida.